ENDING WARS

ENDING WARS

NEJPP Special Issue, Vol 37, Issue 1, 2025 – papers from the 2024 Conference on the Resolution of Intractable Conflict, Oxford

JOHN ALDERDICE AND
PADRAIG O'MALLEY

Published in the New England Journal of Public Policy, Volume 37, Issue 1, 2025

In September during each of the last eleven years, John Alderdice (https://lordalderdice.com) has organized and hosted a **Conference on the Resolution of Intractable Conflict (CRIC)** at Harris Manchester College, University of Oxford. In recent times many of the papers presented at these annual conferences have been published in the New England Journal of Public Policy. In 2023, to celebrate the tenth anniversary conference, Professor Padraig O'Malley, the Editor-in-Chief of the NEJPP invited Lord Alderdice to join him as Guest Editor for a Special Issue devoted to papers from CRIC 2023. The CRIC theme for 2023 was **The Changing Character of War and Peacemaking**.

The original published digital version of that NEJPP Special Issue is available without charge at https://scholarworks.umb.edu/nejpp/vol36/iss1/ and the hard copy format is produced by ARTIS Europe Ltd (https://artiseurope.com) who hold the copyright for the cover design © 2024. Copies of the book are available through Amazon, at bookshops and from the ARTIS (Europe) Ltd on-line bookstore - https://artis-europe-ltd.sumupstore.com/

In September 2024, Lord Alderdice, held the last of the CRIC events that he will organize and again a Special Issue of the NEJPP was produced by Professor Padraig O'Malley and Lord Alderdice, this time on the theme of **Ending Wars** - https://scholarworks.umb.edu/nejpp/vol37/iss1/ and now a hard copy is available in this book – a companion volume to **The Changing Character of War and Peacemaking**.

The book version of this Special Issue has been produced by ARTIS (Europe) Ltd (https://www.artiseurope.com/) in collaboration with The Concord Foundation (https://theconcordfoundation.org/)

The publishers are most grateful to our Manuscript Editor, K. Rhett Nichols and Citation Editor, Erin K. Maher for their marvellous and conscientious work and to our excellent cover designer for both books, Irena Czaplicka-Laskowska - irena.laskowska@gmail.com

We are especially grateful to Dr Moisés and Mrs Mimi Lemlij and their family foundation for their very generous financial support that made both CRIC 2023 and CRIC 2024 and the two hard copy publications possible.

ISBN – e-book 978-1-80541-835-1
ISBN – paperback 978-1-80541-836-8

Copyright © 2025, New England Journal of Public Policy https://scholarworks.umb.edu/nejpp/ Requests for permission to reproduce material from this work should contact the ScholarWorks Administrators at: scholarworks@umb.edu

Special Issue: Ending Wars

Editor's Note vii
Padraig O'Malley

Introduction to the Special Issue on Ending Wars xxxvii
John, Lord Alderdice

What Future for Peace in a World Characterized
by Uncertainty and Fear? 1
Cedric de Coning and John, Lord Alderdice

Ending Wars in Times of Uncertainty:
Moral Leadership, Memory, and the Cost of Peace 11
Eva Grosman

Ending War, but Beginning Peace? 21
Alain Tschudin

Play the Players for Winning Peace:
Complexity Analytics with the UK-Ireland
Good Friday Agreement as a Case Study. 39
Bilal M. Ayyub

Gerald Templer's Leadership in the Malayan Emergency
(1948–1960): Its Enduring Relevance 63
Kumar Ramakrishna

Solving Global Problems Requires Global Cohesion 81
*Harvey Whitehouse, John, Lord Alderdice, Carlos Alvarado Quesada,
Peter Gluckman, Hakima El Haité, and Lukas Reinhardt*

Examining Shifts in Group-Based Motivations
for Civil Conflicts in Libya 97
*Michael D. Buhrmester, William B. Swann Jr., Brian McQuinn,
Alexis Everington, Layal Hafid, and Harvey Whitehouse*

How Gaza Sees the 2023–2025 War and
the Future of the Israel-Palestine Conflict 117
Scott Atran, Laura Rodriguez-Gómez, Kamil Yilmaz, and Ángel Gómez

Understanding the Underlying Motivations
of the Russia-Ukraine War 143
John Bell

Subnational Diplomacy as 'Positive Fragmentation':
Our Best Hope for a Peaceful Collapse of the Nation-State? 151
Alison R. Holmes

Political and Psychological Effects of Political Public Art
in Conflict Zones 177
Leora Sotto and Caryl Sibbett

Preventing War as Ending War: the European Network
Remembrance and Solidarity on Channeling Potential
Conflict through Dialogue on History 199
Rafał Rogulski

EDITOR'S NOTE

Padraig O'Malley
University of Massachusetts Boston, padraig.omalley@umb.edu

All wars end, some with a whimper, some with a bang; some with outright victory for one side and peace agreements reflecting the victor's demands; some with ceasefires where uneasy armistices do not address the root causes of the conflict, ensuring that the conflict will most likely reoccur at a future date; some conflicts grind to a halt, 'frozen conflicts,' often the case with intractable intra-state conflicts; and some end in a stalemate—many "proxy" wars during the Cold War fit this category. And some end with negotiations that frequently call for compromises on core issues on both sides. Peace agreements in themselves often do not bring peace and sometimes contain the seeds of the next war.

As we go to press, in the eightieth anniversary year of the end of the Second World War in Europe, more evidence accumulates that the US international order is over. "Everyone is scrambling to work out what will succeed it," the historian Timothy Garton Ash wrote in the *Financial Times*. "A new multi-polar world? Spheres of influence? A worldwide version of the nineteenth century Concert of Europe?"[1]

"By far the most plausible answer, however," he concluded, "is a prolonged and dangerous period of global disorder." And with disorder comes uncertainty, instability, and heightened interstate tensions. The potential for future conflicts rises when the guardrails that theretofore acted as a brake on emerging conflict have collapsed. In Ukraine, Gaza, Sudan, East Congo, and Libya wars are raging; in nuclear armed India and Pakistan's on-and-off wars over Kashmir, an uneasy ceasefire was reached before the April–May 2025 escalation got out of hand.

Padraig O'Malley is the John Joseph Moakley Professor of Peace and Reconciliation at the John W. McCormack Graduate School of Policy and Global Studies, University of Massachusetts Boston.

On June 21, 2025, the United States joined the Iran-Israel war. B-2 bombers unloaded monstrous 30.6-ton bombs (Massive Ordnance Penetrator bombs) to penetrate Iran's nuclear enrichment facility at Fordow, some 300 feet underground. Initial intelligence reports suggested severe damage to the facility and not the "obliteration" President Donald Trump immediately claimed. Also, some 900 pounds of uranium, enriched to 60 percent, is unaccounted for.[2] As with all wars, there will be unintended consequences—a ceasefire without addressing the root causes of the Iran-Israel conflict invariably leads to a resumption of the conflict. Moreover, whatever they are, the strike at Fordow did not fulfill Israeli Prime Minister Benjamin Netanyahu's obsession with eliminating every trace of Iran's nuclear capabilities, including its nuclear knowledge and know-how. Having effectively destroyed Iran's air defenses, giving it absolute control over Iran's air space, Israel can continue to use precision bombs guided by sophisticated AI systems to target any facility and individual in Iran. Iran's missile response during the twelve-day war was spasmodic, mostly intercepted by Israel's Iron Dome, David's Sling, Arrow, and the US's Terminal High Altitude Area Defense (THAAD). With its decimation of Hamas, flattening Gaza, establishing an extended beachhead in the Golan Heights, destroying Syria's air defenses, militarily neutralizing Hezbollah and establishing a security buffer zone in Lebanon, Israel has emerged as the hegemonic power in the Middle East.

In their article, "What Future for Peace in a World Characterized by Uncertainty and Fear?" Cedric de Coning and John, Lord Alderdice refer us to Albert Einstein's statement that "Past thinking and methods did not prevent world wars. Future thinking must prevent wars."

Much of the rules-based order that provided the paradigm for global governance post–World War II, including the institutions of the United Nations (UN), are dysfunctional and do not reflect today's political realities. The US, Russia, and Israel have abandoned the international norms regarding how wars should be conducted. US President Donald Trump with his America First Agenda driving US foreign policy represents not just an abandonment of the rule-based order, but taking a chainsaw to its institutions and agencies. It is as if they never existed.

Across the globe, and in Europe in particular, countries are diverting public resources into security, forging more security alliances, all at a time when the surge of support for far-right parties is undermining the remnants of the liberal democratic order.

It was never more opportune to publish a volume on ending wars and how they end. De Coning and Alderdice call for a new form of thinking and stress the importance of relationship building and systems analysis. Fortunately, there is a rich literature on the subject of how wars have ended, a repository of wisdom from some of the best thinkers of their age that today's diplomats and security elites can draw on to inform their conflict resolution efforts.

Landmark Treaties

Of particular historical note is the landmark Peace of Westphalia in 1648, which ended the Thirty Years' War. It marked a pivotal shift in European warfare and a framework for conflict resolution that has withstood the test of centuries.[3]

The Thirty Years' War (1618–1648) began as a conflict between Protestant and Catholic states within the Holy Roman Empire; it evolved into a continental power struggle involving most major European powers. The Peace of Westphalia established principles that would shape the international state system for centuries to come and retains its relevance in the twenty-first century.

The peace negotiations, which took place in the German cities of Münster and Osnabrück, lasted for four years (1644–1648). The eventual settlement was reached not because one side had achieved decisive military victory, but because all participants had reached a point of exhaustion. The treaties established the principle of state sovereignty, noninterference in the internal affairs of another country, religious tolerance, and a balance of power mechanism designed to prevent any single state from achieving hegemony.

The Peace of Westphalia exemplifies how wars can end through intricate, painstaking, complex multilateral negotiation when no party can achieve its maximal objectives through continued fighting. It also illustrates that how a war ends can establish new normative frameworks that shape subsequent international relations.

It serves as a warning to parties involved in negotiations to end the war in Ukraine, where Trump's impatience to seal a deal ASAP, if not sooner still, overrides how complex these negotiations are. It cannot end well if the US withdraws military support for Ukraine, if they do not address the interests of both Russia and Ukraine, and if they fail to establish a stable political/security order in Europe.

Of note, too, is the Concert of Europe (1815), another pivotal achievement at preserving peace in Europe. Emerging from the tremendous upheaval caused by the French Revolutionary and Napoleonic Wars, the Concert of Europe framework established for nearly a century a relative peace in Europe through consensus-building among the continent's great powers. This system represented a shift from battlefield confrontations to negotiation tables, creating an institutional approach to managing international conflicts that would influence global diplomacy for generations.[4]

The Concert of Europe was born from the urgent need to establish a new political order. After more than two decades of conflict that had redrawn the map of Europe multiple times, the victorious powers sought a system that could prevent such continental catastrophes from recurring. The defeat of Napoleon created both opportunity and necessity for a new approach to international relations among European states. In short, it called for "new thinking."

The foundations of the Concert were laid at the Congress of Vienna, which began in September 1814 and concluded its "Final Act" in June 1815, shortly before Napoleon's final defeat at Waterloo. This gathering brought together representatives from more than 200 European states and principalities under the chairmanship of Austrian statesman Klemens von Metternich. Unlike previous peace settlements, the Congress aimed not merely to restore pre-war boundaries but to reshape Europe's political landscape to ensure lasting stability.[5]

The format of the Congress itself marked a departure from traditional diplomatic practices. Before the Congress of Vienna, international diplomacy typically relied on exchanges of notes between capitals and separate negotiations in different locations—a cumbersome process that required extensive time and travel. By contrast, the Congress format developed by Metternich brought national representatives and stakeholders together in a single city, establishing a template for future international conferences.

However, while more than 200 delegations attended, real decision-making was concentrated among the major powers—Austria, Britain, Russia, Prussia, and later France. These "great powers" negotiated the main terms and then presented them to the wider assembly for ratification.[6] The large number of delegates reflected the complex and fragmented nature of pre-Napoleonic Europe and the Congress's attempt to be inclusive in legitimizing the new European order.

The primary objective of the Concert of Europe, was not unlike the Peace of Westphalia, to maintain a balance of power that would prevent any single state from achieving hegemony. This meant deliberately "resizing" the major powers so they could effectively counterbalance one another while collectively providing security for smaller states. The principle reflected a pragmatic recognition that European peace required managed equilibrium rather than unchecked competition.

The most innovative aspect of the Concert was its emphasis on regular consultation among the great powers. Though the formal "Congress System" envisioned regular meetings, in practice congresses were convened on an ad hoc basis to address specific crises. This principle of diplomatic consultation before unilateral action represented a significant evolution in international relations, establishing norms that would influence diplomacy long after the Concert itself had dissolved.

The formal Congress System began to disintegrate in the 1820s due to disagreements over intervention in revolutionary movements. However, the broader practice of great power consultation continued throughout the nineteenth century, adapting to new challenges like the rise of nationalism. This evolutionary capacity allowed the Concert to remain relevant despite changing European political landscapes.

The unifications of Italy and Germany fundamentally altered the European balance of power that the Concert had been designed to maintain. Prussia's emergence as the dominant German state upset the careful equilibrium established at Vienna, while the decline of the Ottoman Empire created new tensions in Eastern Europe. These structural changes made it increasingly difficult to preserve the Concert's original arrangements.

The most enduring legacy of the Concert was its establishment of principles that would influence future collective security arrangements. The Concert represented the first systematic attempt to create an institutional framework for managing international conflicts through multilateral diplomacy. These innovations influenced how the missions of the post–World War I League of Nations and post–World War II United Nations were defined, making the Concert an important precursor to modern international organizations.

The slow demise of the Concert also raises important questions about the conditions under which international institutions can successfully maintain peace. Its relative success during the nineteenth century reflects the value of flexible frameworks that balance power politics with diplomatic norms. This "rules-based order" of the nineteenth century struggled and ultimately failed to the accommodate fundamental shifts in power, ideology, and nationalism that accompanied the late decades of that century and the opening decades of the twentieth. The post–World War II rules-based order of this century faces a similar collapse.

The twentieth century introduced the concept of *total war* and unconditional surrender in conflicts like the world wars, but it also saw the rise of multilateral peace efforts. World War I's punitive negotiated peace (the Treaty of Versailles) taught the international community a lesson when its failures led to World War II. In contrast, after World War II, the Allied powers took a more reconstructive approach: Germany and Japan were occupied and reformed rather than simply punished, and massive economic aid (the Marshall Plan in Europe) was deployed. US Secretary of State George Marshall understood that the vindictive Versailles approach after World War I had contributed to German impoverishment and the rise of Adolf Hitler. Thus, a key shift was a move from retribution to rehabilitation—helping former adversaries recover, which contributed to a durable peace. Post–World War II saw the creation of institutions like the United Nations to facilitate dialogue and prevent war, reflecting a new understanding that how a war ends should aim at a stable peace, not just victor's justice. In the Iran-Israel-US war the lessons of Versailles should be kept in mind by Israel and the US. They can bomb Iran back to the Stone Age in response to how it might respond to the destruction of the nuclear site at Fordow, target Ayatollah Khamenei, and impose regime change, and ultimately bring a defeated Iran to the negotiating table. Should draconian measures form the basis of a victors' "peace" agreement, the seeds of a future conflict would be sown: Iran would not forget its humiliation.

During the Cold War (1945–1991), direct great-power wars were avoided, but many proxy wars and civil conflicts raged in Asia, Africa, and Latin America. Superpower involvement often prolonged these wars, and many civil wars in this era ended in one side's victory rather than negotiation. However, as the Cold War waned, negotiated settlements became more common. In the 1990s especially there was a major shift: a much larger proportion of conflicts, especially civil wars, ended at the bargaining table rather than on the battlefield.

How Wars End

The conduct of warfare has evolved immeasurably since the nineteenth century but nevertheless, the tools that produced peace settlements in earlier centuries still have relevance in today's super militarized multipolar world. The evolution of warfare reflects changes in technology, the nature of combatants, international norms, and geopolitical dynamics. The patterns of how wars ended have also evolved: military outcomes, diplomatic interventions, economic pressures, and third-party mediation have influenced the end of conflicts across different historical contexts and geographical regions.

A 2022 analysis by The Hague Centre for Strategic Studies examines how and when wars ended in the past and what they can tell us about war termination.[7]

> In the period 1946–2005, 63 interstate wars have been recorded globally. Only about one fifth (21%) had a decisive outcome in which one party ended up as the victor and the other as the loser (i.e., total victory/defeat). Almost one third (30%) of these wars ended in a ceasefire, while only one sixth (16%) concluded with a peace agreement. The remaining cases had an outcome without either clear victory/defeat nor any type of peace settlement.
>
> Worryingly, of the negotiated peace agreements between 1975 and 2018 almost four out of ten (37%) broke down following a reignition of the war between the same parties. Moreover, more than three quarters (76%) of the peace agreements that broke down did so within two years, 12% lasted for two to five years, and another 12% lasted for more than five years but eventually broke down. Wars that end in a tie as opposed to a decisive victory, where both sides share an acrimonious history, and where one side's existence is threatened, are significantly more likely to be repeated.[8]

"An initial ceasefire agreement between Russia and Ukraine," HCSS warns, "does not mean an end to the war."[9]

Monica Toft's research for *Securing the Peace: The Durable Settlement of Civil Wars* found that while negotiated settlements ended only a handful of civil wars (intra state) between 1940 and 1989, military victory was the dominant mode of ending civil wars, for three-fourths of such wars up to the 1980s. By the 1990s negotiated settlements surpassed military victories, ending 42 percent of all civil wars.[10] Her data reveals that two-thirds of all negotiated settlements occurred during the 1990s.

Other scholars have noted similar trends. In the post–Cold War period, more than half of all insurgencies have been settled through negotiation,[11] and some studies suggest that as much as 50 percent of civil wars ended at the peace table during the 1990s, representing a huge increase over the broad historical average.[12]

These trends were attributable to several factors: the end of superpower proxy competition made compromise more feasible, and international norms evolved to favor mediation and peace processes. For instance, civil wars in El Salvador, Mozambique, and Cambodia were all resolved by peace agreements in the early 1990s, each with extensive United Nations mediation and peacekeeping roles.

In interstate conflicts however, formal peace treaties have become less common in recent decades—many wars now end with ceasefires or informal accords. Tanisha M. Fazal's study *The Demise of Peace Treaties in Interstate War* concluded that since 1950 the rate of interstate wars ending with a signed peace treaty has declined sharply: only about 15 percent of wars since 1950 have concluded with a formal peace treaty; most others ended via ceasefire or unilateral withdrawal without a comprehensive treaty. Approximately 75 percent of nineteenth-century interstate wars ended with formal peace treaties; this figure dropped to 40 percent across the entire twentieth century.[13]

These findings demonstrate a reversal in what was once a standard diplomatic practice for centuries. Fazal notes that "The conclusion of peace treaties following war was a norm of international politics for millennia. Since approximately 1950, however, the rate at which interstate wars have ended with a formal peace treaty has declined dramatically."[14]

Fazal argues that the costs of concluding formal peace treaties have risen significantly with the development of the modern canon of international laws of war. She contends that "states today prefer to avoid admitting to a state of war and risk placing their leaders and soldiers at risk of punishment for any violations of the law of war."[15] Paradoxically, these trends reflect how the evolving international legal framework has made ending wars more difficult despite strengthening humanitarian protections.

Another notable modern trend is the role of international and regional organizations in bringing civil wars to an end. Mediation and peacekeeping missions became far more prevalent after the Cold War. For example, the Dayton Accords of 1995 that ended the Bosnian War were brokered by the United States and backed by NATO peacekeepers to enforce the terms, illustrating how external actors can help craft and uphold a peace deal. Likewise, the Northern Ireland conflict (The Troubles) was settled in 1998 by the Good Friday Agreement, which was achieved through intensive multi-party negotiations with support from outside facilitators, especially the UK, the Republic of Ireland, the US, and the EU. In many contemporary conflicts, the United Nations, the African Union, or other bodies sponsor peace talks and monitor ceasefires, something that was much rarer in earlier centuries. This shift underscores an increasingly globalized approach to ending wars—treating civil conflicts not just as domestic issues but as threats to international peace that warrant collective conflict resolution efforts. However, in the opening decades of the twenty-first century, many of these global institutions are either not working or simply ignored by warring protagonists.

In his introductory article "Introduction to the Special Issue on Ending Wars," John, Lord Alderdice notes that,

> after the relatively peaceful period after World War II, there has been a serious deterioration in global peacefulness, as evidenced by the 2025 Global Peace Index (GPI) published by the Institute for Economics & Peace (IEP).[16] IEP colleagues have been monitoring and publishing objective measures of the level of peacefulness for nearly two decades. This nineteenth report covers 163 independent states and territories containing some 99.7 percent of the world's population and rates their various levels of peacefulness. The GPI is the world's leading measure of global peacefulness and for the sixth year in a row that measure has deteriorated. The average country score on the GPI has also deteriorated for thirteen of the last seventeen years and has not improved on average in any year since 2013.

The Theorists

A.F.K. Organski's Power Transition Theory, expounded in *World Politics* (1958) provided a framework for understanding the conditions under which major wars begin and end. Developed during the Cold War when the US and the Soviet Union were locked in a geopolitical contest to achieve global supremacy, Organski's theory challenged the traditional balance of power view. He argued that peace is best preserved not when power is evenly distributed among states, but when there is a clear hierarchy, with one dominant state holding a preponderance of power.[17] Organski envisioned the global order as a pyramid, with a dominant state at the top, followed by great, middle, and small powers.

Peace is most likely preserved when the dominant state has a clear advantage in power. Wars are most likely when a rapidly rising power, dissatisfied with the status quo, reaches near-equal strength with the dominant state and seeks to revise the international order.[18]

According to Organski, major wars typically end with a decisive outcome that establishes a new hierarchy. If the challenger wins, a new dominant power emerges and sets the terms of the postwar order. If the dominant power prevails, the existing order is reinforced and peace is restored until the next significant shift in relative power.[19]

"Preponderance by the dominant power ensures peace among great powers, while a balance of power may lead to either conflict or peace." Jacek Kugler and Organski write. "Clearly, the necessary but not sufficient conditions for major war emerge only in the rare instances when power parity is accompanied by a challenger overtaking a dominant nation."[20] The theory suggests that negotiated settlements are less likely to produce lasting peace if parity and dissatisfaction persist, as these conditions are inherently unstable.[21] Organski's theory is a variation of Thucydides' Trap—when a rising power threatens a dominant power (Sparta and Athens during the Peloponnesian Wars, the Soviet Union and the US post–World War II, and China and the US today).

William Zartman pioneered the concept of "ripeness"—that conflicts are most likely to end when they reach a "mutually hurting stalemate" (MHS)—a situation where all parties recognize that they cannot achieve their objectives through continued fighting and that the costs of war have become unbearable.[22] This creates a moment ripe for negotiation and settlement.

In "Ripeness: The Hurting Stalemate and Beyond" (2000) Zartman identifies two key elements that make conflict ripe for resolution:[23] A mutually hurting stalemate is one where all parties recognize that they cannot achieve victory through continued unilateral action, and that persisting in the conflict will be painful and costly for everyone involved. The conflict reaches a deadlock where escalation is no longer beneficial, and both sides are suffering losses (though not necessarily equally or for the same reasons). In addition to the stalemate parties must perceive that a negotiated solution is possible—a "way out" of the impasse. This does not require a specific solution to be identified in advance, but rather a shared sense that negotiation could lead to an acceptable outcome and that the other side is also willing to search for a solution.

Zartman emphasizes that ripeness is a necessary but not sufficient condition for negotiations to begin. The presence of a ripe moment does not guarantee that negotiations will occur or succeed; it simply means that the situation is conducive to resolution if seized by the parties or a mediator. Ripeness is not self-fulfilling—it must be recognized and acted upon.

Perceptions of a mutually hurting stalemate and a way out can be influenced by objective events such as military stalemates or impending catastrophes but ultimately depends on the subjective perceptions of the parties involved. Mediators can play a crucial role in helping parties recognize when a conflict is ripe for resolution and encourage them to take advantage of the opportunity.

In short, successful conflict resolution depends as much on timing and the psychological readiness of the parties as on the substance of any proposed solution.

Negotiations are most likely to succeed when parties are trapped in a mutually hurting stalemate and see a way out through negotiation.

The rationalist approach, articulated most prominently by James Fearon, suggests that wars end when the costs of continuing to fight exceed the expected benefits. In "Rationalist Explanations for War," he addresses the question of why rational actors, who should prefer to avoid the costs and risks of war, sometimes fail to reach peaceful settlements and instead resort to conflict.[24] Influenced by Clausewitz's analysis of how wars end, Fearson's analysis is grounded in the bargaining model of war. This model sees war as a bargaining process over disputed issues. Wars end, he concludes, when the underlying causes that prevented a pre-war bargain—uncertainty, commitment problems, or indivisibility—are resolved. (Commitment problems refer to uncertainty over whether adversaries will fully commit to implementing settlements reached; indivisibility refers to issues that cannot be split, leaving no room for compromise. Both can explain why rational states might still end up at war, despite the existence of mutually preferable bargains.) The process of war itself often provides the information or shifts in power needed to enable a negotiated settlement or impose a unilateral outcome.[25]

Fearon argues that, in theory, there is always a range of possible settlements ("bargaining range") that both sides should prefer to the costly alternative of fighting. War should end when the two sides can agree on a settlement within this range. The puzzle is why, if such settlements exist, wars ever occur or persist.

He explains the three main obstacles that can prevent rational actors from reaching a bargain and thus prolong or prevent the end of war: a) States may have private information about their own capabilities or resolve and incentives to misrepresent this information, leading to miscalculations and failed bargaining. War may end when this uncertainty is resolved, often through the costly process of fighting, which reveals true capabilities or resolve. b) Even if a bargain is available, one or both sides may not trust the other to stick to the deal, especially when future shifts in power are expected. Wars may end only when these commitment problems are overcome, often through decisive shifts in power, external guarantees, or the defeat of one side. c) If the issue at stake cannot be divided or compromised upon, bargaining may fail. However, Fearon notes this is rare, as most issues can be made divisible through side payments or creative negotiation. According to Fearon, wars end when one or more of these obstacles is removed.

Dan Reiter's book *How Wars End* builds upon and extends the rationalist bargaining framework of war articulated by Fearson.[26] Reiter identifies two principal factors that determine how wars end: a) Information and uncertainty: Wars begin partly because states are uncertain about each other's military capabilities. As fighting progresses, this information is revealed, potentially allowing for rational settlements when states realize either that defeat is likely or that victory is unnecessary. b) Commitment problems: Even when both sides have sufficient information to reach a settlement, wars may continue if one side fears the other will not honor peace agreements in the future. This credibility deficit can drive conflicts toward absolute victory rather than negotiated settlements.

Reiter argues that commitment problems play a far more significant role in extending wars than previously recognized, demonstrating that states often continue fighting not because they lack information about their opponent's capabilities, but because they cannot trust their opponent to adhere to peace terms.

At its core, Reiter's theory suggests that war termination requires a rebalancing of cost-benefit analysis by the belligerents. When the costs of continuing to fight exceed the benefits that might be gained through victory and when the parties can trust each other to honor agreements-wars can end through negotiation. Otherwise, wars tend to continue until one side achieves a decisive victory that eliminates concerns about future commitment problems. Hence, Ukraine's core demand: a peace agreement with Russia must have ironclad security guarantees to forestall future Russian aggression. Hence, too, in the Iran-Israel War, Israel's press for total victory.

Constructivist perspectives emphasize the role of norms, ideas, and identity in shaping how wars end. Martha Finnemore and Kathryn Sikkink, in their 1998 article "International Norm Dynamics and Political Change," provided a framework for understanding how norms shape state behavior during conflicts, including mechanisms that could lead to conflict de-escalation or resolution.[27]

The article describes the "life cycle of norms," which explains how norms such as humanitarian intervention, laws of war, and bans on specific weapons become established and influence state behavior. 'Norm emergence' can happen when advocacy by transnational actors (e.g., the International Committee of the Red Cross, International Criminal Court) can pressure states to adopt new rules of war, such as the Geneva Conventions. A 'norm cascade' emerges when states adopt norms due to socialization pressures, redefining their identities as members of an international community. This process can lead to shifts in conflict behavior, such as the 1997 Ottawa Treaty banning landmines. And finally, 'norm internalization': over time, norms become taken-for-granted, influencing how states perceive "appropriate" conduct even in war.

The Practitioners

Carl von Clausewitz (1780–1831), a Prussian general, argued in *On War* (1832) that war is not an isolated act but always subordinate to political purpose: "war is nothing but a continuation of policy with other means" and that "in essentials that intercourse [politics] continues, irrespective of the means it employs."[28] Thus, the end of war is not simply a matter of military victory but of achieving the political objectives for which the war was fought. The transition from war to peace is shaped by the same political logic that started the conflict.

Clausewitz also acknowledged that even decisive military victories do not always produce lasting peace, that war rarely produces permanent results, and that the end of one war may plant the seeds for another. He emphasized that the political objectives and considerations that lead to war continue to shape its conduct and its conclusion. "The main lines along which military events progress," he wrote, "are political lines that continue throughout the war into the subsequent peace," meaning that the political underpinnings of the war do not cease with the outbreak of hostilities, nor do they end abruptly with military victory or defeat.[29]

Clausewitz identified several practical conditions under which wars end; a) Breaking the enemy's will: War does not truly end until the enemy's will to resist is broken. This could mean compelling the enemy government and its allies to seek peace or making the population submit. Even after occupying territory and destroying enemy forces, animosity and the potential for renewed hostilities can persist unless the enemy is decisively overcome. b) Wars might end not only through the total defeat of one side but when continued resistance becomes either improbable or too costly to bear. If one side demonstrates to the other that victory is unlikely or that the price of continuing the fight is unacceptable, this can force a move toward peace treaties and political settlement. Here, the formal conclusion of war typically comes with a peace treaty, which serves to extinguish ongoing conflict and stabilize relations, even if underlying tensions may persist. Clausewitz noted, however, that not every war leads to a final or permanent settlement—hostilities can resume if the underlying issues are not resolved.[30] The Oslo Accords (1993), intended to be the first step on the path to Palestinian statehood are a case in point.

Otto von Bismarck (1815–1898), the "Iron Chancellor" who orchestrated German unification in 1871 wrote frequently about how wars end. He warned, "Woe to the leader whose arguments at the end of a war are not as plausible as they were at the beginning."[31] He argued that the justifications for initiating conflict must withstand the public scrutiny that follows its conclusion.

Bismarck's cautioned against ill-considered wars where there is a disconnect between decision-makers and those who bear war's burden. "It is easy for a statesman in his office or his chamber to blow the trumpet with the breath of popularity and all the time to sit warming himself by his fireside," he wrote, "while he leaves it to the rifleman, who lies bleeding on the snow, whether his system attains victory and glory."[32]

Will war advocates, he asked, "have the courage to go to the peasant by the ashes of his cottage, to the cripple, to the childless father, and say: 'You have suffered much, but rejoice with us, the Union is saved.'"[33] Bismarck was acutely aware of war's human toll and his belief that leaders must justify this sacrifice with meaningful outcomes.

Bismarck approached warfare with strategic vision. According to his biographer, the historian Jonathan Steinberg, "In international relations, [this] meant absolutely no emotional commitment to any of the actors. Diplomacy should, he believed, deal with realities, calculations of probabilities, assessing the inevitable missteps and sudden lurches by the other actors, states, and their statesmen. The chessboard could be overseen and it suited Bismarck's peculiar genius for politics to maintain in his head multiple possible moves by adversaries...He had his goals in mind and achieved them. He was and remained to the end master of the finely tuned game of diplomacy."[34] This deliberate approach ensured that Prussia's wars served specific purposes rather than ambiguous or emotional causes.

In recent times, models of how wars end continue to incorporate much of both Von Clausewitz's and Bismarck's thinking.

George F. Kennan (1904–2005), the architect of Cold War containment policy, articulated a vision of how conflicts conclude, emphasizing non-military strategies, internal systemic pressures, and the dangers of escalation. Kennan's 1947 *Foreign Affairs* article, "The Source of Soviet Conduct" (published under the pseudonym "X") posited that sustained containment of Soviet influence would "promote tendencies which must eventually find their outlet in either the breakup or the gradual mellowing of Soviet power."[35] He rejected direct military confrontation in favor of political, economic, and psychological pressure. By countering Soviet expansionist efforts at strategic points, Kennan argued that the US could exhaust the USSR's ideological and institutional coherence, leading to internal reform or collapse.

His analysis drew from historical precedents of imperial overreach, noting that no regime—no matter how outwardly formidable—could indefinitely withstand the strain of systemic contradictions. For the Soviets, these included the inefficiencies of centralized planning, nationalist dissent in Eastern Europe, and the moral bankruptcy of Marxist-Leninism.[36] Kennan predicted that containment would exacerbate these weaknesses, forcing either liberalization or dissolution—a prophecy fulfilled in 1991 with the USSR's collapse.

Kennan opposed conflating containment with militarization. In his view, wars often spiral beyond their original objectives, as seen in his critique of US interventions: "War has a momentum of its own and carries you away from all thoughtful intentions... You never know where you are going to end."[37] He warned that military solutions risked hardening adversarial stances, as demonstrated by NATO's expansion and the rearmament of West Germany, which he believed unnecessarily provoked Soviet insecurities.[38] He opposed the Vietnam War, and at close to 100 years of age argued vociferously against the Iraq War, writing that the 2003 invasion of Iraq "bore no relation to the post 9/11 war on terrorism" and criticized efforts by the Bush administration to link Saddam Hussein with al-Qaeda as "pathetically unsupportive and unreliable."[39]

Central to Kennan's strategy was the use of "measures short of war"—economic aid (e.g., the Marshall Plan), cultural diplomacy, and covert operations—to undermine adversaries without direct combat. He advocated for policies that allowed hostile regimes to "save face," believing that rigid ultimatums only fueled resistance. For instance, he later argued that offering the Soviets a neutral, unified Germany in the 1950s might have eased tensions and accelerated reform.[40]

Kennan also emphasized the importance of understanding an adversary's historical and psychological drivers. His "Long Telegram" attributed Soviet aggression to a mix of Marxist ideology, Russian imperial traditions, and Stalin's personal paranoia—factors requiring tailored responses rather than blanket militarization.[41] By addressing root insecurities (e.g., through economic stabilization in Western Europe), the US could reduce the appeal of Soviet expansionism.[42]

Kennan tied the success of containment to America's moral and institutional vitality. He argued that defeating authoritarianism required demonstrating the superiority of democratic values through domestic progress: "The United States need only measure up to its own best traditions" to repel Soviet influence.[43] Corruption, inequality, or social fragmentation, he warned, would undermine global credibility and embolden adversaries. In many respects he advocated a foreign policy that presaged Joe Nye's concept of "soft power," in the 1980s that became the bedrock of US foreign policy until Donald Trump took an axe to the institutions and agencies that underpinned it.

Henry Kissinger (1923–2023) as National Security Adviser and later Secretary of State under Presidents Nixon and Ford, pioneered the policy of détente, a pragmatic strategy that sought to manage tensions with the USSR through a combination of cooperation and competition rather than confrontation.[44] His theory about how wars end emphasized strategic foresight, political realities, and the paramount importance of planning for conclusion before engaging in conflict.

He observed that "the test of policy is how it ends, not how it begins," reflecting his belief that political leaders often enter conflicts without adequate consideration of exit strategies.[45] In this regard, Kissinger, born Germany, echoed Bismarck. This principle emerged from his analysis of American military interventions, where he noted that "in my life, I have seen four wars begun with great enthusiasm and public support, all of which we did not know how to end and from three of which we withdrew unilaterally."[46] These wars, he concluded, ended in "national trauma," and that "America struggles to define the relationship between its power (still vast) and its principles."[47]

His analysis suggests that American foreign policy makers consistently fail to develop comprehensive strategies for determining when its wars should end, leading to prolonged entanglements that ultimately undermine both military objectives and domestic political stability. The lesson Kissinger drew was that successful wartime leadership required not just the ability to wage war effectively, but the wisdom to conclude it on favorable terms.

Kissinger's views on war endings were shaped by his academic research at Harvard, studying power dynamics in international relations, and by America's experience in Vietnam. He used the term "realpolitik" to describe a policy that emphasizes practical considerations over ideological principles or moral considerations.[48]

His Soviet policy emerged from his rejection of what he viewed as American foreign policy's excessive moralism. Rather than approaching the Soviet Union through the lens of anti-Communist ideology, Kissinger advocated for a realist framework that recognized the USSR as a rival superpower requiring careful management rather than simple opposition.[49] During the 1970s this approach represented a transformation in Cold War diplomacy, reshaping the strategic landscape between the Soviet Union and the United States. His realpolitik framework led to arms control agreements and a temporary stabilization of the nuclear balance of power.[50]

As the leading US negotiator at the Paris Peace talks that ended American involvement in Vietnam, Kissinger's interactions with North Vietnamese representative Le Duc Tho encapsulated the complexity of transitioning from military conflict to political settlement.[51] The process itself required orchestrating "a complex negotiation campaign with multiple fronts: North Vietnam, the US public and Congress, China, the USSR, West Germany, and South Vietnam."[52]

The breakthrough in talks came when both sides recognized that they could separate the political and military terms of an armistice and negotiate an agreement that addressed the latter while leaving longer-term political questions for future resolution.[53] This separation of immediate and ultimate objectives became a hallmark of Kissinger's diplomatic approach.

The eventual signing of the Paris Peace Accords in January 1973 represented both the possibilities and limitations of negotiated war endings. While the agreement successfully ended direct American military involvement, it only "held for about two years before collapsing in the wake of Watergate."[54] TV images of US personnel on the embassy rooftop scrambling to get aboard the last helicopter to leave Saigon before the Viet Cong breached the embassy compound encapsulated America's humiliation, the one thing Kissinger had hoped to avoid. Successful war termination, he concluded, required not just reaching agreements but ensuring their long-term sustainability through continued political commitment and strategic engagement.

Central to Kissinger's understanding of war's end was his recognition that modern conflicts are fundamentally political rather than purely military endeavors, here echoing von Clausewitz, another German. His analysis of the Vietnam War exemplified this perspective. "We fought a military war; our opponents fought a political one." he said. "We sought physical attrition; our opponents aimed for our psychological exhaustion. In the process we lost sight of one of the cardinal maxims of guerrilla war: the guerrilla wins if he does not lose. The conventional army loses if it does not win. The North Vietnamese used their armed forces the way a bullfighter uses his cape—to keep us lunging in areas of marginal political importance."[55]

Hence the challenge facing superior military forces when confronting non-state actors, where the mere ability to continue fighting represents a form of victory for the weaker party—the challenge facing Israel in the current Gaza war. Both Israeli and

US intelligence estimate that for every Hamas member killed, another has stepped up to take his place.[56]

Kissinger argued that conventional military superiority did not automatically translate into political success, and that achieving sustainable conclusions to conflicts required understanding the political objectives and constraints of all parties involved.[57]

His experience during the Vietnam era convinced him that domestic political considerations played a crucial role in determining how wars end, particularly in democratic societies. Thus, the importance of maintaining domestic consensus throughout military engagements. He argued that "the most important thing we need in the current situation [the Afghan War during the Obama administration] is, whatever disagreements there may be on tactics, that the legitimacy of the war itself does not become a subject of controversy."[58]

The erosion of public support for military interventions created what Kissinger saw as a fundamental constraint on American strategic options. When wars have become domestically controversial, political leaders have faced increasing pressure to conclude conflicts quickly, often on less favorable terms than might otherwise be achievable. This dynamic has created a strategic vulnerability that adversaries could exploit by prolonging conflicts until domestic pressure forced American withdrawal.

Throughout his long life, Kissinger, who lived to be 100, continued to address contemporary conflicts. In the opening months of the Russia-Ukraine conflict, he argued that "negotiations need to begin in the next two months before it creates upheavals and tensions that will not be easily overcome," advocating for a return to "the status quo ante" rather than pursuing "a new war against Russia itself."[59] In essence, Ukraine would have to concede some territory. His position reflected his consistent emphasis on avoiding conflicts that lacked clear termination strategies. He argued that "there are three possible outcomes to this war," and warned that pursuing maximalist objectives could lead to uncontrolled escalation.[60]

Zbigniew Brzezinski, a Polish American who was National Security Advisor to President Jimmy Carter (1924–2024), brought his own countervailing theories on how wars should end to the job. He strongly opposed the Nixon-Kissinger policy of over reliance on détente, and advocated a hardline, strategic, and multifaceted approach for dealing with the Soviet Union. It called for exploiting the USSR's vulnerabilities, leveraging proxy conflicts, manipulating geopolitical dynamics to force it into unsustainable positions, combining containment with ideological competition, and selective engagement. He also viewed the promotion of human rights as a powerful tool to put the Soviet Union on the ideological defensive, arguing that highlighting American freedoms and the USSR's internal weaknesses could mobilize global support.

Brzezinski viewed ending war through the lens of systemic competition, arguing that conflicts conclude when one side's political or economic infrastructure collapses under the weight of its contradictions. In *The Grand Chessboard* (1997), he argued that the Soviet Union's demise resulted not from military defeat but from its inability to adapt to the "technetronic era."[61] This analysis framed ending a war as a process of accelerating an enemy's internal decay rather than achieving traditional military objectives.

After the Soviet bloc disintegrated in 1991, Brzezinski attributed its collapse to this principle: "The Cold War came to an end because the Soviets lost… Their system could not compete economically or politically."[62] He rejected the notion of a "victory" in conventional terms, instead emphasizing the cumulative impact of ideological, economic, and military pressure over decades.[63]

Brzezinski's most explicit articulation of how to end a war emerged from his orchestration of US support for Afghan mujahideen during the Soviet-Afghan War. In a 1998 interview with *Le Nouvel Observateur*, he admitted to having told President Carter: "We now have the opportunity of giving to the USSR its Vietnam War… [The conflict] brought about the demoralization and finally the breakup of the Soviet empire."[64] This statement encapsulates his belief in proxy warfare as a tool for inducing systemic collapse. The US began funneling covert aid to the mujahideen in July 1979—six months before the Soviet invasion. "[On] July 3, 1979," he recalled, "President Carter signed the first directive for secret aid to the opponents of the pro-Soviet regime in Kabul. And that very day, I wrote a note to the president in which I explained to him that in my opinion this aid was going to induce a Soviet military intervention."[65]

This strategy relied on asymmetric warfare: the mujahideen exploiting terrain to negate Soviet conventional superiority, and global perception management, framing the conflict as a Soviet "quagmire" to undermine Moscow's international standing and increasing the strain on its faltering economy.[66]

Brzezinski dismissed concerns about arming Islamist militants, arguing that the geopolitical payoff—the Soviet Union's dissolution—justified the means: "What is more important in world history? The Taliban or the collapse of the Soviet empire?"[67] Yet, there were lasting unintended consequences. Osama Bin Laden's road to 9/11 began with his radicalization in Afghanistan where he played an active role in the mujahideen insurgency, and 9/11 transformed the United States and led to the misbegotten Iraq War that followed, including an ongoing war on terror. (Brzezinski regarded the American response to 9/11 as an overreaction giving Osama Bin Laden a major tactical victory, and diverting US attention from other more pressing security concerns. He opposed the Iraq War, arguing not to repeat the counterinsurgency and state building failures of Vietnam in Iraq.)[68]

Brzezinski viewed arms control agreements not as endpoints but as tools for managing conflicts toward favorable conclusions. During the strategic arms limitation talks (SALT II), he advocated for treaties that would "stabilize the strategic competition" while maintaining US technological advantages. His approach combined verifiable limitations on destabilizing weapons systems (e.g., anti-ballistic missiles) and linkage strategies tying arms control progress to restraining Soviet action in conflicts in the developing world.

He emphasized narrative control as critical to managing the termination of a war. During the rise of the Polish Solidarity movement (1980–81), he advised President Carter to publicly support dissidents while privately warning Soviet leaders against intervention. When the Soviet Union threatened intervention in Poland in 1980, Brzezinski coordinated an international response, mobilizing global opinion and warning Moscow of severe diplomatic and economic consequences.[69]

This dual-track approach aimed to legitimize opposition movements as expressions of popular will, frame Soviet repression as morally indefensible, and exploit ideological contradictions within Marxist-Leninist regimes.

He later credited this strategy with making Poland the "first domino" in communism's collapse, demonstrating how narrative warfare could achieve outcomes unattainable through physical force. Even after the collapse of the Soviet Union, he remained deeply skeptical about the possibility of the Soviet Union (and later Russia) transitioning to a Western-style democracy, warning the West to remain cautious and prepared for assertive Russian behavior.[70] "It cannot be stressed enough," he wrote in 2012, "that without Ukraine, Russia ceases to be an empire, but with Ukraine suborned and then subordinated, Russia automatically becomes an empire."[71]

Recurring Themes

Despite the diverse ways wars can end, several recurring themes emerge across history. These themes highlight critical lessons about the war-to-peace transition:

Ending Fighting vs. Building Peace

A core lesson is that ending a war is not the same as securing a lasting peace. History is replete with "ended" wars that soon reignited because the underlying issues were left unresolved. Many peace agreements only offer a temporary pause in violence. For example, the armistice that halted World War I did stop the fighting, but the subsequent peace terms failed to settle grievances or ensure a just order, leading to World War II two decades later. If a treaty or settlement does not tackle core political and ethnic disputes, or if it humiliates one side, it may merely postpone conflict. The "how" a war ends and conflict resolution must go hand in hand.

The Terms of Peace Matter

The nature of the settlement—whether magnanimous or punitive, inclusive or one-sided—profoundly affects postwar stability. A punitive peace that imposes harsh penalties on the loser can breed long-term bitterness (as with Versailles in 1919, which fueled German resentment and the rise of fascism). By contrast, a conciliatory approach that respects the enemy's basic dignity and addresses their concerns can foster durable peace. A peace agreement should seek a balance of justice and reconciliation. Victors who are too harsh risk sowing the seeds of the next war, while a fair peace that all sides can accept creates a stronger foundation for lasting stability.

"Ripeness" and Willingness to End War

This pattern has appeared from ancient wars to modern ones. For instance, the protracted Iran–Iraq War in the 1980s only ended after eight brutal years once both regimes realized neither could win a decisive victory and international pressure mounted. The lesson is that timing and context are crucial: peace deals typically emerge only when the parties are ready to accept them. Effective diplomacy may help hasten this recognition by highlighting the painful stalemate and offering a face-saving way out.

The Role of External Actors

A frequent theme in modern war endings is the influence of third-party mediators and guarantors. International involvement can be decisive in bringing combatants to the table and in ensuring agreements stick. Neutral mediators can broker compromises that the parties alone could not. For example, US mediation was critical in achieving the Camp David Accords (1978) that ended open hostilities between Egypt and Israel. Similarly, the Dayton peace conference ending the Bosnian War was orchestrated by great-power diplomats and enforced by NATO troops. United Nations peacekeepers have supervised many ceasefires and elections (as in Cambodia in 1993 or Liberia in 2003), providing security guarantees that build trust among former enemies. The involvement of respected external actors can lend credibility to a peace process, but it also matters that these actors remain even-handed and committed. The lesson here is that peacebuilding often requires international support, especially in civil wars where the combatants need security assurances that neither side will exploit the peace to dominate the other. However, outside powers must also respect local ownership of peace; externally imposed deals can fail if they lack local legitimacy.

No One-Size-Fits-All Outcome

History demonstrates that there is no single "right" way for a war to end—victory, partition, power-sharing, and other outcomes have all worked in some cases and failed in others. Decisive military victory can create a clear endpoint (as in World War II or the Sri Lankan Civil War's end in 2009 with the Sinhalese government's victory over the Tamils; such outcomes often correlate with a lower risk of immediate recurrence of that same conflict). Yet victory can come at a high human cost and may introduce new grievances (a victor's domination can spark insurgencies). Negotiated settlements, on the other hand, can save lives and address some root issues, but they carry the risk of unraveling if parties sign under duress or use talks to re-arm. Some studies of civil wars find that conflicts ending in negotiated peace have been more prone to relapse than those ending in outright victory, highlighting the fragility of compromise if not buttressed by strong institutions.[72]

Whether through victory or negotiation, what ultimately counts is ensuring that the war's end removes (or at least sufficiently mitigates) the causes of war and creates incentives to maintain peace. In practice, this means postwar power arrangements must be perceived as legitimate and secure by all key stakeholders.

In modern times, how a war ends is seen not as just an end but as a transition—from war to peace—that must be managed. International law has evolved to support this, from the Geneva Conventions (to humanely manage surrender and treatment of combatants) to UN peacebuilding commissions. Yet, as conflicts in the twenty-first century like Syria until 2025, Yemen, East Congo, Sudan, Israel-Palestine, Ukraine-Russia, and Israel-Iran show, achieving a definitive end to war is difficult when interests are complex and external actors are involved. Understanding how wars have ended—through negotiated settlements, territorial concessions, military defeat, or stalemate—is crucial, because the way a war ends can profoundly influence the peace that follows. Each ending carries lessons for future peacemakers: the importance of inclusive dialogue, the need for magnanimity in victory, and the value of addressing grievances to prevent the cycle of war from repeating.

The articles in this issue of the journal complement the previous issue, *The Changing Character of War and Peacemaking*.

Notes

[1] Timothy Garton Ash, "Brace for Disorder as the Great Power Shifts Begin," *Financial Times*, May 9, 2025, https://www.ft.com/content/e45091ae-31c7-46b2-95bb-b8197655cd33.

[2] David E. Sanger, "Officials Concede They Don't Know the Fate of Iran's Uranium Stockpile," *New York Times*, June 22, 2025, https://www.nytimes.com/2025/06/22/us/politics/iran-uranium-stockpile-whereabouts.html.
Jim Sciutto, Katie Bo Lillis, and Natasha Bertrand, "New Intelligence Suggests Israel Is Preparing Possible Strike on Iranian Nuclear Facilities, US Officials Say," *CNN*, May 20, 2025, https://www.cnn.com/2025/05/20/politics/intelligence-israel-possible-strike-iran-nuclear-facilities.

[3] Derek Croxton, "The Peace of Westphalia of 1648 and the Origins of Sovereignty," *The International History Review* 21, no. 3 (1999): 569–91, https://doi.org/10.1080/07075332.1999.9640869.

[4] *Britannica*, "Concert of Europe," last updated December 7, 2023, https://www.britannica.com/event/Concert-of-Europe.

[5] More than 200 states, princely houses, and other entities were present at the Congress of Vienna because, prior to the Napoleonic Wars, Europe was a patchwork of many small states, principalities, free cities, ecclesiastical territories, and other political units, especially within the former Holy Roman Empire. The Congress aimed to redraw the map of Europe and restore the political order disrupted by Napoleon, so virtually every state in Europe, regardless of size, sent a delegation to protect its interests and claim its rights. In addition to sovereign states, there were also representatives from cities, corporations, religious organizations (such as abbeys), and special

interest groups. "The Congress of Vienna," in *Boundless World History* (Lumen Learning, n.d.), http://courses.lumenlearning.com/tc3-boundless-worldhistory/chapter/the-congress-of-vienna/; Britannica, "The Congress of Vienna and the Hundred Days," last updated June 11, 2025, https://www.britannica.com/event/Napoleonic-Wars/The-Congress-of-Vienna-and-the-Hundred-Days.

[6] Randall Lesaffer, "The Congress of Vienna (1814–1815)," Oxford Public International Law, https://opil.ouplaw.com/page/477.

[7] Tim Sweijs and Mattia Bertolini, "How Wars End: War Terminations; Insights for the Russia-Ukraine War," Hague Center for Strategic Studies, 2022, https://hcss.nl/wp-content/uploads/2022/05/How-Wars-End-HCSS-2022.pdf.

[8] Ibid., 2.

[9] Ibid., 2.

[10] Monica Duffy Toft, *Securing the Peace: The Durable Settlement of Civil Wars* (Princeton University Press, 2010); Toft, "Peace Through Victory: The Durable Settlement of Civil Wars," paper presented at the 99th annual meeting of the American Political Science Association, Philadelphia, August 2003; Monica Duffy Toft, "Peace Through Security: Making Negotiated Settlements Stick," https://www3.carleton.ca/csds/docs/Toft%20PTS.pdf.

[11] Colin P. Clarke and Christopher Paul, "From Stalemate to Settlement: Lessons for Afghanistan from Historical Insurgencies That Have Been Resolved Through Negotiations," RAND National Defense Research Institute, 2014, https://www.rand.org/content/dam/rand/pubs/research_reports/RR400/RR469/RAND_RR469.pdf.

[12] Timothy D. Sisk, "Peacemaking in Civil Wars: Obstacles, Options, and Opportunities," working paper (Joan B. Kroc Institute for International Peace Studies, March 2001), https://ciaotest.cc.columbia.edu/wps/sit02/.

[13] Tanisha M. Fazal, "The Demise of Peace Treaties in Interstate War," *International Organization* 67, no. 4 (2013): 695–724, https://doi.org/10.1017/S0020818313000246.

[14] Ibid, 695–724.

[15] Ibid, 695.

[16] Institute for Economics & Peace, *Global Peace Index 2025: Identifying and Measuring the Factors that Drive Peace* (IEP, 2025), available from http://visionofhumanity.org/resources.

[17] A. F. K. Organski, *World Politics* (Alfred A. Knopf, 1958). See also Organski, *The Stages of Political Development* (Alfred A. Knopf, 1965); Organski, *World Politics*, 2nd ed. (Alfred A. Knopf, 1968); Organski and Jacek Kugler, *The War Ledger* (University of Chicago Press, 1980).

[18] Carsten Rauch, "Realism and Power Transition Theory: Different Branches of the Power Tree," *E-International Relations*, February 3, 2018, https://www.e-ir.info/2018/02/03/realism-and-power-transition-theory-different-branches-of-the-power-tree/.

[19] Charles J. Koch, "Testing the Power Transition Theory with Relative Military Power," *Journal of Strategic Security* 14, no. 3 (2021): 86–111, https://doi.org/10.5038/1944-0472.14.3.1884.

[20] Jacek Kugler and A. F. K. Organski, "The Power Transition: A Retrospective and Prospective Evaluation," in *Handbook of War Studies*, ed. Midlarsky Manus (Routledge, 1989), 179.

[21] Rauch, "Realism and Power Transition Theory."

[22] I. William Zartman, *Ripe for Resolution: Conflict and Intervention in Africa* (Oxford University Press, 1989).

[23] I. William Zartman, "Ripeness: The Hurting Stalemate and Beyond," in *International Conflict Resolution After the Cold War*, ed. Paul Stern and Daniel Druckman (National Academy Press, 2000).

I. William Zartman, "The Timing of Peace Initiatives: Hurting Stalemates and Ripe Moments," *The Global Review of Ethnopolitics* 1, no. 1 (2001): 8–18, https://thehagueinstituteforglobaljustice.org/files/sites/peacemaker.un.org/files/timingofpeaceinitiatives_zartman2001.pdf.

24 James D. Fearon, "Rationalist Explanations for War," *International Organization* 49, no. 3 (1995): 379–414, https://doi.org/10.1017/S0020818300033324.

25 Ibid.

26 Dan Reiter, *How Wars End* (Princeton University Press, 2009).

27 Martha Finnemore and Kathryn Sikkink, "International Norm Dynamics and Political Change," *International Organization* 52, no. 4 (1998): 887–917, https://www.jstor.org/stable/2601361.

28 Carl von Clausewitz, "What Is War?," in *On War*, rev. ed., trans. J. J. Graham, ed. F. N. Maude, book 1, chapter 1 (Kegan Paul, Trench, Trubner & C., 1918), https://clausewitzstudies.org/readings/OnWar1873/BK1ch01.html.

29 Clausewitz, "War Is an Instrument of Policy," *On War*, book 8, chapter 6B, https://clausewitzstudies.org/readings/OnWar1873/BK8ch06.html.

30 Clausewitz, *On War*.

31 Otto von Bismarck, *Bismarck: The Man and the Statesman; Being the Reflections and Reminiscences of Otto, Prince von Bismarck*, vol. 2, trans. A. J. Butler (Harper & Brothers, 1898), 265.

32 Bismarck, *Bismarck*, 308.

33 James Wycliffe Headlam, *Bismarck and the Foundation of the German Empire* (G. P. Putnam's Sons, 1899), 83.

34 Jonathan Steinberg, *Bismarck: A Life* (Oxford University Press, 2011), 472.

35 George F. Kennan (as "X"), "The Sources of Soviet Conduct," *Foreign Affairs* 25, no. 4 (1947): 566–82, https://www.foreignaffairs.com/articles/russian-federation/1947-07-01/sources-soviet-conduct.

36 Geoffrey Roberts, "What George Kennan Can Teach us About US–Russia Relations," *Responsible Statecraft*, October 25, 2021, https://responsiblestatecraft.org/2021/10/25/what-george-kennan-can-teach-us-about-us-russia-relations/.

37 George F. Kennan, "The Two Planes of International Reality," in *Realities of American Foreign Policy* (Princeton University Press, 1954), 4.

38 Roberts, "What George Kennan Can Teach Us."

39 George F. Kennan, *The Kennan Diaries*, ed. Frank Costigliola (W. W. Norton, 2014), quoted in Ivor Roberts, "Unhappy Warrior," *Dublin Review*, October 2014, https://drb.ie/articles/unhappy-warrior/.

40 Roberts, "What George Kennan Can Teach Us."

41 F. Kennan's "Long Telegram" was sent from the US Embassy in Moscow to the Secretary of State on February 22, 1946. The telegram provided a comprehensive analysis of Soviet policy and recommended a strategy of "containment," which became the foundation of US policy toward the Soviet Union during the Cold War. George F. Kennan, "The Long Telegram," telegram from Moscow to the Secretary of State, February 22, 1946, US Department of State, Central Decimal File, 1945–1949, 861.00/2-2246, https://nsarchive2.gwu.edu/coldwar/documents/episode-1/kennan.htm; reprinted in *Foreign Relations of the United States, 1946, Volume VI, Eastern Europe; The Soviet Union* (United States Government Printing Office, 1969), 696–709.

42 "George Kennan and Containment," US Department of State, Office of the Historian, https://history.state.gov/departmenthistory/short-history/kennan.

43 Frank Costigliola, "'My Voice Now Carried': George F. Kennan's Long Telegram," Wilson Center, February 19, 2021, https://www.wilsoncenter.org/blog-post/my-voice-now-carried-george-f-kennans-long-telegram.

44 Niall Ferguson, "Kissinger and the True Meaning of Détente: Reinventing a Cold War Strategy for the Contest with China," *Foreign Affairs*, March/April 2024, https://www.foreignaffairs.com/united-states/kissinger-and-true-meaning-detente.

45 Council on Foreign Relations, "Henry A. Kissinger Looks Back on the Cold War," November 4, 2014, https://www.cfr.org/event/henry-kissinger-looks-back-cold-war-0.

46 Ibid.

47 Henry Kissinger, *World Order: Reflections on the Character of Nations and the Course of History* (Viking: 2014), 8.

48 Wikipedia, "Henry Kissinger," last modified June 15, 2025, https://en.wikipedia.org/wiki/Henry_Kissinger.

49 "Henry A. Kissinger," Nixon's China Game, PBS, https://www.pbs.org/wgbh/americanexperience/features/china-kissinger/.

50 Ibid.

51 US Department of State, Office of the Historian, *Foreign Relations, 1969–1976, Volume XLII, Vietnam: The Kissinger-Le Duc Tho Negotiations*, https://history.state.gov/historicaldocuments/frus1969-76v42/preface.

52 James K. Sebenius and Eugene B. Kogan, "Henry Kissinger's Negotiation Campaign to End the Vietnam War," Working Paper No. 17-053 (Harvard Business School, December 2016), 1.

53 Wikipedia, "Henry Kissinger and the Vietnam War," last modified April 28, 2025, https://en.wikipedia.org/wiki/Henry_Kissinger_and_the_Vietnam_War; Stanley Karnow, *Vietnam: A History* (Viking, 1983).

54 Sebenius and Kogan, "Henry Kissinger's Negotiation Campaign," 1.

55 Henry Kissinger, *Ending the Vietnam War: A History of America's Involvement in and Extrication from the Vietnam War* (Simon & Schuster, 2003), 54; Ferguson, "Kissinger and the True Meaning of Détente."

56 US intelligence assessments indicate Hamas has recruited 10,000–15,000 new fighters since the war began, nearly offsetting Israel's claimed death toll of 20,000 militants. "US Intel Figures Show Hamas Has Recruited up to 15,000 New Fighters During Gaza War," *The Times of Israel*, January 24, 2025, https://www.timesofisrael.com/us-intel-figures-show-hamas-has-recruited-up-to-15000-new-fighters-during-gaza-war/. Secretary of State Antony Blinken emphasized this parity in January 2025, stating Hamas had replaced "almost as many fighters as Israel killed" during its offensive. Sean Mathews, "US Says Hamas Has Replaced Almost All Killed Fighters in Gaza with New Recruits," *Middle East Eye*, January 14, 2025, https://www.middleeasteye.net/news/us-says-hamas-has-replaced-almost-all-killed-fighters-gaza-new-recruits; Ida Rosdalina, "U.S. Says Hamas Gains New Recruits in Gaza, Replacing Fighters Killed by Israel," *Tempo*, January 15, 2025, https://en.tempo.co/read/1964262/u-s-says-hamas-gains-new-recruits-in-gaza-replacing-fighters-killed-by-israel. Israeli security sources corroborate this trend, reporting 4,000 new recruits monthly in early 2025, primarily drawn from displaced Gazan youth offered financial incentives or humanitarian aid access. Yonah Jeremy Bob, "Hamas Forces Are Making a Substantial Comeback in the Gaza

Strip," *The Jerusalem Post*, January 2, 2025, https://www.jpost.com/middle-east/article-835754; Yoni Ben Menachem, "Hamas Recruits Thousands of New Fighers in Gaza," Jerusalem Center for Security and Foreign Affairs, January 7, 2025, https://jcpa.org/hamas-recruits-thousands-of-new-fighters-in-gaza/. The Saudi-backed Al Arabiya channel further reported a surge of 30,000 new recruits by April 2025, though many lacked advanced training beyond basic guerrilla tactics. Nurit Yohanan, "Hamas Said to Recruit 30,000 Gaza Youths into Its Military Wing," *The Times of Israel*, April 20, 2025, https://www.timesofisrael.com/hamas-said-to-recruit-30000-gaza-youths-into-its-military-wing/.
While these figures include untrained personnel, they demonstrate Hamas's capacity to regenerate forces even under siege. Notably, the US Office of the Director of National Intelligence noted that recruitment has kept Hamas's total fighting force stable at 20,000–23,000 militants—comparable to pre-war estimates.
Patrick Kingsley and Adam Rasgon, "Militant's Death Would Be Blow to Hamas, but May Have Limited Long-Term Consequences," *New York Times*, May 14, 2025, https://www.nytimes.com/2025/05/14/world/middleeast/muhammad-sinwar-hamas-leader-gaza-israel.html.

[57] Henry Kissinger, "The Viet Nam Negotiations," *Foreign Affairs* 48, no. 2 (1969): 214.
[58] Jon Meacham, "Interview with Newsweek," *Newsweek*, December 12, 2009, https://www.henryakissinger.com/interviews/interview-with-newsweek/.
[59] Tom Porter, "Kissinger Says Ukraine Must Give Up Land to Russia, Warns West Not to Seek to Humiliate Putin with Defeat," *Business Insider*, March 2022, https://www.businessinsider.com/kissinger-ukraine-give-up-land-russia-not-humiliate-putin-2022-5.
[60] Henry Kissinger and Andrew Roberts, "'There Are Three Possible Outcomes to This War': Henry Kissinger Interview," *The Spectator*, July 2, 2022, https://www.spectator.co.uk/article/there-are-three-possible-outcomes-to-this-war-henry-kissinger-interview/. In the interview he says,

> If Russia stays where it is now, it will have conquered 20 per cent of Ukraine and most of the Donbas, the industrial and agricultural main area, and a strip of land along the Black Sea. If it stays there, it will be a victory, despite all the setbacks they suffered in the beginning. And the role of Nato will not have been as decisive as earlier thought.
> The other outcome is an attempt is made to drive Russia out of the territory it acquired before this war, including Crimea, and then the issue of a war with Russia itself will arise if the war continues.
> The third outcome, which I sketched in Davos, and which, in my impression, Zelensky has now accepted, is if the Free People can keep Russia from achieving any military conquests and if the battleline returns to the position where the war started, then the current aggression will have been visibly defeated. Ukraine will be reconstituted in the shape it was when the war started: the post-2014 battleline. It will be rearmed and closely connected to Nato, if not part of it. The remaining issues could be left to a negotiation. It would be a situation which is frozen for a while. But as we've seen in the reunification of Europe, over a period of time, they can be achieved.
> **AR:** Could it be another North/South Korea kind of situation where it solidifies into 70 years of statis?
> **HK:** Well, we are talking about only 2½ per cent of the country and Crimea, which is another 4½ per cent, whose relationship to the region is different than that of the pure

Ukrainian, because it has been Russian for hundreds of years. I won't pass a judgment on what the outcome of a negotiation should be. But if the allies succeed in helping the Ukrainians in driving the Russians out of the territory they have conquered in this war, they will have to decide how long the war should be prolonged.

AR: But none of those three outcomes, Henry, really punishes Putin for his aggression, do they?

HK: Quite the contrary. If the war ends as I sketched at Davos, I think it will be a substantial achievement for the allies. Nato will have been strengthened by the addition of Finland and Sweden, creating the possibility of defence of the Baltic countries. Ukraine will have the largest conventional ground force in Europe linked to Nato or a member of it. Russia will have been shown that the fear that has hung over Europe since World War 2, of a Russian army descending – the conventional army descending into Europe across established borders – can be prevented by Nato conventional action. For the first time in recent history, Russia would have to face a need for coexistence with Europe as an entity, rather than America being the chief element in defending Europe with its nuclear forces."

[61] Zbigniew Brzezinski, *Between Two Ages: America's Role in the Technetronic Era* (Viking Press, 1970). This concept represented Brzezinski's vision of a new phase of human civilization that would emerge beyond the industrial age, fundamentally shaped by the convergence of technology and electronics, particularly in computers and communications. The term has become one of Brzezinski›s most significant intellectual contributions to understanding societal transformation in the modern era, representing his attempt to conceptualize how advanced societies would evolve in response to technological revolution. "The technetronic era involves the gradual appearance of a more controlled society. Such a society would be dominated by an elite, unrestrained by traditional values. Soon it will be possible to assert almost continuous surveillance over every citizen and maintain up-to-date complete files containing even the most personal information about the citizen. These files will be subject to instantaneous retrieval by the authorities."

[62] "Cold War Ended Because USSR Lost, Brzenzski Says," *Deseret News*, February 28, 1991, https://www.deseret.com/1991/2/28/18907881/cold-war-ended-because-ussr-lost-brzezinski-says/.

[63] Frederick Kempe, "Zbigniew Brzezinski on the End of the Cold War," *Atlantic Council*, November 4, 2009, https://www.atlanticcouncil.org/blogs/new-atlanticist/zbigniew-brzezinski-on-the-end-of-the-cold-war/.

[64] "1998 Interview with Zbigniew Brzezinski on Afghanistan in *Le Nouvel Observateur*," https://dgibbs.arizona.edu/content/brzezinski-interview-2.

[65] Ibid.

[66] "Cold War Ended Because USSR Lost."

[67] "1998 Interview with Zbigniew Brzezinski."

[68] Richard Falk, "On Zbigniew Brzezinski: Geopolitical Mastermind, Realist Practitioner," *Global Justice in the 21st Century* (blog), June 3, 2017, https://richardfalk.org/2017/06/03/on-zbigniew-brzezinski-geopolitical-mastermind-realist-practitioner/.

[69] Ian Brzezinski, "NATO Thwarted a Russian Invasion in 1980. Could Its Playbook Work Today?," *Atlantic Council*, November 19, 2021, https://www.atlanticcouncil.org/blogs/new-atlanticist/nato-thwarted-a-russian-invasion-in-1980-could-its-playbook-work-today/.

[70] Zbigniew Brzezinski, *Strategic Vision: America and the Crisis of Global Power* (Basic Books, 2012).

[71] Ibid, 95.

[72] The proportion of civil wars that relapse after a negotiated settlement varies by study and methodology, but several key findings emerge from the literature. According to Monica Duffy Toft's analysis of civil wars from 1940 to 2000, 29.2 percent (7 out of 24) of wars ended by negotiated settlements recurred, compared to only 12 percent of those ended by military victory. Ceasefires and stalemates had an even higher recurrence rate, at 33.3 percent. Toft, "Peace Through Security." Toft's data also show that wars ended by negotiated settlement are about three times more likely to reignite than those ended by military victory. A broader survey of nearly 200 civil war peace agreements negotiated from 1975 to 2011 found that 60 percent of those agreements ended armed conflict for at least five years, implying that up to 40 percent relapsed within five years. This suggests that, while negotiated settlements are increasingly common and more successful than in the past, a substantial risk of relapse remains. Michael Quinn and Madgav Joshi, "Is the Sum Greater Than the Parts? The Terms of Civil War Peace Agreements and the Commitment Problem Revisited," *Negotiation Journal* 31, no. 1 (2015): 7–30, https://direct.mit.edu/ngtn/article/31/1/7/121729/Is-the-Sum-Greater-than-the-Parts-The-Terms-of.

The risk of relapse is higher in identity-based wars and in states with weak capacity or high infant mortality. The quality and comprehensiveness of peace agreements, as well as international mediation and enforcement, can affect the likelihood of sustained peace.

INTRODUCTION TO THE SPECIAL ISSUE ON ENDING WARS

John, Lord Alderdice
Pembroke College, University of Oxford; Senator George J. Mitchell Institute for Global Peace, Security, and Justice at Queen's University, Belfast; Global Humanity for Peace Institute, University of Wales Trinity Saint David; House of Lords, UK Trade Envoy to Azerbaijan and Central Asia and Select Committee on International Relations and Defence; The Concord Foundation

Ending Wars

> *I will never know how men can see the wisdom in a war.*
> —Chris de Burgh (1982) from his song, *Border Line*

In September 2014 the Centre for the Resolution of Intractable Conflict, which had been founded the previous year at Harris Manchester College, Oxford,[1] organized a conference bringing together an international group of scholars from different disciplines including psychology, anthropology, political science, and theology for a two-day seminar. The goal was to take forward our thinking about religious fundamentalism by examining, from different academic perspectives, the commonalities

---

John, Lord Alderdice is an Honorary Fellow of Pembroke College, Oxford and a professor of practice at the Senator George J. Mitchell Institute for Global Peace, Security and Justice at Queen's University, Belfast and at the Global Humanity for Peace Institute, University of Wales Trinity Saint David. A life member of the House of Lords, he is currently the UK Trade Envoy to Azerbaijan and Central Asia and a member of the House of Lords Select Committee on International Relations and Defence. He is the Founder and Chairman of The Concord Foundation, and as Leader of the Alliance Party of Northern Ireland, he was one of the negotiators of the 1998 Belfast/Good Friday Agreement.

of the form of thinking and experiencing of identity, of individuals in large groups, and to explore the evidence for how far the thinking and identity were related at that time to political radicalization and violence. I organized this conference along with my Oxford colleagues, Harvey Whitehouse, Scott Atran, and Richard Davis. It was a successful meeting and from then until 2024, at the same time every year, we had a follow-up Conference on the Resolution of Intractable Conflict (CRIC).

As the years passed an increasing number of the papers that emerged from these CRIC events were published, particularly in the *New England Journal of Public Policy*, whose Editor-in-Chief, Padraig O'Malley, took a great interest in our proceedings and was a regular attender at CRIC events. This volume entitled *Ending Wars* includes articles based on many of the presentations at or emerging from CRIC 2024, the conference held in September 2024, and along with *The Changing Character of War and Peacemaking*, articles based on significant presentations from CRIC 2023, these two volumes represent the approach to thinking about war and violent political conflict that developed through those eleven annual international residential conferences.[2]

While I do not intend to organize further annual conferences myself, it is likely that this responsibility may be picked by colleagues at the Global Cohesion Lab in the Centre for the Study of Social Cohesion at the University of Oxford.[3] In any case the work will continue to be taken forward through The Concord Foundation, ARTIS International, and ARTIS Europe, as well as the rest of the network of colleagues and organizations around the world that have worked together for more than a decade.[4]

Ending individual wars has always been a preoccupation for those embroiled in them, but as Michael Howard, the doyen of military history in Britain, has noted, "throughout history the overwhelming majority of human societies have taken war for granted and made it the basis for their legal and social structures."[5] However, addressing the problem of ending wars as a damaging phenomenon of human society has become ever more urgent and challenging in recent years, not only because of the existential threat posed by nuclear weapons, but because, after the relatively peaceful period after World War II, there has been a serious deterioration in global peacefulness, as evidenced by the 2025 Global Peace Index (GPI) published by the Institute for Economics & Peace (IEP).[6] IEP colleagues have been monitoring and publishing objective measures of the level of peacefulness for nearly two decades. This nineteenth report covers 163 independent states and territories containing some 99.7 percent of the world's population and rates their various levels of peacefulness. The GPI is the world's leading measure of global peacefulness and for the sixth year in a row that measure has deteriorated. The average country score on the GPI has also deteriorated for thirteen of the last seventeen years and has not improved on average in any year since 2013.

Efforts to address the ending of wars came to the fore in political and intellectual circles at the end of World War I, but these were by no means the first attempts. Arguably the Westphalian settlement of 1648 was the most significant earlier attempt to construct a system of agreements that would obviate the possibility of wars between the major state powers in Europe at the time. However, the wars between European states and the bloody revolution in France in 1789 led Immanuel Kant to pen his essay *Perpetual Peace: A Philosophical Sketch* a few years later, setting out what one might call a 'democratic peace theory.'[7] He believed that however long and difficult the road, if people were freed from monarcho-aristocratic regimes, the public engagement and debate that would result from the democratic republican form of government would eventually lead people to conclude that they should manage their differences in a different and non-violent way. As Michael Howard noted, Kant was not an optimist about human nature, and in this he differed from most of the 'philosophes' of his time, who believed that humankind was naturally good, but corrupted by malign leaders. However, Kant saw that war was so horrifying and costly in both 'blood and treasure' that he believed that, in the end, rationality and a moral imperative would ensure the adoption of a new and more peaceful way of living.

The Enlightenment thinkers challenged the old ways of thinking in almost every area of life including the view that wars were an inevitable element in the human condition. They were convinced that the success that 'rationalism' had brought to so many other aspects of human endeavor could surely apply to war and that the adoption of rational thought, and the establishment of rational social organization, would banish pointless and destructive violent conflict to history. It seemed that considerable, albeit not entirely linear, progress was being made along that path until the outbreak of World War I. The massive slaughter between 1914 and 1918 punctured that liberal optimism, however, many believed that the end of empires and the expansion of liberal democracy would protect future generations, while others hoped that research and education held the key to a more peaceful and prosperous world. The International Committee on Intellectual Cooperation that was established in Paris in 1922 brought together some of the greatest minds of the day, including Albert Einstein, Marie Curie, Gilbert Murray, and Henri Bergson. In addition to publishing books and papers, and organizing courses and university exchanges in Europe, they engaged in discussions with some of the most eminent thinkers in the world of the time. One of the first, best-known of these exchanges is found in the letters between Albert Einstein and Sigmund Freud, published under the title *Why War?*[8]

Einstein laid out with impressive clarity the challenge as he saw it and Freud's response is worth reviewing because little advance in understanding has been made since his summation.

Freud started by saying, "It is a general principle, then, that conflicts of interest between men are settled by the use of violence…domination by brute violence, or by violence supported by the intellect."[9] The rule of law then comes about when several weaker individuals come together to confront the power of an individual. Freud pointed out that this needs to be maintained as a stable community of interests if it is to provide for a culture of lawfulness, but if this is the case, such an agreement may lead to the growth of emotional ties that strengthen the agreement and provide stability. A significant historical example of such a process was the meeting and negotiation between King John and the barons at Runnymede in June 1215, when the king was pressured to sign what became known as the Magna Carta, a document that became the basis for much subsequent Anglo-Saxon law.

Freud went on to point out that the key to further development is the extent to which the rule of law in such an agreement applies equally to all. If it does not, this issue may become the cause of a return to violent struggle, either because the powerful do not want to relinquish the power they have had, or from dissatisfaction on the part of the less powerful who want equality. This use of violence, or threat of violence, tends to lead to partial or temporary solutions, but the result has been that many minor wars have been replaced by 'wars on a grand scale'—less common but more destructive.

Freud agreed with Einstein about the principle of setting up a global authority to which all would agree to submit. However, he was doubtful that it could be done in practice. It would need to have more power than the League of Nations that was in place at the time, and it was his view that it could only be held together by the force of violence or strong emotional ties (identifications) between its members. Unlike the religious and nationalist identifications of the past there did not seem to be a big idea that exerted a sufficient unifying authority, and of course his views were prescient given what happened in Europe shortly afterward.

Freud then set out in a simplified form his developing ideas about the life and death instincts —Eros and Thanatos—and interestingly he referred to the power and the necessity of the interaction of love and hate, though not of love simply being better than hate but rather of the importance of a combination or admixture of these drives—the combination of idealistic and destructive impulses. Regarding the latter, he remarked that the death drive preserves itself by projecting its destructiveness onto another. It was his view that it was not possible to get rid of human aggressive instincts but rather we could re-direct or re-deploy them in what he described as the 'evolution of culture/civilization.' He spoke of strengthening the intellect that governs the instincts, and the need to internalize aggression, and warned that there were various advantages and dangers in this necessary but constant dynamic struggle. He believed that humanity would both benefit and suffer from civilization and while "whatever fosters the growth of civilization works at the same time against war," such evolutionary developments could, paradoxically, lead to the extinction of humanity.[10] He also spoke of religion and psychoanalysis using the same word, love, to describe these attachments between people and quoted the commandment from both the Old and New Testaments, "Love your neighbor as yourself."

At the end of his message Freud said that he felt that he had given a disappointing answer to Einstein, for much of what he said simply repeated Einstein's own observations and the two factors that he said that he believed might ultimately lead humankind along a more pacifist road were not commonly held by people. Adopting them would require a change in the cultural attitude as well as the dread of the consequences of a future war. As we will see later, while Einstein, and perhaps Freud himself, may have hoped for an easier solution to the question, these are indeed the two factors that we must return to consider almost a century later.

Einstein already realized that science and technology would take humankind along a road to the development of atomic and nuclear weapons so powerful and destructive as to be beyond imagination, and perhaps even beyond survival, and he continued to devote himself to thinking, speaking, and writing about the dangers for the future of humankind. In "The Real Problem Is in the Hearts of Men," in 1946, he said, "Past thinking and methods did not prevent world wars. Future thinking must prevent wars."[11] Is there any indication of what such thinking might look like?

'Complexity thinking' may be the 'future thinking' to which Einstein was referring. It was to this approach that many colleagues in the CRIC network found themselves being drawn, not just in terms of the problems that they were investigating, but also in the way they needed to work.

After the invention of 'the bomb' and its further development as a hydrogen bomb and beyond, the scientists at Los Alamos had continued their more general research and began to realize that there were limitations to the way they had been thinking about mathematics and physics. They realized that in breaking everything down into fundamental components, they lost a sense of structure, data, and organization. These observations set the scene for the elaboration of systems theory and later complexity thinking. Social scientists and psychologists also began to appreciate that addressing individuals and their functioning failed to explain many of the problems they were trying to understand, or to bring about therapeutic change and betterment, unless the context and relationships in which those individuals, families, or societies lived was taken into consideration. This exploration came to be known as complexity thinking. Scientific analysis had involved breaking things down into their more fundamental elements, but also splitting knowledge and scientific activity into very specialized silos. While directing experimentation into ever more refined areas of analysis had been incredibly successful both as a scientific method and as an approach to technological development, as Einstein suggested, we may have come to the point where it no longer answers the questions we need to ask, and so a new approach is needed.

Complex systems exist at every level of organization but instead of seeing the commonalities we have tended to focus on the differences between subjects, levels, and disciplines. In working with human beings, for example, we may see the study of psychology that works to understand and address individual function and dysfunction, as quite separate from politics. But politics may be best understood as the psychology of 'large groups' and how we function, not as individuals but as communities, large and small.

Religion is often regarded, both by those who study it and those who disregard it, as a something completely separate from other more scientific enterprises in human knowledge. However, as the twentieth-century Irish theologian, J. Ernest Davey defined it, "Religion is the most ultimate, the most real and the most compelling form in which we conceive the social or universe relationships and obligations of our lives; and in the case of those who may be called non-religious it is only necessary to invert the form of the sentence; the most ultimate, real and compelling form in which they conceive their social or universe relationships and obligations is their true religion."[12] In an earlier book, *The*

Changing Vesture of the Faith, he wrote about his view that authority structures, doctrinal and belief statements, and liturgical forms of worship in the different religions were all the 'vestures' or external garments that we put on and later discard, while underneath is the fundamental body of engagement or relationship with society and the universe.[13] In other words, if psychology is the study of the individual and how people manage their own contrary internal wishes and impulses—often loving and hating the same person (which could be themselves) at the same time—and politics is how as communities we manage the contrary wishes and impulses of our communities, both within large groups and between them—then religion, in Davey's understanding, is the way we manage the wider, and even universe relations and obligations as we construe them in the face of a degree of complexity, contradiction, and mystery that is beyond our understanding. I remember as a young physician, psychiatrist, and psychoanalyst being told by my mentor that it was so difficult to get patients better that one had to use whatever instruments one could find in one's therapeutic quiver. Given the difficulty and complexity of the challenge of Ending Wars we will require every possible understanding, and we will need to hold together both the simplicity and complexity of our task.

The simplicity may be stated as follows. Wars arise because there are human beings. Without human beings there would be no human conflict. Human beings have differing wishes, interests, and desires, even within themselves, but certainly between themselves and others. When some human beings decide to impose their will on others and the victims resist, there is a conflict. If the former group is prepared to use physical force and the latter group resists with physical force, there is a fight, which may escalate, cause enough casualties, and last long enough to qualify as a war.

The complexity arises when individuals and groups apply their intelligence, ingenuity, and creativity to the development of tools and instruments of war to enable them better to impose their will on others, and if necessary, eliminate them. Until 1945 the limits of our capacity to destroy our enemies and wreak havoc, ensured that after a violent conflict the world could repair itself. Since that time, there is no such reassurance. In addition, outside the context of conflicts and without the intention of harm, human activity has increasingly impacted the systems of the natural world and damaged its capacity to repair itself. We are therefore faced with the prospect of both nuclear holocaust, what Freud called 'the consequences of a future war,' and environmental catastrophe. There is only modest evidence of humanity taking either threat sufficiently seriously.

Taking the second of Freud's two factors, what kind of change in the 'cultural attitude' might be possible to mitigate disaster and potentially the end of humanity?

Alfred, Lord Tennyson was Britain's poet laureate during the nineteenth century imperial reign of Queen Victoria and though he was called upon to celebrate military events, he wrote much about peace.

In December 1899, on the brink of the new century he published in *The Advocate of Peace* (a publication of the American Peace Society) a section of his much longer poem, "Locksley Hall Sixty Years After."[14] I am very familiar with this piece because it was a favorite poem of my father and often quoted by him.

> After madness, after massacre, Jacobinism and Jacquerie,
> Some diviner force to guide us through the days shall I not see?
> When the schemes and all the systems, kingdoms and republics fall,
> Something kindlier, higher, holier - all for each, and each for all?
> All the half-brain, full-brain races led by armistice, love and truth?
> All the millions filled, at length, with all the visions of my youth?
> All diseases quenched by science, no man halt or deaf or blind;
> Stronger ever born of weaker, larger body, lustier mind?
> Earth at last a warless world, a single race, a single tongue?
> I have seen her far away, for is not Earth as yet so young?
> Every tiger-madness muzzled, every serpent-passion killed;
> Every grim ravine a garden, every blazing desert tilled;
> Robed in universal harvest up to either pole she smiles,
> Universal ocean softly washing all her warless isles.

This vision of global peace was what inspired those imperialists who believed their nation to have the best religion, government, and culture—British, French, German, and others. Later it was the vision that inspired those who believed that they had the best political system and philosophy and that others should grasp the opportunities of liberal democracy, or socialism, or communism, or whatever political program they espoused. As these all proved insufficient to prevent war, and even became a cause of it, structural organizational and systemic solutions were espoused: the post-war, liberal, rules-based international order that we now see dissolving before our eyes.

If the ending of war is not to be found in identifying a religion, nation, political philosophy, or system that can create Tennyson's 'warless world' where do we turn?

If war represents a disturbance in relations between communities, then what would repair that breakdown? Instead of hoping or working for "a single race, a single tongue," as was Tennyson's dream, should we not recognize that we have different visions and values and that these will inevitably conflict, just as we have wishes in each of ourselves that clash, and which we must find a way to accommodate? Isaiah Berlin recognized "that all cultures were not ultimately commensurable and that there were not objective ahistorical answers to the perennial questions facing us" and also that "our values conflict and compete with each other." This realization led him to develop the idea of value pluralism.[15] It is not the case that all values are of the same order, nor is there a simple hierarchy, but rather we must hold to our different perspectives even though they conflict with each other, but without violence. We used to say in Northern Ireland that the 1998 Belfast/Good Friday Agreement was an agreement to disagree without killing each other. At an individual human level, we know that relationships are never 'sorted.' Even at a point where they are on a relatively even keel, they are vulnerable to internal disruption and external pressures. Relationships are 'organic,' fluid and constantly adapting to the changing environment. This does not mean that we cannot have trust that a relationship is stable, dependable, supportive, and trustworthy, but these qualities cannot be taken for granted without constant nourishing of the relationship. Such a recognition begins to change our perspectives about Ending Wars. It implies that there is no specific formula for ending wars and no structure or process that inevitably brings peace, stability, and reconciliation between enemies.

Instead of being willing to keep repeating the French Revolutionary rallying cry of "Liberty, Equality, and Fraternity," we may have to substitute it with the much less simplistic "Freedom, Fairness, and Community." Freedom may be a more complex concept than liberty. Equality is unachievable and therefore a false prospectus. Fraternity suggests a relationship with those who identify with each other, but when we live in a community that is not homogeneous, we must develop a working relationship with those around us, whether they are friends or not.

It is not that we should abandon the search for agreement. It is essential that we continue to develop workable structures and negotiation processes that allow enemies to find a way to the table and away from the battlefield. Our CRIC colleague, Sundeep Waslekar, has described in detail an updated version of such an approach in his book,

A World without War.[16] It could be seen as one response to Tennyson's plea, "Warless? war will die out late then. Will it ever? late or soon?" However, following the process outlined in the book will not bring a result without the development of positive working relationships between the participants. The best result that can be hoped for is not agreement all round, but rather a sufficient agreement to allow political institutions to function with a sufficient disagreement to realistically reflect the genuine cultural differences that exist.

The aim of conflict resolution is not therefore the reaching of agreement and satisfaction about all the social, political, economic, and legal issues. It is rather getting to a place where those who differ deeply, can agree to disagree without killing each other. If any particular war, or war as a means of resolving differences, can be brought to closure in this way, then there can be some hope that a sufficient set of relationships can be established and then nourished so that the parties concerned can abandon war as a way of addressing their differences.

Notes

[1] John, Lord Alderdice, "Why We Have the Center for the Resolution of Intractable Conflict in Oxford," *New England Journal of Public Policy* 29, no. 1 (2017): Article 3, http://scholarworks.umb.edu/nejpp/vol29/iss1/3.

[2] John, Lord Alderdice and Padraig O'Malley, eds., "The Changing Character of War and Peace-Making," special issue, *New England Journal of Public Policy* 36, no. 1 (2024), https://scholarworks.umb.edu/nejpp/vol36/iss1/; repr. ARTIS (Europe) Ltd, 2024.

[3] Global Cohesion Lab, https://www.cssc.ox.ac.uk/the-global-cohesion-lab.

[4] The Concord Foundation, https://theconcordfoundation.org; ARTIS International, https://artisinternational.org; and ARTIS Europe, https://artiseurope.com.

[5] Michael Howard, *The Invention of Peace: Reflections on War and International Order* (Yale University Press, 2000), 1–2.

[6] Institute for Economics & Peace, *Global Peace Index 2025: Identifying and Measuring the Factors that Drive Peace* (IEP, 2025), available from http://visionofhumanity.org/resources.

[7] Immanuel Kant, *Perpetual Peace: A Philosophical Sketch* (F. Nicolovius, 1795).

[8] Albert Einstein and Sigmund Freud, "Why War?," in *The Revised Standard Edition of the Complete Psychological Works of Sigmund Freud*, vol. 22, ed. James Strachey and Mark Solms (Rowman & Littlefield, 2024).

[9] Ibid, 215.

[10] Ibid, 225.

[11] Albert Einstein, "The Real Problem Is in the Hearts of Men," *New York Times Magazine* June 23, 1946, 7.

12 J. Ernest Davey, *Religious Experience – Its Nature, Validity, Forms and Problems,* (ARTIS Europe, 2021), 7.
13 J. Ernest Davey, *The Changing Vesture of the Faith: Studies in the Origins and Development of Christian Forms of Belief, Institution and Observance* (James Clarke & Co., 1923).
14 Alfred, Lord Tennyson, "Locksley Hall Sixty Years After," in *The Works of Tennyson*, vol. 6, ed. Hallam, Lord Tennyson (Macmillan, 1908).
15 Johnny Lyons, *The Philosophy of Isaiah Berlin* (Bloomsbury Publishing, 2020), 200, 234; Isaiah Berlin, "The Pursuit of the Ideal," in *The Proper Study of Mankind: An Anthology of Essays*, ed. Henry Hardy and Roger Hausheer (Pimlico, 1998), 10.
16 Sundeep Waslekar, *A World Without War* (HarperCollins, 2022).

WHAT FUTURE FOR PEACE IN A WORLD CHARACTERIZED BY UNCERTAINTY AND FEAR?

Cedric de Coning
Norwegian Institute of International Affairs; African Centre for the Constructive Resolution of Disputes

John, Lord Alderdice
Pembroke College, University of Oxford; Senator George J. Mitchell Institute for Global Peace, Security, and Justice at Queen's University, Belfast; Global Humanity for Peace Institute, University of Wales Trinity Saint David; House of Lords, UK Trade Envoy to Azerbaijan and Central Asia and Select Committee on International Relations and Defence; The Concord Foundation

ABSTRACT

After World War II the leading victorious powers put in place a series of structures that became known as the 'rules-based international order.' Its purpose was to prevent another global conflict, and for Western countries the method was the promotion of liberal democracy. During succeeding decades, the commitment to building and securing a more peaceful world order saw the establishment of political, security, and economic institutions and civil society organizations that worked to implement it. However, the

---

Dr. Cedric de Coning is a Research Professor with the Norwegian Institute of International Affairs (NUPI) and a Senior Advisor for the African Centre for the Constructive Resolution of Disputes (ACCORD).

John, Lord Alderdice is an Honorary Fellow of Pembroke College, Oxford and a professor of practice at the Senator George J. Mitchell Institute for Global Peace, Security and Justice at Queen's University, Belfast and at the Global Humanity for Peace Institute, University of Wales Trinity Saint David. A life member of the House of Lords, he is currently the UK Trade Envoy to Azerbaijan and Central Asia and a member of the House of Lords Select Committee on International Relations and Defence. He is the Founder and Chairman of The Concord Foundation, and as Leader of the Alliance Party of Northern Ireland, he was one of the negotiators of the 1998 Belfast/Good Friday Agreement.

last decade has seen the increasing fragmentation and dissolution of this rules-based order and those who worked to develop it are having increasing difficulty in raising the resources and support necessary for their activities. Many of them are also questioning the assumptions on which it was based. Following the Conference on the Resolution of Intractable Conflict (CRIC 2024) with its focus on Ending Wars, the authors brought together twenty leading scholars and practitioners from around the world for a colloquium at Harris Manchester College, Oxford, March 20–22, 2025, to discuss the role of peace practice and research in a time of global disruption, fragmentation, and insecurity and to explore whether 'complexity thinking' provides a possible way forward. This article is based on the key insights they took away from these meetings.

In an accelerating trend over recent years, months, and even days, there is a shift in government policies, resources, and public debate from global peace, peacebuilding, and development to national security and defense. This transition is driven by long-term changes in the global political-economy, especially the rise of China; the defection of Russia, Israel, and the United States from a rules-based world order; climate change; and the influence of new technologies such as artificial intelligence (AI). These trends have been stimulated by frustration with the slow progress in fulfilling the so-called Enlightenment expectations of a global society characterized by liberty, equality, and fraternity, and have been accelerated by the significant disruption to long-standing US and international norms and institutions since the January 2025 inauguration of President Donald Trump for his second term.

The behavior of Russia, Israel, and the United States has irreparably displaced core elements of the post–World War II rules-based international order, including the inviolability of national sovereignty, the pursuit of national interests through the force of law rather than the law of force, the accepted norms of what is permissible in the conduct of war, and the responsibilities required of occupying powers. As a result, for the foreseeable future, we will have to cope with a global system where at least two of the major powers that are permanent members of the UN Security Council, as well as several other regional powers and states, are choosing to operate outside the parameters of what had come to be known as the international rules-based order.

Many of the other states around the world, including the remaining permanent members of the UN Security Council, are trying to uphold what is left of the multilateral system, however some, especially in the industrialized West, are at the same time shifting significant resources and attention to strengthening their national defense and security capabilities in the hope of deterring potential aggression from 'defector' states.

The Rise and Fall of Peace as a Priority

Not only is the number of conflicts increasing, but there is also less policy space for 'peace work' today than at any point since the beginning of the twenty-first century, or perhaps even since the end of World War II. Instead, the focus seems to be on maintaining national and international security through investments in military and related defense capabilities. Policy interest and budget allocations for peacemaking, peacekeeping, and peacebuilding institutions, programming, and research funding has been in sharp decline, as resources have shifted to countering hybrid threats to national security and strengthening military alliances. A young military officer in Europe today is far more likely to be training or advising Ukrainian forces in the conduct of a full-scale war with Russia or engaging in NATO or European exercises to defend their country from a Russian attack than to be deployed as a United Nations peacekeeper.

By the end of World War II, throughout the period of the Cold War, and in the decades after the collapse of the Soviet Union, maintaining international peace and security and preventing another world war was the central focus of international diplomacy and the global multilateral system. The United Nations' 1992 *An Agenda for Peace* had introduced the operational concepts of peacemaking and preventive diplomacy, peacekeeping, and peacebuilding.[1] Many state and civil institutions were dedicated to promoting peace, developing mediation, peacekeeping, and peacebuilding capabilities, and investing in knowledge about how to achieve and sustain peace.

This peace ecosystem had developed as a collective response to the two terrible global conflicts of the twentieth century, and the primary aim was the prevention of another war on this scale, especially because there was now the potential for mutually assured nuclear destruction. Adolf Hitler had been defeated by a conventional war, somewhat similar in its modality if not in its technology, to the defeat of Napoleon one hundred thirty years before, but the first use of nuclear weapons radically changed the likely outcome of any similar global conflict in the future. Such a war would likely end in one of three ways. Either there would be a negotiated outcome (possibly after a ceasefire that facilitated the negotiations) or there would be a collapse of one side through internal disintegration, or there would be a global nuclear catastrophe. The purpose of having nuclear weapons was the deterrence of any attempt to defeat the regime that possessed them. If the regime believed that they faced an existential threat from outside the state, they were likely to press the nuclear button, with catastrophic consequences. The theory behind the rules-based international order was that if all states signed up to the rules and could engage as members of the United Nations, a large-scale war would be prevented by the universal acceptance of the rules and the availability of recognized processes of negotiation. For the next seven decades confidence grew that while there were still regional wars, they could be managed so that no emerging conflict would scale up to become a threat to global peace and security.

As the memory of the world wars of the twentieth century faded, the attention and resources of states shifted, from maintaining the postwar peace through the period of the Cold War, to the 'global war on terror,' and more recently the priority given to preventing and countering violent extremism, and subsequently what was termed 'stabilization.' The more recent wars in Ukraine and Gaza represent a tipping point where the focus on national and regional ambitions by some powerful states has displaced the commitment to maintain international peace and security. What is left of the peace ecosystem, will have to adapt to significant cuts in the funding of political and economic development assistance and peacebuilding, with a pivot in government attention and public debate to defense and related national security capabilities.[2]

Disruption and Resilience

Over the postwar decades there was an increase in knowledge about the factors that influence systemic resilience and societal stability. There was substantial development of capacities in conflict analysis, mediation, and institution-building and the United Nations showed that it could deploy ceasefire verification and other peace operations. Insofar as this 'peace ecosystem' remains, it is of great value as we navigate the uncertainties and the challenges of the transition to a new international arrangement. In addition, some of the capabilities and lessons that may appear less relevant just now, in the context of inter-state war and the focus on national interest, may be needed again downstream, and if this knowledge and capacity are lost our national, regional, and international security and defense systems will be less resilient.

Not all resilience is good, nor is all disruption negative. Many national, regional, and international peace and development institutions have become inefficient, and vested interests have made them resistant to change. Resilience can be understood as the capacity of a system to maintain or return to its previous stability in the face of a disruptive impact. Where the steady state is an undesirable one, its resilience makes it difficult to effect lasting change for the better. Contrariwise, new technologies that alter the type and balance of military hardware and the conduct of war, even though they can produce terrible destruction, can make systemic shifts more possible. New systems have often been simply an addition to the armamentarium rather than a replacement of the old weapons, and so fundamental systemic change is not always the result of technological advances. However, if directed thoughtfully, wisely, and creatively, resources and other pressures, including technological advances, can not only create an opportunity and a stimulus for those who conduct wars, but may also encourage those committed to peacebuilding and development to find ways to make international peace efforts more lean, agile, flexible and creative, as they are forced to adapt to the needs and realities of the twenty-first century.

Countries such as Japan that frequently experience natural disasters, and the people and institutions of the 'Global South' who have been on the periphery of the rules-based international order, may have valuable experiences that can guide more developed industrialized societies in how to manage in these times of uncertainty and insecurity and navigate a way forward to a new resilience that accepts systemic change while maintaining and even bettering the well-being of their people.

"A New Type of Thinking is Essential..."

The challenges we face are not only to be found in adapting or updating our techniques and technologies. In the aftermath of the first use of nuclear bombs at Hiroshima and Nagasaki, Albert Einstein insisted that we had now entered an era where new ways of thinking were essential. In an article entitled "The Real Problem Is in the Hearts of Men," published in *The New York Times Magazine* on June 23, 1946, he expanded on this theme and said,

> Many persons have inquired concerning a recent message of mine that "a new type of thinking is essential if mankind is to survive and move toward higher levels." [...] Past thinking and methods did not prevent world wars. Future thinking must prevent wars.[3]

During subsequent decades, some other nuclear physicists who had worked on the Manhattan Project at Los Alamos began to realize that to find explanations for new observations they were making in physics they had to move beyond linear thinking to an appreciation of how, from the smallest elements up to the largest, the universe seemed to be constructed as systems of systems. The question then became how these systems related to each other. Initially it was suggested that there seemed to be a hierarchy of systems with the higher and more complex systems being affected by the lower-level structures and being vulnerable to a return to that lower level when there was some breakdown. When it became apparent that the lower-level systems could also be impacted by higher-level functioning, a simple hierarchical structure was no longer convincing, and so an appreciation began to emerge that all aspects of science had to consider a greater complexity than had been anticipated. This complexity thinking or complexity science has opened up new ways of thinking, with studies that showed how complex adaptive systems and other complex systems respond to changes in their environment. These ideas are now being applied in many areas of science, including in the social sciences. Complexity thinking may be the 'new type of thinking' that Einstein called for and may be particularly relevant for navigating the current period of transition in the global order.

While World War II ended with the victory of the most militarily and technologically advanced alliance, the development and use of nuclear weapons has, somewhat paradoxically, brought to an end the victory of the most powerful and since then, the United States has found it increasingly difficult to win wars. The Korean War ended in a draw; the Vietnam War was a humiliating defeat, as were the wars in Afghanistan, Libya, and Syria. In Iraq and elsewhere the more technologically and militarily powerful states have been able to inflict terrible destruction, but the result was not a victory for liberal democracy but a chaotic failed state.[4] Top-down efforts at control are not enough to achieve predictable outcomes and less powerful groups can often bring about the defeat of much more powerful opponents.[5]

One example of a very powerful state being brought to the negotiating table by a terrorist organization can be seen in the Northern Ireland peace process that ended centuries of violent political conflict on the island of Ireland. After decades of failed attempts at bringing peace through the implementation of liberal democratic rules and structures, a lasting peace settlement was achieved through an approach based on addressing the three key disturbed historic communal relationships: between pro-British

Protestant unionists and pro-Irish Catholic nationalists in the north of the island; between the people of the north and the people of the south in Ireland; and between the United Kingdom and the Republic of Ireland. Complexity thinking is characterized by a focus on understanding relationships. In physics it has become evident that it is not the study of particles but an understanding of relations at that fundamental level that provides new insights, and the same is true at every other level, including in societal dysfunction.

Bringing about system change also seems to require appropriate interventions at different levels. Top-level political agreements tend not to survive unless there are also changes in relationships on the street, especially between the agents of the state and the population. This can be observed, for example, in changes in relations between the police and the community.

A 'theory of change' informed by complexity thinking will also appreciate the significance of time. Unsatisfactory situations can survive for much longer than one might expect from a rational examination of the pressures for change, but when that change comes, it can be explosive. Dams do not burst gradually. The pressure may build up gradually but go unnoticed until the dam suddenly bursts. Political change is often the same—long delayed, and then unexpectedly dramatic.

It's All About Relationships

Other key insights from complexity thinking include the appreciation that social and other complex systems make sense of and cope with uncertainty by continuously adapting to their environment.[6] They do not do this by working it all out in advance and then implementing 'the plan,' but rather through a 'learning from doing' process that consists of iterative cycles of strategic probing, evidence-based reflection, and purposeful selection or rejection based on the emerging results of each cycle through an ongoing evolutionary process. Those working on sustaining peace, maintaining security, and preventing future wars, including through deterrence, can employ similar adaptive approaches to make sense of, cope with, and proactively navigate the uncertainties of the global transition.[7] It can be difficult to persuade funders to support this approach because they want the plan that is proposed to be fully worked out in advance, and then costed and carried out, with careful monitoring to ensure that the approved scheme is being followed. However rational and apparently reasonable such an approach, the evidence shows that in human affairs, especially complex and conflictual relations, it usually does not work.

Another insight from complexity science or thinking is that networked systems that benefit from the distributed knowledge, burden sharing, and resilience of the larger system, are more robust in managing shocks and setbacks.[8] Investing in mechanisms that facilitate and sustain cooperative relationships among those with shared interests, without limiting the adaptive capacities of the parts or the whole, thus seems key to navigating this new turbulent phase of world history. This is the opposite of the approach being taken by President Donald Trump. He has decided that he has the solution to America's problems through imposing tariffs on other countries and focusing exclusively on American interests. This engagement is transactional rather than relational. Insofar as there is a relational element to his analysis it seems to be what one might characterize as 'Yalta 2.0.' In February 1945 at a meeting in Yalta, Franklin D. Roosevelt, Winston Churchill, and Joseph Stalin, the leaders of the US, Britain, and the Soviet Union, decided among themselves how their spheres of influence in the postwar world would be divided up. It would seem President Trump believes that he and Presidents Vladimir Putin and Xi Jinping can similarly determine how the new post-liberal dispensation can be managed. This will not work.

The Yalta agreement took place in the aftermath of World War II, and everyone was clear about the outcome of the war and who the victors were. When the United Nations was created later in 1945 it was open to all states, but the central role of the UN Security Council, with permanent seats for the US, the Soviet Union, Britain, France, and China, recognized this political reality. In 2025 both the number of wars and related deaths are still increasing, and no process that can reverse this trend, including in Gaza and Ukraine, has emerged yet.[9] In addition the political reality has changed. There are increasingly powerful states, such as India, Brazil, and South Africa, that will not accept decisions being made over their heads, not to mention the states of the European Union who totally reject the new order that Presidents Trump and Putin might wish to see, and are reticent about how to relate with China. In other words, it is a more complex world and governing it will require an understanding of how to influence and manage complex adaptive systems.

Just as the system of global governance will need to take account of these changes, the peace ecosystem will need to undergo significant transformation if it is to be relevant to the new realities of 'peace and security' in the twenty-first century. Much of the knowledge, practices, and institutions that were developed in the aftermath of the wars of the twentieth century remain relevant and valuable, but they need to be adapted and woven into the new realities and emerging needs of the twenty-first century. This is a century that is thus far characterized by a return to great power rivalry and authoritarian governments, rather than more respectful intergovernmental relations between an increasing number of liberal democratic states.[10] One implication of the dissolution of the liberal democratic order and the return of authoritarian governance, albeit with many more players than at the start of the twentieth century, and the resultant accelerating uncertainty and insecurity, is that peace practice and research will need to rethink its models and understandings and become more adaptive and more pragmatically oriented toward resilience and preparedness to respond to future shocks and setbacks.

Notes

[1] Boutros Boutros-Ghali, *An Agenda for Peace: Preventive Diplomacy, Peacemaking and Peace-Keeping; Report of the Secretary-General Pursuant to the Statement Adopted by the Summit Meeting of the Security Council on 31 January 1992* (United Nations, 1992), https://digitallibrary.un.org/record/145749?ln=en&v=pdf.

[2] Roland Paris, "The Future of UN Peace Operations: Pragmatism, Pluralism or Statism?," *International Affairs* 100, no. 5 (2024): 2153–72, https://doi.org/10.1093/ia/iiae182.

[3] Albert Einstein, "The Real Problem Is in the Hearts of Men," *New York Times Magazine* June 23, 1946, 7.

[4] John, Lord Alderdice, "New Insights into the Psychology of Individuals and Large Groups in a World of Changing Conflicts," *International Political Science Review* 45, no. 1 (2023): 94–105, https://doi.org/10.1177/01925121231177444.

[5] Dominic Johnson, *Strategic Instincts: The Adaptive Advantages of Cognitive Biases in International Politics* (Princeton University Press, 2020).

[6] Cedric de Coning, "Coping with the Complexity of the Changing Character of War: Toward a New Paradigm of Adaptive Peace," *New England Journal of Public Policy* 36, no. 1 (2024): Article 9, https://scholarworks.umb.edu/nejpp/vol36/iss1/9.

[7] Cedric de Coning, "Adaptive Peacebuilding," *International Affairs* 94, no. 2 (2018): 301–17, https://doi.org/10.1093/ia/iix251.

[8] Adam Day, *The Forever Crisis: Adaptive Global Governance for an Era of Accelerating Complexity* (Routledge, 2024).

[9] Siri Aas Rustad, "Conflict Trends: A Global Overview, 1946–2024," PRIO Paper, 2025. For more, see "New Data Shows Conflict at Historic High as U.S. Signals Retreat from World Stage," PRIO, June 9, 2025, https://www.prio.org/news/3616.

[10] John Gray, *The New Leviathans: Thoughts After Liberalism* (Allen Lane, 2023).

ENDING WARS IN TIMES OF UNCERTAINTY: MORAL LEADERSHIP, MEMORY, AND THE COST OF PEACE

Eva Grosman
Centre for Democracy and Peace Building

ABSTRACT

In our era of 'liquid modernity,' ending wars requires more than ceasing hostilities—it demands ethical frameworks that address the deeper wounds of conflict. This article examines how peace processes frequently abandon those who sacrificed most, creating narratives of betrayal that undermine future stability. Using Poland's post–World War II experience as a case study, it demonstrates how prioritizing geopolitical expediency over justice creates lasting damage to international order. Drawing on Zygmunt Bauman's concept of liquid times, Anne Applebaum's work on memory and abandonment, and Jonathan Sacks's vision of moral leadership, the article argues that sustainable peace requires attention to dignity, inclusion, and truth and proposes a framework for ethical peacebuilding. Without leadership rooted in ethical responsibility rather than political calculation, the end of war becomes merely the suspension of violence—not the beginning of genuine peace built on restored trust and shared futures.

Eva Grosman is the CEO of the Centre for Democracy and Peace Building and the founder of the Fellowship Programme for leaders in Northern Ireland. She advises Lord Alderdice in the House of Lords, focusing on diplomacy and global conflict. She initiated the Polish Cultural Week and the Polish Film Festival in Northern Ireland and co-founded the Unite Against Hate campaign. Eva served on the board of the Metropolitan Arts Centre Belfast and was an independent member of the Policing and Community Safety Partnership.

Why Ending Wars Matters Now

In the turbulent landscape of contemporary geopolitics, the challenge of ending wars has become increasingly complex. As conflicts continue across the globe, from Ukraine to the Middle East, the international community grapples with a paradoxical reality: our unprecedented interconnectedness exists alongside deepening divisions and mounting instability. This article examines what it means to end wars not merely through cessation of hostilities, but through ethically defensible and sustainable peace processes.

The late Polish philosopher Zygmunt Bauman, celebrated as one of the greatest social thinkers of our times by some, and highly criticized by others, characterized our era as one of "liquid modernity," a time when traditional structures dissolve, certainties evaporate, and change is the only constant. In these "liquid times," wars too have become more fluid, with blurred boundaries between combatants, complex networks of non-state actors, and conflicts that defy traditional diplomatic resolution.[1] As Winston Churchill grimly noted at the Yalta Conference in 1945, "This is a very exclusive club. The entrance fee being five million soldiers or equivalent."[2] The cost of war—and of ending war—remains devastatingly high.

The question at the heart of this article is not simply how to stop conflict, but how to end war well—in ways that prevent future violence, while honoring the dignity of those involved. For as history repeatedly demonstrates, peace processes that prioritize expediency over justice often sow the seeds of future unrest.

Theoretical Foundations

Zygmunt Bauman and Liquid Modernity

Bauman's concept of liquid modernity provides a critical framework for understanding the challenges of peacebuilding in contemporary times. In a world characterized by uncertainty, fluidity, and rapid change, the solid certainties of the past—clear national identities, structured political ideologies, and stable international alliances—have given way to more elusive and fragmented realities.

This liquidity extends to warfare itself. Traditional large-scale state conflicts have increasingly been replaced by ambiguous confrontations involving non-state actors, insurgencies, and terrorist networks. As Bauman observes, we are simultaneously more globally interconnected than ever before yet increasingly uncertain about who our enemies or allies truly are. This ambiguity complicates the process of ending wars, as peace agreements must address not only state interests, but also the complex web of identities, grievances, and power structures that fuel modern conflicts.

Moreover, Bauman warns that this fluidity exacerbates societal insecurity, making war a persistent feature of liquid life. Globalization has spread economic inequality and social dislocation, feeding into both local and international tensions. The solution, according to Bauman, lies not in attempting to restore rigid structures of the past but in developing new forms of solidarity and cooperation. If war in liquid times is fueled by exclusion and alienation, then sustainable peace requires creating communities that foster inclusivity and shared human values, even amid constant change.

Anne Applebaum: Memory, Justice, and Abandonment

Journalist and historian Anne Applebaum's work on the aftermath of World War II provides crucial insights into the long-term consequences of peace settlements that prioritize geopolitical expediency over moral considerations.[3] Her analysis of the "betrayal" of Eastern Europe (particularly Poland) at the Yalta Conference illustrates how the victors' selective memory and pragmatic compromises created lasting wounds in the international order.

In her recent book, *Autocracy, Inc.*, on a global network of authoritarian regimes, Applebaum demonstrates how modern autocrats thrive on conflict and instability.[4] Leaders such as Vladimir Putin use external wars to distract from domestic failures and to project strength. Through disinformation campaigns, electoral manipulation, and the suppression of civil society, these regimes undermine democratic norms both at home and abroad, creating environments where war becomes more likely and peace more fragile.

Applebaum's work emphasizes the critical role of memory and truth in sustainable peacebuilding. When states fail to properly acknowledge past injustices—especially those suffered by smaller or marginalized groups—those grievances fester and eventually resurface, often in destabilizing ways. Peace achieved at the expense of truth tends to be both brittle and morally compromised. In Applebaum's framing, genuine reconciliation requires the dignity of being remembered and heard—a principle essential to ethical conflict resolution.

Jonathan Sacks: Moral Leadership in Times of Chaos

Jonathan Sacks offers a complementary perspective on ending wars through his vision of moral leadership. For Sacks, one of the root causes of modern conflicts is the collapse of shared ethical frameworks and values. In a world increasingly characterized by cultural diversity and moral relativism, he advocates for what he calls "the dignity of difference"—a recognition that our distinctions need not divide us but can enrich humanity's collective experience.[5]

Sacks contends that wars often arise from a failure to appreciate the distinctiveness and dignity of others. In liquid times, where boundaries blur and identities become increasingly hybrid, he calls for leadership that inspires people to look beyond narrow tribal affiliations and foster a sense of common humanity. This leadership must be covenantal rather than merely contractual—rooted in moral responsibility rather than mere political calculation.

Sacks's emphasis on moral leadership challenges the realpolitik approach to ending wars. While pragmatic compromises are often necessary, Sacks argues that leaders must create meaning in peace, not just order. By articulating shared values and ethical principles, moral leaders can guide societies through the difficult transition from conflict to reconciliation, transforming the end of war from the mere absence of violence into the positive presence of justice and mutual respect.

The Aftermath of World War II: Poland and the Politics of Abandonment

The experience of Poland after World War II provides a powerful case study in the consequences of ending war without adequate attention to justice and dignity. Despite Poland's significant contribution to the Allied victory—furnishing the fourth-largest armed force in Europe and suffering enormous casualties—the nation found itself effectively abandoned to Soviet domination at the Yalta Conference in 1945.

As the Red Army completed its offensive on Berlin, the entirety of Poland's territory fell under Soviet occupation, placing the country behind the Iron Curtain despite its sacrifices for the Allied cause. The 200,000 Polish soldiers who had fought alongside Western forces found themselves without a true homeland to return to. In a particularly poignant symbol of this abandonment, Polish forces were excluded from the Victory Parade in London in June 1946—an omission justified by the British government's desire not to offend Joseph Stalin.

The human cost of this betrayal extended beyond geopolitics to individual lives. Consider the fate of Krystyna Skarbek (Christine Granville), Churchill's favorite female spy. This Polish countess had demonstrated remarkable courage throughout the war, serving in Egypt and Hungary, and later parachuting into occupied France. Her intelligence work and her success in securing the defection of an entire Nazi garrison significantly contributed to the Allied war effort, earning her the George Medal, the title of Officer of the Order of the British Empire, and the Croix de Guerre.[6]

Yet after the war, Skarbek found herself adrift—too British to return to Soviet-ruled Poland, yet too Polish to be embraced as a British war hero. The British government initially denied her a passport, which she obtained only after months of struggle and the intervention of Special Operations Executive (SOE) commanders. Unable to find meaningful work, she eventually settled for menial jobs, becoming increasingly desolate and depressed before her tragic murder in 1952. Her story encapsulates the human dimension of political abandonment—the individual lives crushed beneath the wheels of great power politics.

The Polish experience illustrates how peace settlements that prioritize expediency over justice create lasting wounds in the international order. The narrative of betrayal has shaped Polish national identity for generations, fueling both remarkable resilience and lasting bitterness. The slogan "For Your Freedom and Ours" that had inspired Polish resistance took on a tragic irony as Poland's freedom was sacrificed for what Western powers perceived as broader stability.

This underscores a crucial lesson: when ending wars, who is left behind matters. The humiliation and marginalization of entire nations or communities in peace processes sow seeds of future instability; those excluded from peace settlements often become the most potent challengers to fragile post-war orders.

The Hidden Costs of Ending Conflict

The process of ending wars involves complex calculations of the cost and benefit, with consequences that extend far beyond the cessation of direct violence. These costs—human, economic, environmental, and moral—must be carefully weighed in any ethical approach to peacebuilding.

The direct human cost of twentieth and early twenty-first century warfare is staggering: approximately 200 million people have died in wars between 1900 and 2024, with World War I and II alone accounting for 85-105 million deaths.[7]

The ongoing war in Ukraine has resulted in thousands of casualties and the displacement of over 6.7 million Ukrainians. According to the United Nations, the population of Ukraine has declined by over 10 million since the beginning of the war in 2014 and by an estimated 8 million since the beginning of the full-scale invasion in 2022.[8]

The destruction caused by the war has been immense. By December 2023, international institutions estimated the damage at 152 billion USD. In March 2025, the United Nations predicted that the country's reconstruction may cost 486 billion USD.[9]

Yet the hidden costs of ending wars extend beyond these quantifiable measures to include profound moral and psychological dimensions. Peace processes inevitably involve difficult trade-offs between justice and stability, accountability and reconciliation, truth and pragmatism. These compromises often leave certain groups feeling betrayed or forgotten, creating lasting psychological scars and generational trauma.

While the imperative to end violence is urgent, rushing peace processes without adequate attention to inclusion, justice, and dignity can result in settlements that fail to address the underlying causes of conflict. Too often, hasty peace agreements reproduce rather than resolve the conditions that led to war in the first place.

Moral Leadership in Ending War

Ending wars well requires not just strategic acumen but moral leadership—leadership that recognizes the ethical dimensions of conflict resolution and works toward peace grounded in justice rather than mere expediency. Such leadership involves difficult choices, personal risks, and the courage to prioritize long-term reconciliation over short-term political advantage.

Historical examples demonstrate the transformative potential of moral leadership in ending conflicts. Consider figures like Nelson Mandela in South Africa, whose willingness to forgive his oppressors while insisting on truth and reconciliation created space for a peaceful transition from apartheid. Or John Hume in Northern Ireland, whose persistent advocacy for nonviolence and inclusive dialogue helped break cycles of sectarian conflict. These leaders succeeded not by ignoring injustice, but by finding ways to acknowledge past wrongs while creating pathways to shared futures.

Moral leadership in ending wars involves navigating tensions between competing values: justice and mercy, truth and reconciliation, accountability and forgiveness. It requires creating spaces for memory and mourning while preventing these processes from becoming new sources of division. Above all, it demands moral imagination—the ability to envision possibilities for peace that transcend zero-sum thinking and historical enmities.

In the words often attributed to Churchill, "History is written by the victors." Moral leadership challenges this paradigm by ensuring that peace agreements reflect not just the interests of the powerful, but the dignity and needs of all parties to the conflict. It recognizes that sustainable peace cannot be imposed from above but must be built from below, through inclusive processes that engage stakeholders who are marginalized in traditional diplomacy.

Toward a Framework for Ethical Peacebuilding

Building on the insights of Bauman, Applebaum, and Sacks, we can outline a framework for ending wars in ways that are both politically sustainable and ethically defensible. This framework emphasizes inclusivity, truth-telling, and the rebuilding of moral trust in fractured societies.

First, ethical peacebuilding requires inclusive processes that engage all stakeholders in conflict resolution. This means looking beyond official negotiating tables to include civil society organizations, women's groups, religious communities, and other constituencies often marginalized in traditional diplomacy. The experiences of Northern Ireland illustrate the importance of this approach, as the peace process there ultimately succeeded by creating multiple channels for dialogue across sectarian divides.

Second, lasting peace requires truth and the preservation of memory. As Applebaum's work illustrates, when injustices are ignored or left unaddressed, the resulting grievances linger beneath the surface and eventually re-emerge—often with damaging consequences. Mechanisms for truth-telling—whether formal truth commissions, historical documentation projects, or public commemorations—provide essential spaces for acknowledging past wrongs without allowing those wrongs to determine future relationships. By confronting difficult histories honestly, societies can begin to imagine shared futures.

Third, ethical peacebuilding requires attention to transitional justice—mechanisms for accountability that balance the need for justice with the imperatives of reconciliation. This often involves difficult compromises, as societies emerging from conflict must decide how to address past atrocities without triggering new cycles of revenge. South

Africa's Truth and Reconciliation Commission offers one model of prioritizing public acknowledgment of wrongdoing over punitive justice. Other contexts may require different approaches, but all must grapple with the tension between accountability and forward movement.

Fourth, sustainable peace depends on economic inclusion and development. Many conflicts are fueled by social and economic grievances such as inequitable distribution of resources, lack of opportunity, or exploitation by elites. Peace agreements that fail to address these underlying issues often prove fragile, as marginalized groups turn to violence when other avenues for advancement remain closed. Ethical peacebuilding thus requires attention to economic justice alongside political settlements.

Finally, ethical peacebuilding must foster moral trust—confidence that institutions and processes will operate according to shared ethical principles rather than narrow interests or arbitrary power. This trust cannot be decreed but must be built through consistent commitment to transparency, fairness, and accountability. Sacks's emphasis on moral leadership speaks to this dimension of peacebuilding—the need for leaders who inspire trust through ethical consistency rather than mere political calculation.

Conclusion: Peace Worth Having

Ending wars in times of uncertainty requires more than diplomatic skill or military strategy—it demands moral vision and ethical courage. This article has argued that peace processes that prioritize expediency over justice often sow seeds for future conflict. The betrayal of Poland after World War II illustrates the consequences of ending wars without adequate attention to inclusivity, truth, and dignity.

In Bauman's liquid times, where certainty dissolves and change accelerates, the work of peacebuilding must adapt to new realities while remaining anchored in enduring ethical principles. This requires leaders who are not just deal-makers but truth-tellers who can navigate the difficult terrain between acknowledgment of past wrongs and hope for shared futures. It demands peace processes that engage the full range of stakeholders rather than just official negotiators, creating multiple channels for dialogue across divides.

Sustainable peace requires patient attention to both structures and narratives—the institutional arrangements that distribute power and resources alongside the stories that communities tell about themselves and others.

Ultimately, ending wars is not merely about stopping violence, but about healing futures. It requires creating conditions where former enemies can imagine shared destinies, where grievances can be acknowledged without determining future relationships, and where the dignity of all parties is respected. Such peace is difficult to achieve and requires constant renewal, but it represents the only peace truly worth having—peace rooted not just in power but in justice, not just in order but in human flourishing.

As we confront the complex challenges of ending contemporary conflicts, the framework outlined in this article offers a path forward—emphasizing moral leadership, inclusive dialogue, truth-telling, transitional justice, economic inclusion, and the rebuilding of trust. For in the end, how we end wars shapes not just the cessation of violence, but the quality of peace that follows.

Notes

[1] Zygmunt Bauman, *Liquid Times: Living in an Age of Uncertainty* (Polity Press, 2007).
[2] Quoted in "How Churchill, Roosevelt and Stalin Planned to End the Second World War," Imperial War Museums, https://www.iwm.org.uk/history/how-churchill-roosevelt-and-stalin-planned-to-end-the-second-world-war.
[3] Anne Applebaum, *Twilight of Democracy: The Seductive Lure of Authoritarianism* (Doubleday, 2020).
[4] Anne Applebaum, *Autocracy, Inc.: The Dictators Who Want to Run the World* (Doubleday, 2024).
[5] Jonathan Sacks, *The Dignity of Difference: How to Avoid the Clash of Civilizations* (Continuum, 2002); Jonathan Sacks, *Morality: Restoring the Common Good in Divided Times* (Basic Books, 2020).
[6] Clare Mulley, *The Spy Who Loved: The Secrets and Lives of Christine Granville* (Macmillan, 2012).
[7] Statista, "Conflicts Worldwide 2025—Statistics & Facts," March 21, 2025, https://www.statista.com/topics/13125/conflicts-worldwide-2025/.
[8] United Nations, "Ukraine's Demographic Crisis UNFPA," October 22, 2024, https://www.unognewsroom.org/story/en/2394/ukraines-demographic-crisis-unfpa-22-october-2024.
[9] Mario Pianta, "What Has Been the Cost of Ukraine's War—And Who Pays?," Social Europe, March 10, 2025, https://www.socialeurope.eu/what-has-been-the-cost-of-ukraines-war-and-who-pays.

ENDING WAR, BUT BEGINNING PEACE?

Alain Tschudin
Faculty of Arts and Social Sciences, Stellenbosch University; St Edmund's College, University of Cambridge

ABSTRACT

The end of war, conventionally marked by the implementation of a ceasefire agreement, is popularly celebrated and politically lauded in the aftermath of extreme violence. However, the so-called "silencing of the guns" is regarded only as "negative peace" or first steps away from direct violence. What about beginning Peace? Johan Galtung, esteemed for his life work in peace studies, suggests that the situation after the cessation of hostilities might be worse than the status quo ante. With reference to contemporary violent conflict in the Middle East, focusing on hostilities between Israel and Palestine, I suggest that pursuing lasting "positive peace" will in fact turn on whether or not greater attention is afforded to addressing cultural and structural peace, both for survivors and belligerents, through preventative and rehabilitative efforts. The search for narratival convergences between affected parties opens the possibility of a shared language and dialogue between self and other. This recognition can enable a relational ethics with restorative actions. Alternatively, so long as the Thrasymachan mind-blindness of those in power persists among belligerents, ordinary civilians will continue to bear the brunt of the violence, suffer grievously and lose their lives or those of loved ones, while peacebuilding efforts will remain futile.

Professor Alain Tschudin is the UNESCO Gandhi-Montessori-Luthuli Chair on Education for Peace and Transformative Solidarity, hosted by the Faculty of Arts and Social Sciences, Stellenbosch University, and co-hosted by St Edmund's College, University of Cambridge, where he holds a College Fellowship.

The Problem—Might as Right

Early in Plato's *Republic*, Thrasymachus and his interlocutors contend with Socrates in a dialogue on justice, which, based on his observations, Thrasymachus approximates to "nothing else than the advantage of the stronger,"[1] because unjust men profit more greatly than their counterparts; perhaps something akin to the contemporary turn of phrase, "good guys end last." Simon Blackburn characterizes Thrasymachus as a representative of "the Machiavellian men of realpolitik, knowing they live in a dog-eat-dog world and adapting themselves to it."[2]

Socrates uses his "craft" analogy to gradually dismantle this argument, although commentators such as Edward Warren suggest that the analogy is rather more of a profound learning opportunity, a reflection of Plato's "deeper convictions" surrounding his worldview, "not only about justice, but also about man and the cosmos he lives in,"[3] with an adversary who holds a very different, dare one say, counterposed position.

On a Socratic reading, justice renders to each their due and the end of justice, namely "the good," is constant and unwavering. Accordingly, for Socrates, the design of the ruler's craft must be "to guide a community so that its citizens can reach their human good." While Socrates admires the nous of craftsmen, as Warren suggests, he is less enthused by politicians "who have vague opinions and prejudices and cannot explain or defend what they do and frequently are incompetent in reaching whatever goals they do have."[4]

Plato, channeling Socrates, argues that for knowledge as *telos* (end or goal), there must be action. In the Platonic sense, knowing is doing. To know justice means to do justice. However, he recognizes that there will always be a gap between knowledge and action since the human aspires toward the ideal form of the good. Warren recognizes that, "Knowledge is being and power...[t]o have knowledge for Plato means that a person embodies knowledge so that he acts and is the knowledge. In being one's knowledge a person is good."[5]

Hence, "The evil general is one who does not understand that the goal of war is peace and so is a general ambiguously. Justice is a skill that has at its object the securing of the human good by the maintenance of order according to a hierarchy of powers that produce good."[6] Our yardstick for discussion around ending war and beginning peace will be precisely this: what promotes the good, not for the strong man, or woman, but for the shared, universal good?

The Impact of Ending War(s)

I shall argue that the problem outlined above is critically relevant when approaching the theme "Ending War" precisely because many modern-day heads of state, rulers, and generals appear to have lost sight of the fact that the goal of war is peace. Rather, by warmongering, their ambitions are diametrically opposed to advancing the good and much more aligned with the pursuit and maximization their own self-interest or that of their faction. The consequences of such approaches can be witnessed in various contexts around the world, not least of which, in Sudan, the most under-reported current conflict, where, according to Save the Children, as of September 2024, ten million people had been internally displaced, half of which were children.[7] In April 2025, according to the UN Office of the High Commissioner for Refugees (UNHCR), this total figure had risen to thirteen million displaced people.[8]

Likewise, we see this deviance from the good with respect to the ambitions of individual leaders and their regimes, perhaps most visibly exemplified at present by those such as Vladimir Putin in the invasion of Ukraine and Benjamin Netanyahu in the Middle East. Under operating conditions such as these, acts of provocation and escalation are on the rise, whether through a regime's internal acts of terror to quell dissent (consider the murder of Alexei Navalny) or externally, as in aggression aimed at the eradication of peoples. Poignantly, *The New York Times* reports 101-year-old Mrs. Halyna Semibratska of Izium, Ukraine as stating, "I understand, even though I'm old," "I have kept my memory. I remember a lot. But now I can't understand what's going on. It's not a war. It's not a war, it's an elimination."[9]

Consider likewise the extra-judicial state sponsored killings such as witnessed across the Middle East, which have extended from individual assassinations to the mass taking of life in dense civilian populations (e.g., Gaza, the pager incident in Lebanon) and the Israeli Security Forces (ISF)'s repeated military violations of state sovereignty and the laws of war.

Under such conditions, simply put, peace cannot prevail. Ontologically speaking, it is as if Thrasymachus's strong men are lacking the capacity to put themselves in the shoes of the other, because in their mind-blindness, they seemingly have lost their sense of other. What is just for them parts ways from the teleological end of justice, as human good. Instead, we are confronted with an increasingly downward "spiral of violence."[10]

Suffice it to say that the events leading to the outbreak of conflict, whether in Sudan, the invasion of Ukraine, the crisis in the Middle East, and elsewhere, are unique and have their own context, albeit at times being inter-related. Some unpicking of the thread may help us to understand why ceasefires do not necessarily represent the end of war.

Given the gravity of the situation in the Middle East, this article attempts to delimit the topic to concentrate efforts on this context, with an awareness both of its complexity and of limitations of time and scope. At a moment when sensitivities are running high and people are traumatized, and perhaps becoming increasingly polarized, it is difficult to say anything. As Italian antifascist and human rights activist Ginetta Sagan famously remarked, however, "Silence in the face of injustice is complicity with the oppressor."[11] Respected psychologist and social justice activist Anthony Collins recently shared how difficult it is to attempt to say anything on the topic of Israel and Palestine without being accused of anti-Semitism or Islamophobia, depending on which perspective is being advanced.[12]

At the outset, let us acknowledge how terribly devastating the last year and a half has been—and continues to be—for our own friends and colleagues, both Israeli and Palestinian, Jewish and Muslim. One's compulsion to speak, even if awkwardly and despite the challenge of so doing, arises from witnessing the profound impact of the trauma on friends, families, and society at large.

In this endeavor, some acknowledgment of one's own positionality is necessary; Roni Berger, for one, notes the importance of reflexivity in the research process.[13] My own positionality is as a psychologist and applied moral philosopher living in South Africa with conflict zone experience, having served as a humanitarian in Africa and the Middle East. My mother originates from a Maronite Christian background; her grandparents emigrated from Lebanon to South Africa in the late nineteenth century and we still have family there. We are preoccupied about their safety and wellbeing. Mindful of a diverse and inclusive readership, it might be mindful to flag that some content may be triggering while reassuring readers that the framing intention of the article is fraternal, to promote peace for all.

No Peace in the East

In the Middle East, the most recent flare-up was triggered by the mass-coordinated attack on Israel by Hamas and related Palestinian armed groups on October 7, 2023.

The world could not believe, as we watched on livestream, the almost surreal wave of motorized gliders fly by the Nova festival as civilians scattered screaming into the unfolding dust and chaos of the attack. Much as with inflection points such as 9/11, global citizens appeared to take existential pause at the horror being unleashed. I visited a Jewish school in Mexico City on Day 152 after the attack where flowers had been placed in a vase and staff members wore military style dog-tags reading "bring them home." It was a highly emotive experience and very difficult to see affected friends and colleagues taking strain, feeling helpless and traumatized.

The United Nations addresses this attack and related atrocities comprehensively in the report of an Independent International Commission of Inquiry on the Occupied Palestinian Territory, including East Jerusalem, and Israel of June 10, 2024, entitled *Detailed findings on attacks carried out on and after 7 October 2023 in Israel*,[14] which finds Hamas and related armed combatants guilty of war crimes.

In the aftermath of October 7, 2023, the statecraft of the Israeli prime minister ought to have been to secure the release and return of the hostages. Instead, his response became a premise for a full-scale ground offensive in Gaza that as of late September 2024 had claimed more than 41,000 lives and much to the chagrin of the families of the hostages, had little to do with their wellbeing.

In the light of unfolding events, on December 29, 2023, South Africa brought an application to the International Court of Justice (ICJ) against Israel regarding alleged violations by Israel of its obligations under the Genocide Convention pertaining to Palestinians in Gaza. South Africa requested provisional measures in order to "protect against further, severe and irreparable harm to the rights of the Palestinian people under the Genocide Convention" and "to ensure Israel's compliance with its obligations under the Genocide Convention not to engage in genocide, and to prevent and to punish genocide."[15]

The Court issued its Order on January 26, 2024, with additional provisional measures on March 28 and new measures on May 24. The ICJ also declared the occupation of Palestinian territories unlawful in July 2024, opening the way for the UN General Assembly to pass a (non-binding) resolution on September 18 calling for an immediate end to unlawful occupation of all Palestinian territory.[16] In addition to the above, the Prosecutor of the International Criminal Court (ICC) sought arrest warrants for Hamas leaders Yahya Sinwar, Mohammed Diab Ibrahim Al-Masri (Deif), and Ismail Haniyeh and for Israel's Benjamin Netanyahu and Yoav Gallant for war crimes and crimes against humanity.[17]

However, instead of showing restraint after mounting international pressure or expansive domestic protests,[18] Netanyahu, his cabinet, and generals upped the ante, seemingly seeking to provoke war on several fronts while continuously signaling a willingness to persistently violate the international laws of war and international humanitarian law. This has been documented in the "apocalyptic destruction" of Gaza described in the United Nations Independent Commission of Inquiry report of June 10, 2024, entitled *Detailed findings on the military operations and attacks carried out in the Occupied Palestinian Territory from 7 October to 31 December 2023*,[19] which finds the Israeli Security Forces and their commanders to have perpetrated war crimes, as well as crimes against humanity.

At the initial penning of this article, the latest round of explosive carnage in the Lebanon on September 17, 2024 prompted US secretary of state, Antony Blinken, who had been in Cairo working toward a ceasefire, to comment as follows: "We've seen that in the intervening time, you might have an event, an incident - something that makes the process more difficult, that threatens to slow it, stop it, derail it - and anything of that nature, by definition, is probably not good in terms of achieving the result that we want, which is the ceasefire."[20]

Sophisticated Evil

Much as the originally intended topic was a consideration of ceasefires and their aftermath in memory of the late Professor Johan Galtung, it seems as if even this would be a bridge too far, given the present escalation in the Middle East. Galtung himself makes the following realistic observation:

> then comes the basic point: *after the cease-fire the situation may be worse than before the violence erupted.* The direct violence may be the lesser evil, at least in the longer term, than the structural and cultural damage wrought. It is like the way being hospitalized is seen in some societies: like a market. The patient offers one disease and gets two or three iatrogenic diseases in return, one surgical error, one infection; and then "hospitalitis" if only in the form of long-lasting back-sores.
>
> Direct violence may have come to a celebrated end. The direct suffering is over, but the structural and cultural violence have increased in the process. Violence therapy has to learn from disease therapy: include *prevention* – build cultural and structural peace – and include *rehabilitation*, meaning build cultural and structural peace again. And again. And again.[21]

What the latest episode in the Middle East, involving Israel, Palestine, Lebanon, and now Iran, does confirm is the certainty that a ceasefire will not signal a lessening of violence, but on the contrary, and in keeping with Galtung's fears, that things will effectively become worse. And since September, 2024, they unreservedly have.

To make this point, it is necessary to consider the aftermath of the pager attack in Lebanon. United Nations High Commissioner for Human Rights, Volker Türk, comments thus on the atrocity:

> Widespread simultaneous explosions across Lebanon and in Syria yesterday, where detonating pagers killed at least 12 people – including two children – and left thousands of people injured, are shocking, and their impact on civilians unacceptable. The fear and terror unleashed is profound…Simultaneous targeting of thousands of individuals, whether civilians or members of armed groups, without knowledge as to who was in possession of the targeted devices, their location and their surroundings at the time of the attack, violates international human rights law and, to the extent applicable, international humanitarian law. There must be an independent, thorough and transparent investigation as to the circumstances of these mass explosions, and those who ordered and carried out such an attack must be held to account.[22]

William Christou, writing for *The Guardian* on September 18, 2024, entitles his piece "'Sophisticated Evil': Beirut medics and civilians horrified by pager attack."[23] Documenting the shock, trauma, and outrage expressed by survivors and bystanders, he reports a witness comment that, "I saw a man trying to hold his face together; it had completely split. His eyes had popped out of his skull and blood was pouring out." Medics described the mass event as apocalyptic, with an ophthalmic emergency on an unprecedented scale in the Lebanon (and globally, perhaps somewhat reminiscent of the Halifax Explosion of 1917). Comments from two Lebanese civilians aptly illustrate the point:

The first, a mother of two, distributing aid outside a hospital, states, "I'm horrified by the level of sophisticated evil. It's completely crazy," commenting on her existential anxiety as follows, "By doing this today, they can get to anyone. They can get to us in our bedrooms. They breach all laws of war and humanity. And no one is stopping them."

The second, a male medic, while stressing he would hold fast to nonviolent resistance remarked thus, "I am a medical worker, but the grudge I have now ... I will insist on teaching it to my great-great-grandson. I was neutral, but now I'm going to take a side."[24]

Unpacking the term "sophisticated evil," we find the etymological roots of the first word "sophisticated" from the medieval Latin *sophisticatus* 'tampered with,' coming to mean "adulterated or mixed with a foreign substance."[25] "Evil," in turn, stems from *yfel*, in Old English, which stems from Germanic origins *euvel* (Dutch) or *uebel* (German), the proto-Germanic *ubilaz*, signifying the Proto-Indo-European (PIE) $h_2upélos$ "bad, evil" or Hittite "to mistreat, harass" or "throw / cast away" or alternatively from the PIE word *upélos* "literally going over or beyond (acceptable limits)."[26]

Here is an instantiation of the might of the stronger, indiscriminately targeting those representing (and possibly only potentially, if at all) an opposed group, in a flagrant deviation from justice defined as virtue with a morally good end, and without any sanction. Such violent force continues at scale with impunity. Since the original presentation of this article in September 2024, by the end of April, 2025, the death-toll from Israeli strikes in Lebanon had surpassed 4,000 fatalities,[27] with a further 10,000 deaths recorded in Gaza,[28] while the ICJ continues painstakingly to deliberate on whether genocidal actions are underway amid Israel's continued military action and sustained blockade on all humanitarian aid to Gaza.[29]

Tipping Point or Teleological Suspension?

Much like our intuitive recoil at the horror of the Nova livestream, there is something in human nature that finds the industrial-scale cruelty of the response as morally repulsive—alienlike, tampered with and beyond acceptable limits. This is the case because its end is so comprehensively destructive, both physically and directly in the short-term (death, disability, despair, anxiety) and deleterious to the longer-term aim of cessation of hostilities or to any prospects of sustainable peace. Hence, as we heard from the final interviewee, a medic; he was once neutral but this experience has led to a grudge and to the promise of an inter-generational transmission of resentment and hatred, which is, now, not baseless. Herein lies the persistent problem and the impediment to promoting peace.

With reference to the example above, we are already well on the way to ethnic cleansing, if not genocide, and face the real possibility of opposed parties intent on mutual annihilation. The escalation has already transgressed acceptable limits, whether considered from the initial event triggered by Hamas or from the ISF response. We are now into the realm of the surreal.

The only possible way to reason further around unacceptable transgression for either party might be to consider the phenomenon from the angle of the teleological suspension of the ethical. Might we consider the exceptional suspension of normative ethical rules for the achievement of a greater good, as in Søren Kierkegaard's exploration of the story of Abraham and Isaac?[30] As Elmer Duncan puts it, "The question is: is there a higher telos in relation to which ethical duties must be suspended as we go beyond them?"[31]

On Kierkegaard's account, Abraham, faithful to the command of God, is prepared to sacrifice his only son Isaac, willing to violate the command "Thou shalt not kill," to conform himself to divine will. For Kierkegaard, it is only outside of ethics (and not in universal rules because he transgresses these) that Abraham's action can be justified, but only in his individual particularism. This prompts Duncan to refer to Abraham as not an ethical man, but as "a religious man of faith."[32] As Stephen Faison comments:

> Abraham's choice seems quite clear, however distressing: either kill his son or disobey God. As long as he is able to suspend the knife over Isaac, which he cannot do indefinitely, Abraham can remain in the paradox and believe that he will both gain and lose Isaac, but as soon as he must plunge the knife or discard it, then the paradox is broken. If Abraham sincerely believes that he will lose Isaac in the here and now because God ordered the sacrifice, then he thrusts the knife into Isaac's chest, killing his son. If Abraham sincerely believes that he will not lose Isaac in the here and now, then he does not plunge the knife into Isaac's chest, and does not kill his son. Once Abraham's time expires, he must act, and the paradox dissolves.[33]

In the current case, we cannot readily invoke divine command to justify the suspension of the ethical, since the pursuit of the "good" of the one party will obliterate the existence of the other and vice versa. It would be as if both Abraham and Isaac were to turn the knife on each other, believing this to be necessary to fulfill God's will. So long as both parties, in this instance Hamas and the ISF, maintain their course of violence and remain intent to extinguish the other, "ceasefires" will remain cosmetic, advanced only because of the pragmatic gains to be made by swaying global opinion (sanctions, boycotts, avoidance of trials for war crimes) while the underlying ontological and ethical tensions continue to simmer and fester beneath the surface.

A Precondition of Violence: Narratival Divergence

Before exploring alternatives for peace in a fast-dwindling window of opportunity, and mindful of the all-too-human utterance of individuals such as the medic above, we ought to give more consideration to the preconditions for violence. As Dražen Pehar suggests:

> expectedly and normally, we are all against violence. And, of course, violence ought to be condemned and to an extent possible removed from this world. However, an insufficient number of people are aware of the fact that some conditions naturally create in one a need to respond violently; and a few people are indeed willing to try to identify, understand, and scrutinize, such conditions. If something repeatable within a human relationship precedes the outbreak of violence, what is it exactly? Viewed with a cold eye, the violence creating conditions should be deemed morally more problematic than violence itself. However, we don't hear the call, and protest, against 'the violence creating conditions' as often as we can hear one against violence.[34]

Referring to a classical conflict between Sparta and Athens, Pehar posits that war could have been avoided. Both parties were culpable and that while they both rightly pointed out "questionable moves" by their opponents, they erred in "not being able to confess their own errors and seek correction through dialogue and mutual understanding."[35]

To make this point, enter a *ho apolis* (one without a city), a being who, as opposed to a 'citizen,' "cannot co-live with other individuals within a sustainable community, a city," because they lack sociality, disregard justice and impose their unjust will by fear. In diametric contrast to Aristotle's rational citizen or *zoon logon echein*,[36] "the 'non-citizen' is marked by the absence of language that can be valid for the entire city, which is why s/he can protect the injustice only by the force of arms in order to gratify his or her perverted, and self-feeding, lust."[37]

Critically, Pehar makes the observation that much as the direct violence of the 'non-citizen' is problematic, "the more insidious, and persistent, forms of violence…are transmitted, and enabled, by language. However, we cannot respond to violent forms of language by the equivalent means. For instance, a liar is typically immune to lies. Also, one cannot overcome a lie by a lie, or a sophism by a sophism. You overcome it by a truth and a valid form of argument. Hence, in this sense, the key forms of violence in human societies actually tend to produce language constantly."[38]

A Precondition of Peace: Narratival Convergence

The key takeaway on this reading of human interaction is that language can be a medium for creating and sustaining collective life, whether for peace or for violence. This relates to the stumbling block that Pehar identifies: how to establish and maintain the balance between one's own openness to correction and receptivity to the language of others, with the "capacity/gift to create a common and viable language" to address "social-moral-legal-political disputes"?[39] In short, how might we balance and harmonize the self with the other through a shared language?

Given the possibility for human deviation from shared language and a closing off to, or perhaps even splitting off from, the other, if we are to consider an approach of humans away from competition and conflict to cooperation and compassion, we need a common bridge. Faced with a fatalistic and dizzying spiral into violence, Helder Camara presents a refreshing alternative, namely, the need to recognize human universality:

> Whatever the colour of your skin, the shape of your lips or your nose, whatever your height, you are neither a sub-man or a superman; you are a human creature. You have a head, a heart, hopes, dreams. More important still: the creator…has a whole plan of human fulfilment which involves you. If you belong to a tribe, a family, a race, you belong too to the human family. The injustices you encounter in your own environment exist everywhere.[40]

Revisiting Self-Other Relations

In the face of ideologies that seek to divide one from another, the capacity to consider oneself as another is critical. Martin Buber, in his book on I-Thou relations, referred expressly to the Zulu greeting still used where I come from in South Africa, *Sawubona*, literally, "I see you."[41] Much as this was viewed as a primordial or 'primitive' relation by European writers, the capacity to see another, or what in African philosophy we refer to as *ubuntu*, is complex, adaptive, highly evolved and critical to promoting a shared humanity.[42]

On the contrary, if I do not see you, then what are my responsibilities toward you? After all, seeing leads to knowing. As scripture tells us, "Then the Lord said to Cain, 'Where is your brother Abel?' 'I don't know,' he replied. 'Am I my brother's keeper?'" Note the narratival divergence. The Lord said, "What have you done? Listen! Your brother's blood cries out to me from the ground."[43]

Emmanuel Lévinas, sometimes referred to as the philosopher of "exteriority," urges us to consider the nature of encounter, and of relation, with the other. He develops an ethic of responsibility based on our "face-to-face" experience of the other.[44] Basically, I find myself responsible for right action in the "face of the Other." This appears to be promising and can be contrasted with the "interior" emphasis of Martin Heidegger, for example, focused predominantly on "self."[45]

There are some issues associated with this position, however. That 'Other,' on the reading of Paul Ricoeur, is considered by Lévinas to be "Justice, my Master."[46] As Ricoeur notes, this power relation imposed upon me does not establish a bond of genuine relation between us, but rather leads to action out of a forced or contrived "irrelation."[47] Amanda Ford describes the contrast between Lévinas's presupposition of "a primordial injunction initiated by the Other, 'thou shalt not kill'" with Ricoeur's invitation "'love me,' which returns the initiative to the self, acting from solicitude arising from empathy."[48]

For Ricoeur, whereas friendship turns on equality, or shared moral excellence in the Aristotelian sense, justice serves as an equalizer of power inequality. Hence his invocation of the Golden Rule ("Do unto others as you wish done to yourself and refrain from doing unto others that which you would not like done to yourself"). Ontologically, for Ricoeur, the consideration of oneself as another, as formulated above, leads to action, and attestation, "I was there!"[49] While linguistic analysis gives meaning to action, attestation is critical because it mediates between language and action,[50] and enables what we might term a relational ethics.

Such a relational ethics turns on the notion of *recognition*. The moment I recognize you, I must acknowledge your rights and my responsibilities toward you, because wisdom arises from "living well" for and with others. But what about your recognition of me? The issue now becomes one of mutual recognition and how we live, intersubjectively. In contradistinction to a combative Hobbesian struggle of all against all, for Ricoeur the preferred "state of peace," as the apex of mutuality, only arises through the mediation of love and justice. This cannot be reduced to the narrow, self-serving interest of a *homo economicus*, but rather relies on an alternative currency, "the economy of the gift"[51] and a different, more open and generously evolved being, one that we might term a *homo solidaritus*.

Transformative Solidarity

At a time when people are bunkering down while the world explodes, literally and peace implodes, is there the possibility to consider another way of being and right action? It is hard to consider the notion of generosity and gift-giving when so much is being taken, daily, from respective victims and survivors of violence. Specifically, in this analysis, is there a position whereby we can stand for and with the people of Israel and the people of Palestine?

Consider the foreword to *On Palestine*, the dialogue between Noam Chomksy and Ilan Pappé. When asked about his activism, Frank Barat comments:

> We are all born with compassion, generosity, and love for others inside us. We are all moved by injustice and discrimination. We are all, inside, concerned human beings. We all want to give more than we receive. We all want to live in a world where solidarity and companionship are more important values than individualism and selfishness. We all want to share beautiful things; experience joy, laughter, love; and experiment, together. But we have a problem. A big one. We live in a society, and an epoch, where we do not have time to think any longer.[52]

It is true that time on the existential clock for many humans appears to be running low. But to summarize the above argument: any attempt to shift our prevailing reality from war to peace will turn on the notion of recognition. Solidarity implies all of this: I recognize you, I am with you, I accept the negative consequences on your behalf and will bear them with you. However, solidarity can only arise where the other is seen and heard. If the other remains unseen, muted with their stories unspoken, all manner of atrocities remain possible.

For any hope at a ceasefire to be meaningful and lasting, as Galtung recognizes, there needs to be a disproportionate investment in building structural and cultural peace. Currently there is a disproportionate focus on violence, both direct and indirect.

That violence will only cease once there is an openness to the other. At present, the extreme closing off to the other, whether it be the obstinate commitment of Hamas and aligned armed groups to violence, or the retributive rage of the ISF, undercuts this.

Primarily, it will fall on those members of Israeli and Palestinian society who are willing and able to muster the immense courage (and one can only imagine how fraught that must be) and goodwill to lead any initiative for peace, with support from the international community.

While the plural of anecdote is not data, here is a story that illustrates the point: I volunteer with an NGO that focuses on education, peace, and integral human development. A Canadian neuroscientist reached out to our Executive Director in the Netherlands with urgency, having been contacted by an Israeli (Jewish) peace activist to alert them to the fact that the only Palestinian (Muslim) child and adolescent psychiatrist in Gaza and their family were in extreme danger. I was contacted in South Africa to seek out the help of NGOs who might be able to assist via neighboring countries such as Egypt to evacuate the family. This is only one minuscule example, but the empathy shown by the Israeli toward the Palestinian led, literally, to a global response based on whatever resources could be mobilized (time, money, talents, networks) resulting in eight human lives becoming more secure. Only eight lives saved, perhaps, but eight lives that may otherwise have been in jeopardy, albeit that their struggle continues. And all this from one individual's determined initiative, translated into recognition, attestation, and interpersonal solidarity.

I referred earlier to the dialogue between Noam Chomsky and Ilan Pappé, *On Palestine*. In their conversation, much reference is made to South Africa, and the lessons learned from that context, albeit that the two academics have differing interpretations of its use-value. There have been mixed reactions to South Africa's approach to the ICJ ranging along the spectrum from dismissive political grandstanding to the timely assertion of moral right.

As a South African, I feel that it is important to recognize that the country advances its position not based on some pietistic moralizing preaching, but rather given the lived experience of colonial and apartheid atrocities and mindful of the extreme effort taken to engage and move forward from these in an inclusive democracy. At least two of our esteemed colleagues, Liz Carmichael[53] and Padraig O'Malley,[54] both extensively involved in the anti-apartheid struggle, will know what I mean. It takes dialogue partners and actors from diametrically opposed sides of such conflicts with a network of local, regional, and global partners willing to work in solidarity. This is a long-term project and there are no quick fixes. This applies to all protracted conflicts, and all the more so with respect to Israel and Palestine.

To shift from a state of protracted war to lasting peace, as Johan Galtung suggests, prevention and rehabilitation are required. There is a process preceding this and continuing along with it, and this is a transformative strategy, one that considers conflict dynamics, analyzes these, and intentionally shifts the dial. Transformation necessitates understanding the preconditions for both violence and peace and then engaging these, not just the direct violence but its indirect manifestations, culturally, structurally, linguistically. Prevention will turn on viable, humane alternatives to uncertainty, suffering, and violence.

As this article has argued, any advances will hinge on an ethics of relationality, whereby parties and related stakeholders can and will remain committed to seeing the other, even if sitting with and holding space in a very difficult and uncomfortable tension. Within this ethic, if we consider rehabilitation, the notion of transformative solidarity suggests that generosity of spirit will yield a better solution than justice rendered minimally. Such a delicate path suggests that victims, or rather those survivors, and perpetrators are given the possibilities, individually and communally, to attest to their own challenges of being, of processing related trauma and loss. One's hope, no matter how futile, is that this delicate process might lead to the recognition, through shared language and action, mediated where helpful, of what it means to live a good human life together in harmony with others, and not to spite them, in the aftermath of such pervasive dehumanization, death, and destruction.

We are reminded that if we seek peace, we must work for justice.[55]

Notes

[1] Plato, "Republic," Book One in *Plato: The Collected Dialogues*, ed. Edith Hamilton and Huntington Cairns (Princeton University Press, 1999), 588.

[2] Simon Blackburn, *Plato's Republic: A Biography* (Atlantic, 2006), 34. Blackburn also sees them as "the direct ancestors of blitzkrieg, terrorism, the worship of the free market, and the ethics of the business school…also…of American 'neo-conservatism'" (ibid.).

[3] Edward Warren, "Plato's Refutation of Thrasymachus: The Craft Argument," *The Society for Ancient Greek Philosophy Newsletter*, no. 124 (1985): 4, https://orb.binghamton.edu/sagp/124.

[4] Ibid., 9–10.

[5] Ibid., 13.

6. Ibid., 16.
7. Save the Children, "What Is Happening in Sudan?," accessed September 22, 2024, https://www.savethechildren.net/what-we-do/emergencies/what-happening-sudan.
8. USA for UNHRC, "Sudan Crisis Explained," accessed April 30, 2025, https://www.unrefugees.org/news/sudan-crisis-explained/.
9. Emile Ducke and Evelina Riabenko, "A Replay of Childhood Terror," *The New York Times*, May 22, 2024, 1–2.
10. Helder Camara, *Spiral of Violence* (Sheed and Ward, 1971).
11. Lawrence Joffe, "Ginetta Sagan," *The Guardian*, September 14, 2000, https://www.theguardian.com/news/2000/sep/14/guardianobituaries.
12. Anthony Collins, "Irreconcilable Differences: Competing Constructions of Genocide from the West and Global South," in *The Palgrave Handbook of Criminology in the Global South*, 2nd ed. (Palgrave Macmillan, 2025). See also Collins, "Gaza: From Colonial Violence to Peace Action," online seminar, December 12, 2024, International Centre of Nonviolence, Durban University of Technology, YouTube, 50 min., 9 sec., https://www.youtube.com/watch?v=oZuZbmmtPX0.
13. Roni Berger, "Now I See It, Now I Don't: Researcher's Position and Reflexivity in Qualitative Research," *Qualitative Research* 15, no. 2 (2013): 219–34, https://doi.org/10.1177/1468794112468475.
14. United Nations, "Detailed Findings on Attacks Carried Out On and After 7 October 2023 in Israel," A/HRC/56/CRP.3, accessed September 23, 2024, https://www.ohchr.org/sites/default/files/documents/hrbodies/hrcouncil/sessions-regular/session56/a-hrc-56-crp-3.pdf.
15. United Nations, "Application of the Convention on the Prevention and Punishment of the Crime of Genocide in the Gaza Strip (South Africa v. Israel) Decision of the Court on South Africa's Request for Additional Provisional Measures," accessed September 23, 2024, https://www.un.org/unispal/document/south-africa-v-israel-decision-of-the-court-on-south-africas-request-for-addition-16feb2024.
16. United Nations, "Illegal Israeli Actions in Occupied East Jerusalem and the Rest of the Occupied Palestinian Territory," accessed September 23, 2024, https://documents.un.org/doc/undoc/ltd/n24/266/48/pdf/n2426648.pdf.
17. International Criminal Court, "Statement of ICC Prosecutor Karim A.A. Khan KC: Applications for Arrest Warrants in the Situation in the State of Palestine," accessed September 23, 2024, https://www.icc-cpi.int/news/statement-icc-prosecutor-karim-aa-khan-kc-applications-arrest-warrants-situation-state.
18. Martin Bekker, "Protest as an Act of Love," *International Journal of Žižek Studies* 15, no. 1 (2021), https://zizekstudies.org/index.php/IJZS/article/view/1194.
19. United Nations, "Detailed Findings on the Military Operations and Attacks Carried Out in the Occupied Palestinian Territory from 7 October to 31 December 2023," A/HRC/56/CRP.4, accessed September 23, 2024, https://www.ohchr.org/sites/default/files/documents/hrbodies/hrcouncil/sessions-regular/session56/a-hrc-56-crp-4.pdf.
20. Simon Lewis, "Blinken Warns Against Further Middle East Escalation After Lebanon Blasts," Reuters, September 18, 2024, https://www.reuters.com/world/middle-east/egypt-blinken-discuss-bilateral-ties-gaza-ceasefire-2024-09-18/.

21 Johan Galtung, "Violence, War, and Their Impact on Visible and Invisible Effects of Violence," *Polylog: Forum for Intercultural Philosophy*, no. 5 (2004), http://them.polylog.org/5/fgj-en.htm.
22 United Nations Office of the High Commissioner for Human Rights, "Comment by UN High Commissioner for Human Rights Volker Türk on Explosions Across Lebanon and Syria," September 18, 2024, https://www.ohchr.org/en/statements/2024/09/comment-un-high-commissioner-human-rights-volker-turk-explosions-across-lebanon.
23 William Christou, "'Sophisticated Evil': Beirut Medics and Civilians Horrified by Pager Attacks," *The Guardian*, September 18, 2024, https://www.theguardian.com/world/2024/sep/18/lebanon-beirut-medics-civilians-horrified-pager-attacks.
24 Ibid.
25 *The Concise Oxford English Dictionary* (Oxford University Press, 1999).
26 Guus Kronen, "*ubila-," in *Etymological Dictionary of Proto-Germanic* (Brill, 2013), 557.
27 Human Rights Watch, "World Report 2025: Lebanon Events of 2024," accessed April 30, 2025, https://www.hrw.org/world-report/2025/country-chapters/lebanon; "Israel Has Killed at Least 71 Civilians in Lebanon Since Ceasefire, UN Says," *Al Jazeera*, April 15, 2025, https://www.aljazeera.com/news/2025/4/15/israeli-attacks-killed-over-70-in-lebanon-since-ceasefire-un.
28 OCHA, "Reported Impact Snapshot: Gaza Strip (15 April 2025)," accessed April 30, 2025, https://www.ochaopt.org/content/reported-impact-snapshot-gaza-strip-15-april-2025.
29 OCHA, "UN Relief Chief Calls for End to Gaza blockade, Says 'Aid Must Never Be a Bargaining Chip,'" May 1, 2025, https://www.unocha.org/news/un-relief-chief-calls-end-gaza-blockade-says-aid-must-never-be-bargaining-chip.
30 Søren Kierkegaard, *Fear and Trembling*, trans. Walter Lowrie (Princeton University Press, 1941).
31 Elmer H. Duncan, "Kierkegaard's Teleological Suspension of the Ethical: A Study of Exception-Cases," *The Southern Journal of Philosophy* 1, no. 4 (1963): 9–18, https://doi.org/10.1111/j.2041-6962.1963.tb01051.x.
32 Ibid., 9.
33 Stephen Faison, "Faith as Paradox in 'Preamble from the Heart,'" *Florida Philosophical Review* 17, no. 1 (2017): 114–22, https://cah.ucf.edu/fpr/article/faith-as-paradox-in-preamble-from-the-heart/. Faison notes as follows: "the biblical account of Abraham's ordeal is disturbing because it presents Abraham as praiseworthy for being willing to kill his son at God's command. Johannes asks us to consider our reaction if a member of a church congregation upon hearing a sermon were to emulate Abraham. It is problematic to condemn an act of killing as morally wrong and then accept it as somehow right when the only new information is that God commanded the act…So what are we to make of Abraham's ordeal if the standard interpretation and Johannes' description of faith as paradoxical are unsatisfactory? Perhaps Søren Kierkegaard slyly informed us at the outset when he assigned this essay to his pseudonym, Johannes de silentio. Tales such as these, if accepted as true, are incomprehensible, and the best reply, paradoxically, is to remain silent" (120).
34 Dražen Pehar, "Humanity: Language, Conflict, and Violence, Part One," *TransConflict*, April 30, 2020, http://www.transconflict.com/2020/04/humanity-language-conflict-and-violence-part-one/.
35 Ibid.
36 Aristotle, *Ethics*, Book I: xiii, trans. J. A. K. Thomson (Penguin, 1976).
37 Pehar, "Humanity," 32.
38 Ibid., 37.

39 Ibid., 37–38.
40 Camara, *Spiral of Violence*, 60–61.
41 Martin Buber, *I and Thou*, trans. Walter Kaufmann (Scribners, 1970).
42 Pumla Gobodo-Madikizela, "Forgiveness Is 'the Wrong Word': Empathic Repair and the Potential for Human Connection in the Aftermath of Historical Trauma," in *Alternative Approaches in Conflict Resolution*, ed. Martin Leiner and Christine Schliesser (Palgrave Macmillan, 2018).
43 Genesis 4:9–10 (New International Version).
44 Emmanuel Lévinas, *Time and the Other*, trans. Richard A. Cohen (Duquesne University Press, 1987), 78.
45 For an in-depth discussion, see Alain Tschudin, "Being in Communion and Becoming Reconciled: Social Evolution, Interpersonal Ontology and the Ethics of Relationality" (PhD diss., University of Cambridge, 2007).
46 Emmanuel Lévinas, *Totality and Infinity: An Essay on Exteriority*, trans. Alphonso Lingis (Duquesne University Press, 1969), 72.
47 Paul Ricoeur, *Oneself as Another*, trans. Kathleen Blamey (University of Chicago Press, 1992), 189.
48 Amanda K. Ford, "The Self in the Mirror of the Scriptures: The Hermeneutics and Ethics of Paul Ricoeur" (PhD diss., University of Nottingham, 2012), 61.
49 Paul Ricoeur, *Memory, History, Forgetting*, trans. Kathleen Blamey and David Pellauer (University of Chicago Press, 2004).
50 Ibid., 64.
51 Paul Ricoeur, *The Course of Recognition*, trans. David Pellauer (Harvard University Press, 2005).
52 Frank Barat, introduction to *On Palestine*, by Noam Chomsky and Ilan Pappé (Penguin Random House, 2015), 1–2.
53 Liz Carmichael, *Peacemaking and Peacebuilding in South Africa: The National Peace Accord, 1991–1994* (James Currey, 2022).
54 Padraig O'Malley, "Northern Ireland and South Africa: 'Hope and History at a Crossroads,'" *John M. McCormack Graduate School of Policy and Global Studies Publications* 27 (2000), https://scholarworks.umb.edu/mccormack_pubs/27.
55 Pope Paul VI, "If You Want Peace, Work for Justice," January 1, 1972, https://www.vatican.va/content/paul-vi/en/messages/peace/documents/hf_p-vi_mes_19711208_v-world-day-for-peace.html.

PLAY THE PLAYERS FOR WINNING PEACE: COMPLEXITY ANALYTICS WITH THE UK-IRELAND GOOD FRIDAY AGREEMENT AS A CASE STUDY

Bilal M. Ayyub

Center for Technology and Systems Management, University of Maryland; Imperial College London; National Institute of Standards and Technology; International Joint Research Center for Resilient Infrastructure, Tongji University

ABSTRACT

This article presents an innovative framework for analyzing and resolving intractable conflicts through the lens of complexity analytics. By conceptualizing conflicts as complex adaptive systems with fractal properties, we introduce a multifaceted methodology that integrates game theory, network analysis, cognitive science, and artificial intelligence (AI) to comprehend and influence conflict dynamics across multiple scales. The approach emphasizes 'playing the players' rather than focusing solely on the immediate conflict situation, drawing insights from poker strategy and AI-driven decision-making processes. This strategy involves understanding the psychological profiles, risk attitudes, and decision-making patterns of key actors, allowing for more nuanced and effective interventions.

Bilal M. Ayyub is a Professor and the Director of the Center for Technology and Systems Management at the University of Maryland, College Park. He is also a Visiting Professor in the Department of Civil and Environmental Engineering at the Imperial College London, a Senior Economist in the Applied Economics Office of the National Institute of Standards and Technology (NIST), and Co-Director, International Joint Research Center for Resilient Infrastructure, Tongji University.

We demonstrate how mapping rationality spectrums, from extreme conditions to calculated trade-offs, can inform negotiation strategies. The framework incorporates market-based risk attitude quantification and memetic techniques to analyze information propagation and cultural influences in conflict zones. By treating conflicts as fractals, the methodology allows for the analysis of self-similar patterns across different scales, from local disputes to international conflicts. This approach enables policymakers and negotiators to identify critical intervention points and develop strategies that address the conflict's underlying structure.

The framework provides practical tools for conflict resolution practitioners, including network topology analysis, Bayesian updating of conflict assessments, and AI-driven scenario modeling. These tools are designed to enhance decision-making in complex, high-stakes environments where traditional approaches often fall short.

To validate the framework, we present a detailed case study of the 1998 Good Friday Agreement, demonstrating how complexity analytics can be applied to real-world conflict resolution processes. This case study illustrates the framework's potential for achieving sustainable peace in seemingly intractable conflict situations.

1. Background

1.1. Key Attributes of Intractable Conflicts

The resolution of intractable conflicts presents one of the most complex challenges in modern international relations. Traditional approaches often fail to capture the multifaceted nature of conflicts and their resolution mechanisms. This article presents a novel analytical framework that combines complexity science, game theory, strategic thinking drawn from poker, a game that has influenced political leaders' decision-making for generations, and artificial intelligence (AI).

Complexity science reveals conflicts as dynamic systems with multiple interacting elements, rather than simple binary oppositions.[1] These conflicts often exhibit fractal properties with self-similar partial or full nesting across different scales, from interpersonal power disputes, partisan politics, bilateral tensions or disputes, to contentious international relations at regional and global levels.[2] Some aspects of conflict resilience can be measured through its fractal dimensions, providing quantitative metrics for conflict persistence.[3] By incorporating elements of poker strategy, the framework aims to enhance the understanding of strategic interactions, bluffing, and risk assessment in conflict scenarios. Additionally, the integration of AI methodologies allows for more sophisticated analysis of complex conflict dynamics and potential resolution strategies.

1.2. System and Conflict-Related Terminology

Systems thinking provides a crucial foundation for understanding conflicts. A system is defined as a regularly interacting or interdependent group of elements forming a unified whole. This definition encompasses both complicated systems (large, static, many items) and complex systems (large, dynamic, many interactive and adaptive agents). The terminology provided in this section enables the development of appropriate analytical methods rooted in measurement science.[4]

The distinction between complicated and complex systems is vital for developing appropriate analytical methods: (1) Complicated systems are large, static systems with many items and interactions. These can be understood through reductionist approaches. (2) Complex systems are dynamic with many interactive and adaptive agents, exhibiting emerging properties. These require holistic analysis that accounts for emergence and adaptation.[5]

Complex systems are of particular interest in conflict analytics, where elements form patterns and react to emerging patterns. Such systems are often described as networked adaptive agents, studied for management strategies that influence agents through internal powers, leading to favorable emergent outcomes.

System complexity is often described by the order or structure defining a system and classified as either of the following: (1) Complexity with structure that is analytically addressable by computer models and numerical methods; (2) Complexity without structure that can be understood subjectively and is analytically addressable by expert opinions and AI methods.[6] These types are associated with limitations of computational power and information overload, respectively, and sometimes jointly exist by being not mutually exclusive.

The term "conflict" is preferably defined as peoples' disagreement with opposing opinions or principles. This definition provides an entry point for cooperation and enables the understanding of social processes, particularly among nations. It recognizes that conflicts arise from competing interests, often rooted in resource scarcity, addressing the fundamental questions of "who gets what, when, and how?"

This definition acknowledges that while conflicts may be unavoidable, wars should be preventable. By framing conflicts in this manner, the framework aims to identify opportunities for cooperation and peaceful resolution, even in seemingly intractable situations.

2. A Proposed Methodological Framework

Building upon the background section, this article proposes a comprehensive framework based on complexity analytics that employs multiple interconnected methods to analyze and resolve intractable conflicts. This framework is designed to be flexible and adaptable, allowing for the selection and tailoring of methods to meet the specific characteristics of each conflict situation, including the parties involved, underlying value systems, and objectives of the players.

2.1. Bayesian Networks for Dynamic Conflict Analysis

One key component of this framework is the use of Bayesian networks for conflict analysis. This approach utilizes a fundamental model for updating beliefs:

$$P(H|E) = P(E|H)P(H)/P(E) \tag{1}$$

where H represents hypotheses about conflict evolution, E represents new evidence, P denotes probability, and | indicates a conditional probability. This model enables dynamic updating of conflict assessments as new information becomes available, allowing for real-time adaptation of strategies.[7]

2.2. State-Based Methods for System Tracking

Complementing the Bayesian approach, state-based methods track system variables through transition matrices among system states. These matrices use pairwise probabilities to model transitions from one state to another, providing a structured way to analyze the evolution of conflict situations over time.[8]

2.3. Complex Network Theory and Hypergraph Analysis

Recent developments in network science have significantly enhanced our understanding of conflict dynamics. The application of complex network theory and hypergraph analysis allows for modeling of intricate relationships beyond simple binary connections.

For instance, in analyzing multi-party conflicts, the relationship between actors A, B, and C can be represented as a hyperedge (E):

$$E = \{e_1, e_2, ..., e_n\} \quad (2)$$

where each e_i represents a hyperedge connecting multiple nodes simultaneously.[9] This approach is particularly useful in identifying hidden alliance patterns and complex stakeholder relationships.

2.4. AI-Driven Conflict Analytics

The framework can incorporate AI architectures to process and analyze vast amounts of conflict-related data including (1) transformer networks that utilize multi-head attention mechanisms to analyze conflict-related communications, enabling the detection of subtle patterns in diplomatic exchanges and public statements; (2) graph neural networks to process structural information about conflict networks, revealing key influencers and potential points of intervention; and (3) reinforcement learning for optimizing intervention strategies through "Quality" Q-learning and policy gradient methods, allowing for adaptive conflict resolution approaches.[10]

2.5. Applicability to Resource Disputes Including Integration with Traditional Methods

The framework can also incorporate game theory for addressing preferences in resource-sharing or allocations related to disputes. This approach offers valuable strategies for resolving regional conflicts by modeling complex multi-party negotiations and identifying mutually beneficial solutions. By integrating these diverse analytical methods, the proposed framework provides a comprehensive toolkit for understanding and addressing intractable conflicts. It allows for a nuanced analysis of conflict dynamics across multiple scales, from individual actors to complex international systems, while remaining adaptable to the unique characteristics of each conflict situation.

For example, in the Ethiopian peace process (2022–2023), AI-driven analysis of social media patterns helped identify potential spoilers and supporters of the peace process, informing traditional mediation efforts.[11] Another example is the Yemen

Conflict (2015–2023) that exhibited complexity, demonstrating limitations of traditional analytical approaches, being treated by network analysis in this case to reveal distinct stakeholder groups with varying degrees of influence and interconnection. The application of hypergraph theory can help identify previously unrecognized alliance patterns, particularly in tribal areas. Market-based alliance analytics including in neighboring countries can provide early warnings of conflict escalations. Recent developments in network science have enhanced our understanding of conflict dynamics.

3. Analytical Methods for Conflict Resolution

This section provides details on selected methods presented under the methodological framework as illustrations.

3.1. Game Theory and Decision-Making

The Cold War arms race demonstrates various game-theoretical models that remain relevant today.[12] Recent applications of game theory to the Syrian conflict reveal how multiple actors with competing interests create a complex web of interactions. For example, the Prisoner's Dilemma model exemplifies how rational actors may choose mutual defection despite the clear benefits of cooperation; for instance, in nuclear deterrence scenarios, nations often maintain aggressive postures even when mutual disarmament would benefit all parties.[13] Game-theoretical models provide crucial insights into conflict dynamics based on mixed strategies using the following mindsets: (1) the Prisoner's Dilemma that explains mutual defection despite benefits of cooperation, (2) the Chicken game that models brinkmanship and escalation risks, (3) Deadlock, which illustrates preference for domination over cooperation, and (4) the Stag hunt that reflects assurance and reciprocity. The perceptual dilemma[14] shows how misperceptions prevent mutual disarmament. Figure 1 provides examples.

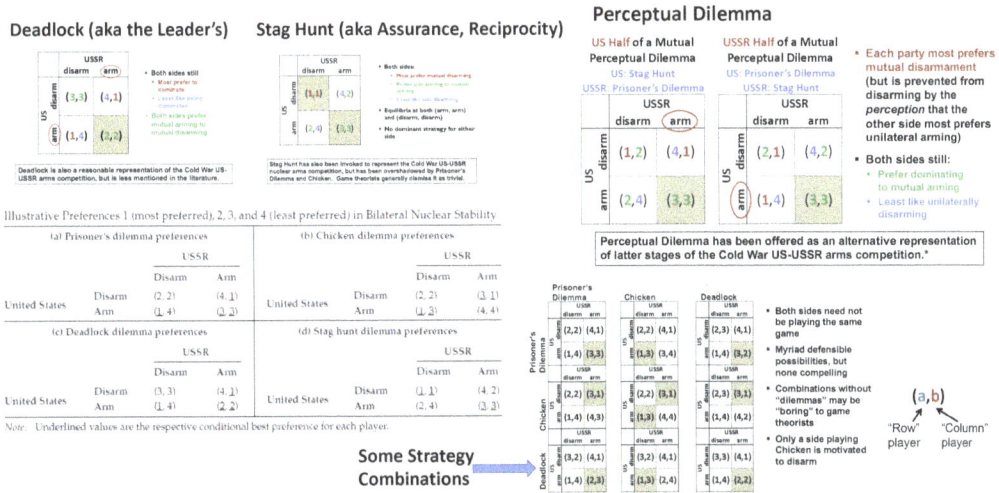

Figure 1: Bilateral Stability Models Showing Game-Theoretical Conflict Scenarios in Payoff and Preferences on a Scale of 1 to 4.

3.2. Bayesian Networks and State-Based Methods

Bayesian networks is an approach based on the probabilistic Bayes' theory for modeling causal relationships in conflicts through directed acyclic graphs (DAGs) capturing dependencies among variables and allowing for updating beliefs based on new evidence. The mathematical foundation builds on conditional probability theory among random variables such as X_1, X_2, and X_3:

$$P(X_1, X_2, X_3) = P(X_3|X_1)P(X_2|X_1)P(X_1) \qquad (3)$$

This formulation allows analysts to update probability assessments as new information becomes available during peace negotiations as illustrated in Figure 2.[15] This approach has proven particularly valuable in analyzing causality,[16] offering potential applications including the Colombian peace process (2012–2016), where multiple stakeholder interactions required continuous reassessment of negotiation strategies. Recent applications also include modeling insurgency dynamics in Afghanistan (2004–2009) and predicting conflict escalation points in South Sudan (2023–2024). For example, the 2012 peace negotiations between the Colombian government and the Revolutionary Armed Forces of Colombia (FARC) offered a rich context for complexity-based modeling of post-conflict dynamics. Stability analysis of the agreement revealed that long-term success depended not only on the disarmament process, but critically on the reintegration pathways for former combatants, the responsiveness of state institutions in rural territories, and the evolution of political inclusion mechanisms.

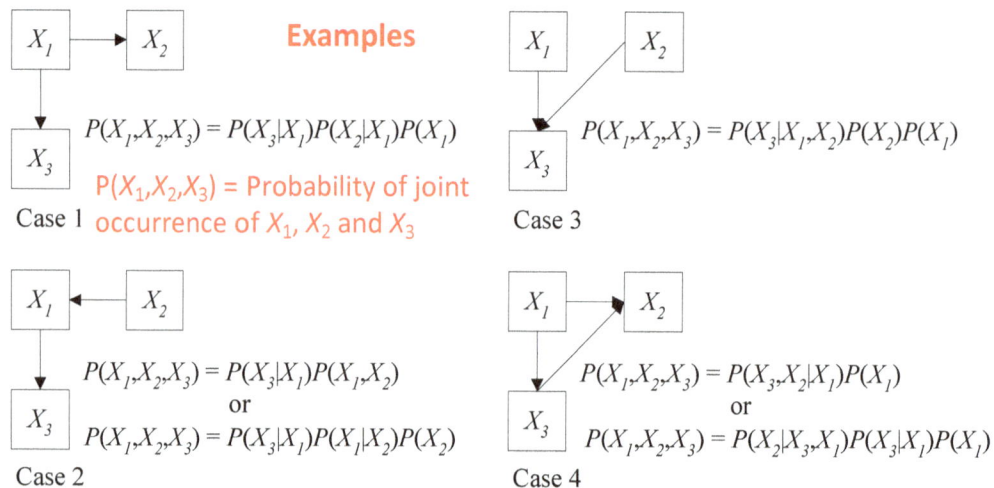

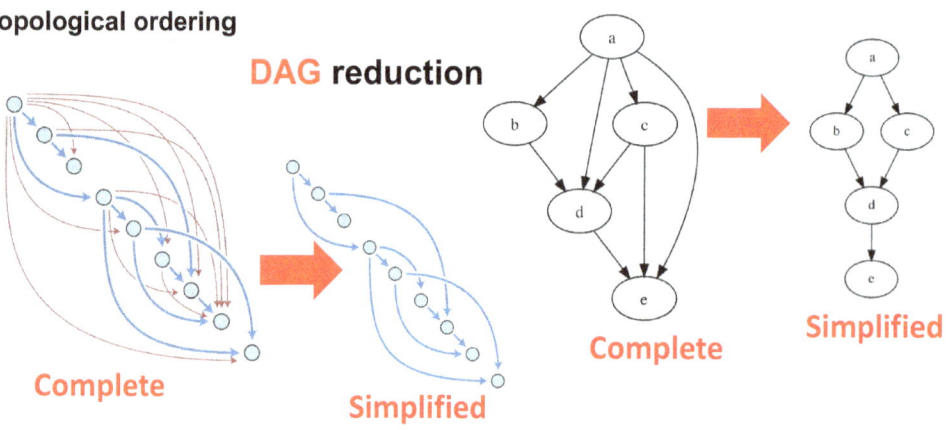

Figure 2: Bayesian Network Example Demonstrating Conflict Variable Relationships.

3.3. Network Analytics from Complexity Science Perspectives

Complex network theory can reveal hidden structures in conflicts and identify critical nodes and links of the networks through the analysis of interconnected relationships of underlying topological structures. Hypernetworks integrate multi-layered connections among entities, exposing centers of influence and communication pathways as illustrated in Figure 3. The 4D/RCS (real-time control system) architecture provides a framework for understanding hierarchical control in complex conflict situations, particularly valuable when analyzing insurgencies and asymmetric warfare.[17] Complex network theory reveals hidden structures in conflict systems through (1) hypernetworks integration, (2) multi-layered connections, and (3) centers of influence identification.

The resilience of conflicts is defined as the persistence of conflict despite resolution and control efforts. Some aspects of conflict resilience can be measured through its fractal dimensions, providing quantitative metrics for conflict persistence.[18] This approach has revealed remarkable similarities between conflicts at different scales, from local insurgencies to international wars. Network analysis has demonstrated that conflict structures often exhibit scale-free properties, meaning that intervention strategies must account for both highly connected hubs and peripheral actors.[19]

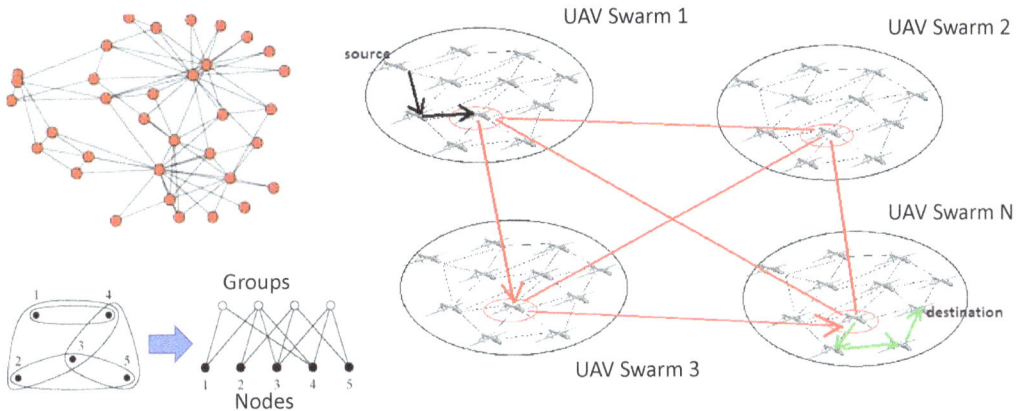

Figure 3: Network and Hypernetwork Topology Illustrated Using Communication, Command, and Control.

4. Rationality in Decision-Making

4.1. Rationality as a Spectrum

Decision-making in conflicts occurs along a spectrum of rationality that can conveniently be defined as (1) redline practices under extreme conditions with potential hysteria by killing and war as witnessed in recent wars, sometimes called a devoted actor mindset, and (2) calculated trade-offs under normal conditions with varying risk attitudes. The US Supreme Court's Industrial Union Department AFL-CIO v. American Petroleum Institute decision (1980) provides a framework for understanding threshold-based decision-making in high-stakes situations.[20] This ruling established a two-step process:

(1) use scientific evidence to identify significant safety concerns that require a regulatory action to set thresholds to be met at any cost, and (2) after meeting basic thresholds, applying trade-off and benefit-cost analysis to achieve economic efficiency. These two steps correspond to the division established under the notion of the spectrum of rationality as illustrated recently in wildfire risk rulemaking.[21]

4.2. Risk Attitudes, Market Mechanisms, and Psychological Factors

4.2.1. Market-Based Risk Attitudes

The quantification of risk attitudes in conflict situations has evolved significantly through market-based indicators and psychological analysis. Insurance markets in conflict zones provide particularly valuable data through premium/loss ratios that reflect both actual and perceived risks. Risk attitudes in conflict situations can be quantified through market mechanisms like insurance and catastrophe bonds. Recent studies of catastrophe bond and risk-transfer pricing in unstable regions have revealed sophisticated correlations between market assessments and hazards perceptions.[22] They reveal (1) risk comfort levels, from intolerable to comfortable, and group dynamics factors, such as leadership, cultural conformity, etc., (3) temporal aspects of risk perception, and (4) market-based loss amplification factors.

4.2.2. Psychological Factors

Psychological risk factors include group dynamics, cultural influences, and temporal aspects as illustrated in Figure 4. Group dynamics in decision-making demonstrate consistent patterns across different conflict scenarios. Cultural influences on risk perception play a crucial role, particularly in multi-ethnic conflicts.

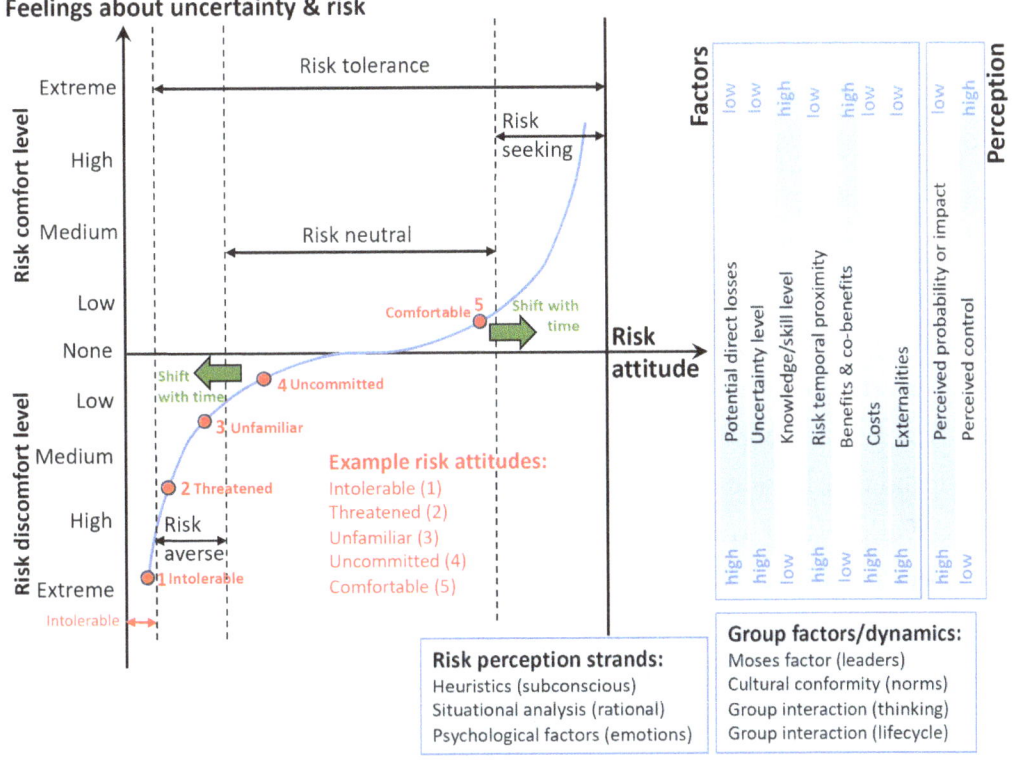

Figure 4: Risk Attitude Spectrum.

4.3. Memetics and Control

Memetics offers a scientific approach to information operations and psychological peacemaking or warfare. Peacemaking or military memetics, a subset of neuro-cognitive methods for behavioral change, studies how information propagates and persists in conflict situations. This understanding can be leveraged through functional magnetic resonance imaging (fMRI), psychological testing, behavioral measures, and neuro-chemical analysis.

5. Playing the Players as a Strategy Suitable for Implementation

5.1. Historical Diplomacy Perspectives

The approach emphasizing engagement by constructively "playing the players" rather than just addressing the immediate conflict situation, draws insights from poker strategy and AI with the requirement of having roots in an honorable value system. An honorable value system defines winning based on integrity, respect, and communication for achieving peace. It starts by defining the situation from the collective perspectives of key players, and subsequently defines the space to operate and engage the players for winning peace.

The application of poker strategy to international relations has a rich history. President Richard Nixon (1969–1974) explicitly connected poker principles to foreign policy strategy. In a 1983 interview, he explained that successful poker required establishing credibility, noting that "this is very important in foreign policy, too."[23] His approach to Vietnam negotiations demonstrated careful opponent observation combined with selective aggression, applying poker psychology to diplomatic strategy. Nixon was known to have connected poker strategy to anti-Communist foreign policy, emphasizing the importance of keeping opponents uncertain about one's intentions and capabilities. President Franklin D. Roosevelt (1933–1945) utilized poker games during World War II as sophisticated tools for wartime alliance building. His poker tables became informal diplomatic venues where crucial relationships were forged and tested, particularly in managing the complex dynamics between Winston Churchill (1940–45 and 1951–55) and Joseph Stalin (1924–53). Other key leaders who used poker in diplomacy or to forge political relationships include presidents Abraham Lincoln (1861–65), Ulysses S. Grant (1869–77), Theodore Roosevelt (1901–09), Harry Truman (1945–53), Dwight Eisenhower (1953–61), and Lyndon Johnson (1963–69). Churchill applied bluffing strategies with Stalin, built allied relationships through games, and examined the correlation between poker and diplomatic success.[24]

5.2. Trends in Poker Analytics

Contemporary poker analytics, particularly through AI applications, e.g., PioSOLVER and PokerSnowie,[25] demonstrate how optimal decision-making can be achieved in complex, incomplete-information environments. These insights apply directly to international negotiations where information is incomplete, multiple stakeholders have competing interests, psychological factors influence outcomes, and risk assessment is critical, represented analytically over time (t) as follows:

$$dx/dt = f(x,u,t) \qquad (4a)$$

$$y = g(x,u,t) \qquad (4b)$$

where x represents the state vector of conflict variables, u represents control inputs (intervention strategies), y represents measurable outputs, and g is the functional interactions.

5.3. AI Applications in Strategic Conflict Analysis

Recent developments in artificial intelligence have started to revolutionize conflict analysis. Machine learning algorithms now process vast amounts of conflict-related data to (1) predict conflict escalation points, (2) identify optimal intervention timing, (3) analyze social media for early warning signs, and (4) model population displacement patterns. AI systems employ architectures for conflict analysis by utilizing a combination of the following processes that were introduced earlier in this article: transformer networks, graph neural networks, and reinforcement learning.

The "play the players" approach draws insights from poker strategy and artificial intelligence with the word "play" intended to be associated with a value system to "engage" for achieving peace. It includes a traditional poker strategy of focus on psychological profiling, metaphorically reading body language and tells, and table talk mastery, and adapts features from game theory optimal (GTO) poker such as mathematical probability-based decisions, Nash equilibrium strategies, and AI-driven analysis, e.g., using the AI-platform PokerSnowie.

5.4. A Proposed Implementation Plan

An implementation plan is proposed below based on the play-the-player strategy defined in a four-phase approach that integrates both individual and system-level perspectives, aiming to address conflicts comprehensively and sustainably. The phases of the plan with details are shown in Figure 5. The plan draws additionally in its details on poker by focusing on understanding and influencing the motivations, behaviors, and relationships of key stakeholders involved as provided in the following steps:

- A. Identify and assess key players by mapping out all the stakeholders involved in the conflict, including primary parties, secondary influencers, and external actors, e.g., governments, NGOs, and community leaders, to identify and engage key ones. This step involves understanding motivations and determining what each player values most—whether it is power, resources, security, recognition, or ideological goals. In poker terms, understand their "hand," i.e., what they are working with, and their "tells," i.e., how they communicate their intentions. Additionally, the relationships between players, including alliances, rivalries, and dependencies should be examined in predicting how they might react to different moves.

B. Assess the conflict dynamics, akin to reading the "table" in poker, to understand the context of the conflict, including historical, cultural, and structural factors, i.e., knowing the environment in which the game is being played. This step includes identifying patterns, recurring behaviors, communication, and decision-making among the players. This can help predict future actions and reactions. It is essential to stay attuned to shifts in the conflict dynamics, such as changes in leadership, external interventions, or emerging issues that could alter the balance of power.

C. Develop strategic communication in terms of controlled disclosure by sharing information selectively to influence perceptions and behaviors, akin to poker where players bluff to mislead opponents. Strategic information releases can be used to create uncertainty or redirect focus. This step includes developing and promoting narratives that align with the desired outcomes. These narratives can shape how players perceive the conflict and their roles within it. The strategic communication uses ambiguity in an advantageous manner by introducing new ideas or proposals that challenge existing assumptions and force players to reconsider their positions.

D. Play the long game by having patience and deciding on timing with a special attention to building trust gradually with key players over time, even if progress seems slow. In poker, patience is crucial; similarly, in conflict resolution, rushing can lead to missteps. Also, timing is key to choosing the right moment to make moves, such as proposing peace talks or introducing new initiatives. Timing can be as important as the move itself. It is important to adapt, iterate, and be prepared to adjust your strategy as the conflict evolves. Flexibility and adaptability are essential in both poker and conflict resolution.

E. Leverage alliances through coalition-building on a strategic level with players who share common interests or goals. In poker, forming alliances can help you control the game; in conflict resolution, it can help you build momentum toward peace. Neutralize adversaries by identifying and engaging them to understand their resistance to outcomes and eventual peace. Using diplomacy, incentives, or pressure can help to reduce their opposition or bring them into the process. Empower moderates to support and amplify the voices of moderate players who are more likely to advocate for compromise and reconciliation.

F. Know when to fold as a strategic withdrawal to cut losses by recognizing that certain strategies or engagements are not working and being willing to disengage or change course. In poker, knowing when to fold is crucial to preserving your resources; in conflict resolution, it is important to avoid escalating tensions or wasting efforts on unproductive paths. In such cases, reassessing and regrouping will make a withdrawal an opportunity to reevaluate the situation, gather more information, and develop new strategies.

G. Aim to win the pot by achieving sustainable outcomes based on an honorable value system, and by securing commitments from all key players to the peace process with enforceable and sustainable agreements. Establishing or strengthening institutions can support long-term peace, such as governance structures, legal frameworks, and reconciliation mechanisms. Celebrating successes provides opportunities to acknowledge milestones in the peace process to build momentum and reinforce positive behavior among the players.

By applying the principles of poker—understanding the players, reading the table, bluffing strategically, playing the long game, leveraging alliances, knowing when to fold, and ultimately winning the pot—a nuanced and effective strategy for managing complex conflicts and achieving sustainable peace can be developed.

These steps can be enhanced further by AI-powered stakeholder analysis and predictive modeling in the form of player profiling including identifying hidden motivations, predicting future actions, and uncovering potential alliances or rivalries. AI-driven natural language processing (NLP) can be used to monitor social media, news, and communication channels to gauge stakeholder sentiment and detect shifts in public opinion or emerging grievances. Complex network theory can be used for mapping and influencing relationships by identifying key nodes (influential actors), clusters (alliances or factions), and weak ties (potential bridges between groups). Analyzing how information, resources, or influence flow through the network will identify which actors are most central or have the highest "betweenness centrality" with the ability to connect disparate groups and target them for engagement or coalition-building. Such analyses will inform the assessment of the resilience of the conflict network to external shocks or interventions. Lastly, memetic technologies can be used for narrative shaping and behavioral influence, such as memetic engineering for developing and disseminating memes-—ideas, symbols, or narratives—that resonate with stakeholders and promote peacebuilding. Memes can be tailored to specific cultural, social, or ideological contexts to maximize their impact. AI and network analysis can be used to design and deploy memetic campaigns that spread rapidly through social networks. For example, a meme promoting reconciliation or highlighting the costs of conflict could go viral, shifting public opinion. In a similar manner, counter-memes can be used to counteract harmful or divisive narratives propagated by adversarial groups. Using AI-enhanced strategic communication and deception can power dynamic messaging, controlled disclosure, and identifying and countering deepfake and synthetic media. Combining game theory with AI can help to model stakeholder interactions and predict outcomes. This combination will help with adaptive learning and creating decentralized intervention strategies to strengthen the network's resilience to future conflicts by fostering connections among previously isolated groups, promoting trust, and creating shared goals and a cultural shift through sustained engagement.

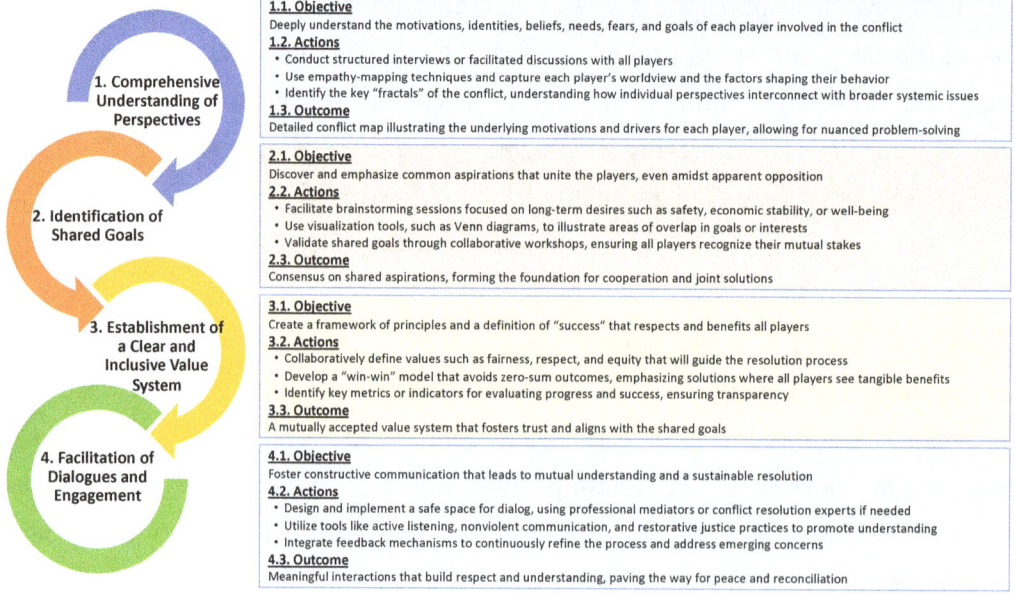

Figure 5: A Proposed Implementation Plan in Four Phases.

6. Case Study: The UK-Ireland Good Friday Agreement—A Practical Application of Engaging the Players for Winning Peace

6.1. Introduction

The Good Friday Agreement (GFA), signed in 1998, marked a significant turning point in the conflict known as the Troubles between Northern Ireland's unionist and nationalist communities, as well as the British government and the Irish Republic. This peace agreement has been widely celebrated as a successful resolution to a deeply entrenched and violent conflict.[26] From the perspective of the framework presented here, the Good Friday Agreement can be seen as a model of how engaging the players—understanding their dynamics, risk attitudes, and rationality—can lead to sustainable peace in a complex and fractal conflict system. This case study explores how the principles of complexity analytics were applied in the negotiation process to achieve the GFA.

6.2. The Complexity of the Northern Ireland Conflict

The Northern Ireland conflict was not simply a dispute between two sides but a multi-layered, multi-actor conflict, involving local players (unionists and nationalists), external actors (the governments of the United Kingdom and Ireland), and international stakeholders such as the United States. The nature of the conflict was deeply embedded in historical, religious, and cultural divides, complicated by issues of identity, territory, and political legitimacy.[27]

From the complexity analytics perspective, the Northern Ireland conflict can be viewed as a complex adaptive system, where the actions of one actor affected the behavior of others in a non-linear fashion. The system's fractal nature meant that tensions and resolutions at the local level mirrored those at the national and international levels, creating a dynamic interplay of multiple layers of conflict and potential resolutions.

6.3. Engaging the Players: The Strategic Application of Complexity Analytics

The process leading up to the Good Friday Agreement illustrates a sophisticated use of the framework's principles of "playing the players." Key actors in the conflict displayed varied risk attitudes, ranging from the highly risk-averse (e.g., the British government and moderate unionist leaders) to those willing to gamble with the status quo (e.g., radical nationalists and Sinn Féin).

Understanding the risk profiles of each of the main players was crucial to shaping the negotiation process. The unionists, particularly the Democratic Unionist Party (DUP) and Ulster Unionist Party (UUP), were traditionally very conservative in their approach to political compromise, fearing that any concession would lead to the erosion of Northern Ireland's union with Britain. Conversely, Sinn Féin, representing the more radical nationalist position, was willing to accept certain risks to secure a long-term political victory for the Irish republican cause, including the possibility of power-sharing arrangements with unionists. The complexity analytics framework suggests that negotiators can engage in dialogue by understanding these varying levels of risk tolerance. In the case of the GFA, this meant crafting solutions that mitigated the risks for both sides, such as the inclusion of a devolved government, which allowed both unionists and nationalists to share power in Northern Ireland without compromising their essential identity and political goals. By engaging and playing the players, the negotiators helped shift the actors' perceptions of risk and gain, enabling them to come closer to a resolution that was mutually acceptable.[28]

6.4. The Role of Identity and Memetics

The role of identity in the Northern Ireland conflict cannot be overstated. The fractal nature of the conflict meant that local identities (Catholic vs. Protestant, Irish vs. British) mirrored larger national and international identities. A key element of the negotiation process was the use of memetic techniques—the strategic communication of ideas and symbols—to shift entrenched positions. For instance, the British government and Sinn Féin used the symbolism of "peace" and "democracy" to create a new narrative that could transcend the polarized identities that had fueled violence for decades. The negotiations drew heavily on symbolic gestures, such as the recognition of Northern Ireland's place within the United Kingdom while simultaneously creating an opportunity for Irish nationalists to express their aspirations for closer ties with the Republic of Ireland. These memetic tools helped both sides navigate their cognitive biases and find common ground without directly confronting each other's most deeply held identity beliefs.

6.5. External Involvement and Hypernetworks

The involvement of external parties played a critical role in addressing two key challenges of historic resilience of the conflict, and the hidden structure of a nested conflict that can be understood and represented by fractals. In shaping the Good Friday Agreement, the United States, under President Bill Clinton, provided diplomatic leverage and acted as a mediator, signaling to all parties that a negotiated settlement, from a higher scale in self-similarity, was in their best interest at all scales. This third-party involvement also introduced a form of a hypernetwork where the actions of external actors influenced the dynamics and emerging post-conflict system state. By engaging external players who were viewed as neutral (or at least less biased), the UK and Irish governments were able to increase the perceived legitimacy of the negotiation process. Furthermore, the inclusion of international peacekeepers, the role of the European Union as another scale in nesting, and even private sector initiatives helped reinforce the stability of the agreement.

6.6. The Success of the Good Friday Agreement

The Good Friday Agreement can be seen as a case study in the successful application of complexity analytics to conflict resolution. The negotiators understood that the conflict was not merely about opposing ideologies but about the players' perceptions of risk, identity, and power. By carefully designing the peace process to address these dynamics—while incorporating mechanisms for power-sharing, disarmament, and the protection of human rights—the agreement created a structure where even deeply opposed groups could find ways to coexist peacefully. The success of the Good Friday Agreement lay not in an absolute resolution of all underlying tensions, but in the creation of a system that allowed for ongoing negotiation, adaptation, and conflict management. It established a framework for peace that recognized the fractal nature of the conflict, allowing for continuous engagement with the various players in the years following the agreement.

6.7. Takeaways and Lessons for Future Conflict Resolution

The Good Friday Agreement provides a compelling example of how complexity analytics can be used to understand and resolve intractable conflicts. By "engaging and playing the players" and recognizing the diverse risk attitudes, rationalities, and identity structures of the key actors, negotiators were able to craft a peace agreement that balanced competing interests and provided a foundation for sustained peace.[29]

The Northern Ireland peace process has since become a model for conflict resolution worldwide. Its success demonstrates the potential for local-to-local connections to support ongoing learning within peace processes. The educative-psychological approach, which has been the dominant mode of lesson learning and sharing in Northern Ireland, shows how peace processes can continue to evolve and adapt long after the initial agreement is signed.

In complex conflicts such as Northern Ireland, success lies not only in the resolution of immediate disputes but in the ability to engage the full spectrum of players and influence their behaviors in ways that lead to lasting peace. The GFA's approach to addressing societal trauma and moving from outright antagonism to a form of agonism—where conflict is addressed while respecting the "other's" entitlement to hold a radically different position—offers valuable lessons for other intractable conflicts.

As we reflect on the twenty-seventh anniversary of the Good Friday Agreement, it is clear that its international significance extends beyond the immediate resolution of the Northern Ireland conflict. The lessons learned from this process continue to inform and inspire peace efforts around the world, demonstrating the enduring value of complexity analytics in navigating the challenges of conflict resolution.[30]

7. Observations and Conclusion

The integration of complexity analytics, game theory, and artificial intelligence offers a powerful framework for understanding and resolving intractable conflicts. This approach recognizes conflicts as complex adaptive systems with fractal properties, exhibiting self-similar patterns across different scales, from within-country disputes to international conflicts.

This article provides foundational elements by setting clear, cross-disciplinary definitions to ensure consistency across various fields of study; providing a nuanced understanding of the rationality spectrum in decision-making, from extreme conditions to calculated trade-offs; and offering foundations for measurement science for quantifying conflict attributes, including resilience and persistence.

It offers analytical approaches including network theory to map and analyze the intricate relationships between conflict actors; game-theoretical models to understand strategic interactions and predict outcomes; and risk attitude analysis inspired by economic strategy analytics, including market-based loss amplification factors. These approaches are provided with technological integration by an innovative methodological framework with special attention to artificial intelligence applications, such as machine learning algorithms for processing vast amounts of conflict-related data, and advanced computational models for simulating complex conflict scenarios.

Success in conflict resolution requires grounding the process in an honorable value system. This ethical foundation ensures that peacebuilding efforts are guided by principles of integrity, respect, and effective communication. The framework emphasizes the importance of defining "winning" in terms that prioritize sustainable peace rather than short-term gains for any single party.

The future of conflict resolution lies in effectively combining traditional diplomatic wisdom with cutting-edge analytical tools. As artificial intelligence continues to evolve, its integration with human expertise will become increasingly crucial for successful peace processes. This synergy between human insight and computational power has the potential to enhance predictive capabilities for conflict escalation and de-escalation, identify novel intervention strategies tailored to specific conflict contexts, and facilitate real-time analysis and decision-making in dynamic conflict situations.

The framework's versatility allows for its application across various scales of conflict, from local disputes to international crises. By treating conflicts as fractals, practitioners can identify critical intervention points and develop strategies that address the conflict's underlying structure rather than just its surface manifestations.

In conclusion, this integrated approach to conflict resolution, grounded in complexity science and enhanced by artificial intelligence, offers a promising path forward in addressing some of the world's most intractable conflicts. Refining these tools and methodologies has the potential to achieve sustainable peace in even the most challenging situations. Some insights offered by George Mitchell clearly demonstrate the importance of engaging the players:

> The most difficult obstacle to overcome is the lack of trust. You can rebuild buildings, you can replace vehicles, you can put bridges back up, but the really important thing to change what is in peoples' hearts and minds takes much longer. … Hope and opportunity are essential to political stability and peace in every society. Whatever people's differences, they want the same thing. They want to get their children off to a good start in life, they want to have a chance for a decent job, and so what is necessary in all of these conflict societies is to create a sense of hope, a vision, a possibility of the future. Without that hope, without that opportunity, peace is in peril everywhere.[31]

Acknowledgments and Disclaimer

The author expresses sincere gratitude for the financial support provided by the Ettore Majorana Foundation and Centre for Scientific Culture in Sicily, Italy. This support has been instrumental in facilitating the research and development of the framework presented in this article. The author also extends special acknowledgment to John, Lord Alderdice for his support and invaluable insights, engagement, and expertise in conflict resolution that have significantly enriched the conceptual development of this work. The author's communication with Senator George Mitchell on the case study was inspirational. It is important to note that the opinions, analyses, and conclusions expressed in this article are solely those of the author and do not necessarily reflect the views of the sponsoring organizations or individuals mentioned above.

Notes

[1] Yaneer Bar-Yam, "Complexity Rising: From Human Beings to Human Civilization, a Complexity Profile," in *Encyclopedia of Life Support Systems* (UNESCO/EOLSS, 2002), http://www.necsi.edu/projects/yaneer/Civilization.html.

[2] Benoit Mandelbrot, "How Long Is the Coast of Britain? Statistical Self-Similarity and Fractional Dimension," *Science* 156, no. 3775 (1967): 636–38. https://www.science.org/doi/10.1126/science.156.3775.636; Bilal M. Ayyub and George J. Klir, *Uncertainty Modeling and Analysis in Engineering and the Sciences* (CRC Press/Chapman & Hall, 2006).

[3] Donald A. Dzedzy and Bilal M. Ayyub, "Fractal Dimensions for Freight Railroad Network Resilience Analysis," *ASCE-ASME Journal of Risk and Uncertainty in Engineering Systems Part A: Civil Engineering* 11, no. 3 (2025), https://ascelibrary.org/doi/full/10.1061/AJRUA6.RUENG-1461.

[4] Ayyub and Klir, *Uncertainty Modeling and Analysis in Engineering and the Sciences*.

[5] George J. Klir, *An Approach to General Systems Theory* (Van Nostrand Reinhold Company, 1969).

[6] Ayyub and Klir, *Uncertainty Modeling and Analysis in Engineering and the Sciences*.

[7] Judea Pearl and Dana Mackenzie, *The Book of Why: The New Science of Cause and Effect* (Basic Books, 2018).

[8] Ronald A. Howard, *Dynamic Probabilistic Systems, Volume II: Semi-Markov and Decision Processes* (Dover Publications, 2007).

[9] Federico Battiston, Giulia Cencetti, Iacopo Iacopini, et al., "Networks Beyond Pairwise Interactions: Structure and Dynamics," *Physics Reports* 874 (2020): 1–92, https://doi.org/10.1016/j.physrep.2020.05.004.

[10] Allan Dafoe, Yoram Bachrach, Gillian Hadfield, Eric Horvitz, Kate Larson, K., and Thore Graepel, "Cooperative AI: Machines Must Learn to Find Common Ground," *Nature* 593 (2021): 33–36, https://doi.org/10.1038/d41586-021-01170-0.

11. Jemal Mohammed Haile, "Social Media for Diffusion of Conflict & Violence in Ethiopia: Beyond Gratifications," *International Journal of Educational Development* 108 (2024): 103063, https://www.sciencedirect.com/science/article/abs/pii/S0738059324000853.
12. Frank C. Zagare, *Game Theory, Diplomatic History and Security Studies* (Oxford University Press, 2019); Stephen L. Quackenbush, "Game Theory and Interstate Conflict," *Oxford Bibliographies*, 2014, https://doi.org/10.1093/obo/9780199743292-0071; Bilal M. Ayyub, *Risk Analysis in Engineering and Economics*, 2nd ed. (Chapman & Hall/CRC, 2014).
13. Thomas C. Schelling, *The Strategy of Conflict* (Harvard University Press, 1960).
14. S. Plous, S. "Modeling the Nuclear Arms Race as a Perceptual Dilemma," *Philosophy and Public Affairs* 17, no. 1 (1988): 44–53, https://philpapers.org/rec/PLOMTN.
15. Ayyub and Klir, *Uncertainty Modeling and Analysis in Engineering and the Sciences*.
16. Pearl and Mackenzie, *The Book of Why*.
17. David S. Alberts and Richard E. Hayes, *Understanding Command and Control* (CCRP Publication Series, 2006).
18. Dzedzy and Ayyub, "Fractal Dimensions for Freight Railroad Network Resilience Analysis."
19. Albert-László Barabási, *Network Science* (Cambridge University Press, 2016).
20. US Supreme Court, "Indus. Union Dept. v. Amer. Petroleum Inst., 448 U.S. 607 (1980)," Industrial Union Department, AFL-CIO v. American Petroleum Institute, No. 78-911.
21. Bilal M. Ayyub, Ramsay Sawaya, David T. Butry, Yumi Oum, Vincent Loh, and Jennifer Helgeson, "Risk Tolerance and Attitude Quantification in the Economics of Electric Power and Gas Utilities: Case of Wildfire for Community Resilience," *ASCE-ASME Journal of Risk and Uncertainty in Engineering Systems Part A: Civil Engineering* (2024), https://ascelibrary.org/doi/10.1061/9780784485163.110.
22. Ayyub et al., "Risk Tolerance and Attitude Quantification."
23. Richard Nixon Foundation, "Unpredictability: A Tenet of a Strong Foreign Policy," July 1, 2016, https://www.nixonfoundation.org/2016/07/unpredictability-a-tenet-of-a-strong-foreign-policy/.
24. Albert Resis, "The Churchill-Stalin Secret 'Percentages' Agreement on the Balkans, Moscow, October 1944," *American Historical Review* 83, no. 2 (1978): 368–87, https://www.jstor.org/stable/1862322.
25. PioSOLVER, https://piosolver.com/; PokerSnowie, https://www.pokersnowie.com/.
26. Peter F. Doran, "Navigating Complexity and Uncertainty After the Belfast–Good Friday Agreement: The Role of Societal Trauma?," *Northern Ireland Legal Quarterly* 71, no. 4 (2020), https://nilq.qub.ac.uk/index.php/nilq/article/view/919.
27. Doran, "Navigating Complexity and Uncertainty."
28. Lord John Alderdice, "Conflict, Complexity, and Cooperation," *New England Journal of Public Policy*: 33, no. 1 (2021): Article 9, https://scholarworks.umb.edu/nejpp/vol33/iss1/9.
29. David Mitchell, "The International Significance of the Northern Ireland Peace Process: Revisiting the Lessons 25 Years After the Good Friday Agreement," *Politics* 45, no. 2 (2025): 258–73, https://doi.org/10.1177/02633957231175616.
30. Mitchell, "The International Significance of the Northern Ireland Peace Process."
31. "George Mitchell Transcript," United States Institute of Peace, Washington, DC, 2023, https://web.archive.org/web/20241104225401/https://www.usip.org/public-education-new/george-mitchell-transcript.

GERALD TEMPLER'S LEADERSHIP IN THE MALAYAN EMERGENCY (1948–1960): ITS ENDURING RELEVANCE

Kumar Ramakrishna

S. Rajaratnam School of International Studies, Nanyang Technological University

ABSTRACT

This article explores the leadership contributions of General Sir Gerald Templer, who was both High Commissioner and Director of Operations, during the counterinsurgency campaign waged by the British colonial authorities in Malaya against the Malayan Communist Party, between 1948 and 1960. This campaign has become known as the Malayan Emergency. The article explores how Templer's leadership—marked by a combination of high intellect, sound practical nous, and the ability to galvanize governmental action and ultimately inspire the population to eventual victory—was instrumental in transforming the nature of the problematic initial British response to the Communist insurgency. The article suggests that Templer's leadership contributions in Malaya may be useful for modern analysts and practitioners charged with dealing with complex conflicts today.

In his excellent memoir, *Call Sign Chaos*, General James Mattis asserts that "[H]istory teaches that we face nothing new under the sun." He adds that by "traveling into the past, I enhance my grasp of the present."[1] In this respect, the Malayan Emergency (1948–1960) not only represents a significant chapter in the history of

Kumar Ramakrishna is Professor of National Security Studies, the Provost's Chair in National Security Studies, and Dean of the S. Rajaratnam School of International Studies, Nanyang Technological University.

post-colonial Southeast Asia, it offers useful learning points for modern practitioners and analysts who seek to navigate complex conflicts in the current era. The Malayan Emergency (or "the Emergency") refers to the armed insurrection waged by the Malayan Communist Party (MCP) against the British colonial authorities in Malaya. There have been numerous accounts of the Emergency, which remains widely regarded as perhaps the lone successful counterinsurgency campaign in the wider context of the global Cold War between the Western-led liberal democratic bloc and the Soviet and Chinese-led Communist bloc.[2] Historians and contemporary observers have argued that central to the eventual British success in quelling the MCP insurgency was the leadership of General Sir Gerald Templer.[3] He has been credited with popularizing the phrase "winning hearts and minds" in the context of counterinsurgency campaigns.[4] Templer's leadership – marked by a combination of high intellect, sound practical nous, the ability to galvanize governmental action and ultimately inspire the population to eventual victory - were instrumental in transforming the nature of the problematic initial British response to the Communist insurgency. This article employs much primary source material, including declassified confidential correspondence of officials and commanders involved in the conflict, to explore the historical context of the Malayan Emergency, the leadership style of General Templer, and how his policies and strategies helped pave the way to the eventual defeat of the MCP. The final section briefly reviews Templer's leadership in the Emergency and outlines the key takeaway for the modern context.[5]

Historical Context

By the end of the Second World War in September 1945, the Indigenous ethnic Malays represented 44 percent of the then–five million population in the Malay peninsula. The rest of the population was dominated by the increasingly settled and large immigrant ethnic Chinese community and the smaller immigrant ethnic Indians. The Chinese and Indians had been brought in by the British since the late nineteenth century, to provide labor for the booming Malayan rubber and tin industries. This Malayan demographic backdrop by the 1930s had implications for the MCP. Ever since its founding in 1930, the largely ethnic Chinese Communists had had little sustained success in establishing themselves in a body politic dominated by the ethnic Malay majority population. The crushing defeat of British forces in Malaya and Singapore at the hands of the Japanese army in February 1942, however, heralded a change in MCP fortunes. During the Japanese occupation, the fledgling Malayan People's Anti-Japanese Army (MPAJA), the armed wing of the MCP, with clandestine British support, emerged. With the surrender of the Japanese and the inauguration by the returning British of the Malayan Union government in April 1946, the Communists intensified subversion of Malayan labor unions. By February 1948, as the constitutionally unitary Malayan Union gradually transitioned to the looser political arrangement known as the Federation of Malaya, the MCP's activists had secured a strong footing among urban and rural Chinese workers. At the same time, however, Communist-inspired disturbances and violence on economically vital rubber estates and tin mines provoked strong responses from the British colonial authorities in Kuala Lumpur, prompting the imposition, on June 18, 1948, of a State of Emergency throughout Malaya. Thereafter, the MCP's leaders and most of its rank and file fled to the ubiquitous jungles lining the western Malayan peninsula. They reorganized as the Malayan Races Liberation Army (MRLA), essentially the wartime MPAJA.

To be sure, the relatively politically sophisticated, better educated, and richer urban Chinese represented by the Malayan Chinese Association (MCA) political party, played a key role in constitutional advancement toward Malayan independence by the mid-1950s. However, as far as the shooting war in the jungle with the MRLA was concerned, the rural Chinese community represented the center of gravity.[6] Internal MCP documents conceded by 1949 that it had failed to make headway with the "city population," and had to rely for its supplies on the "Chinese rural population."[7] The latter consisted of the tin miners, rubber workers on plantations and in factories, unskilled and semi-skilled workers, and the "genuine squatters" engaged in full-time farming. While the MRLA tried to portray itself as a champion of these rural Chinese masses, its over-reliance on coercion and even terrorism, not just against the British colonial authorities but also against these rural Chinese, basically alienated the latter.[8] By the end of 1949, one and a half years after the declaration of the Emergency, MRLA insurgents had killed 655, abducted 250, and wounded 360 civilians. In the following two years, moreover, they perpetrated 10,400 terrorist-inspired incidents.[9] MRLA terrorism was calculatedly brutal: in Plentong in Johor State insurgents shot dead a Chinese squatter, hacked his wife to death, set alight their hut, and flung their eight-year-old daughter into the flames. In Kampar, Perak State, a Chinese girl was murdered by having a nail driven through her head. A 1952 police report asserted that such "senseless cruelty" was not "isolated," but typical of "hundreds of similar incidents" throughout the country.[10] Importantly, the rural Chinese community bore the brunt of Communist terror, "presumably because they presented both the greatest hope and the greatest danger."[11]

The British colonial response initially relied on coercive measures as well, which also alienated the very rural Chinese population they sought to win over. On the one hand, British military operations up to about 1951 tended to be large scale, involving troops engaged in seek-and-destroy missions in the jungle, always after bombing and strafing by the Royal Air Force (RAF). Such operations were found to be inefficient: the RAF bombing alerted the MRLA insurgents of the army presence, generated negligible insurgent casualties, and inadvertently served as "battle inoculation" for the MRLA forces.[12] Worse, RAF bombing was also on occasion inaccurate. Five children were killed when a Chinese school was accidentally bombed in February 1950, creating even more anger at the authorities.[13] More fundamentally, the prevailing assumption in government circles up to 1952 was that because of a supposed "streak of hysteria" in rural Chinese psychology and the so-called "secret society complex," the only way to extract compliance from them was to make them "fear Government more than they fear the Communists."[14]

This "bashing the Chinese"[15] mentality ultimately precipitated not merely security force excesses as at Batang Kali in December 1948,[16] but also the application of harsh Emergency Regulations that fell largely on the rural Chinese. These included individual detention and deportation; mass detention and deportation, and by the end of 1950, collective punishment, involving communal fines and curfews.[17] By February 1951, 2,800 Chinese had been deported to China, and by the end of that year, of 25,641 Malayans detained over more than twenty-eight days under the Emergency Regulations, 22,667 were Chinese.[18] Concerned Chinese leaders such as MCA President Dato Tan Cheng Lock implored the government to not just reduce "the number of offences committed by the Security Forces against the general public especially in the rural areas," but to work much harder to "build up an attitude of love, confidence and trust of the people as a whole toward itself and avoid doing anything to antagonize them or alienate their sympathies in any way."[19]

People-oriented policing in the early days of the Emergency was conspicuous by its relative absence.[20] This was due in no small part to a severe shortage of Chinese-speaking personnel in a mainly European-officered Malay force, creating a communication and affective gap between the police and the rural Chinese in which crass stereotyping soon flourished. Because most MRLA insurgents were Chinese, ordinary Chinese villagers tended to be regarded as "hostile" and were often treated roughly, regardless of their innocence or guilt. Hence British colonial officials cautioned that new police officers especially ought to be educated "to correct false impressions and prevent many serious mistakes in the future through ignorance."[21] In 1950, a study mission from London added that "training for jungle operations can do little or nothing to develop the habits of thought and action required for ordinary police work."[22] Additionally, the average Chinese peasant deeply distrusted a colonial government that not only "ran a Malay police force," and ordered him "not to help the terrorists," but "failed to protect him."[23] Until the end of 1951, British colonial government missteps, exacerbated by the assassination of British High Commissioner Henry Gurney by a MRLA hit squad in October 1951, precipitated widespread low morale and operational paralysis across the government machinery. Hence while the MCP was not exactly winning, neither was the government. All this changed with Templer's appointment as High Commissioner in 1952.

General Templer and the Briggs Plan

The arrival in Malaya in February 1952 of General Sir Gerald Templer, in his important integrated civil-military role as both High Commissioner and Director of Emergency Operations, represented the turning point in the Emergency. Between his arrival in 1952 and the end of his tenure in May 1954, "two-thirds of the guerrillas were wiped out, the incident rate fell from 500 to less than 100 per month, and the civilian and security force casualties from 200 to less than 40."[24] According to contemporary observers, Templer's achievement was to have "taken a difficult, deteriorating situation, checked it, and turned it around."[25] To be fair, Templer did not exactly start from scratch. He had a good strategic blueprint to work with, developed earlier by his predecessor as Director of Operations, General Sir Harold Rawdon Briggs. This blueprint became known as the famous "Briggs Plan." Briggs had recognized that the "uncontrolled squatter areas, unsupervised Chinese estates and small holdings" were the key source of sustenance for the Communists. Neutralizing these areas required resettlement of these rural Chinese away from the exposed jungle fringe. Briggs understood that the first-order aim was to create "a feeling of complete security" among the exposed Chinese, by physically separating them from MRLA insurgents lurking in the jungle.[26] Complementing this thrust was Briggs's encouragement of the British military to cut back on "RAF attacks, artillery fire and large-scale 'fire brigade' operations" that were not only militarily ineffective, but also alienated the rural Chinese. Instead, Briggs had urged army commanders to focus on "a large number of small, harassing patrols in the jungle over a period of days or weeks" operating on good intelligence on MRLA movements. Small-unit patrolling was promoted in tandem with food control operations that significantly restricted the circulation of rice and other foodstuffs in the rural areas. For instance, villagers leaving for work during the day were only permitted to carry liquids and were searched at gates to ensure this. Such food control operations that Briggs formalized were to have a huge physical and psychological impact on MRLA morale.[27]

Another very important feature of the Briggs Plan was the creation of joint civil-army-police headquarters at federal, state, and district levels in Malaya to facilitate closer civil-military integration in the overall conduct of counterinsurgency operations. In addition, to implement federal plans at all levels, existing ad hoc local defense committees were formalized into State War Executive Committees (SWECs) and District War Executive Committees (DWECs). The basic SWEC structure consisted of the State Chief Minister, the British Advisor, the Chief Police Officer, and the senior army commander in the area. The DWEC comprised the District Officer (DO), the Officer Commanding Police District (or Officer Superintending Police Circle) and the local army commander.[28]

While Briggs had gotten the basic blueprint right, the problem was that of implementing it. Briggs had complained that his plan was being implemented "far too slowly," and that there was still "a lack of urgency and the will to seek and solve difficult problems."[29] He lamented that "the whole thing is being run as though it were a discussion group" instead of a "WAR with innumerable people being killed."[30] Templer's ability to breathe life into and electrify the Briggs Plan was therefore a critical element. Briggs had certainly come up a "counter-guerrilla classic,"[31] but as noted, his war committee system was not operating optimally, as it was hamstrung by bureaucratic inertia and a lack of urgency.[32] Templer grasped the complex situation in Malaya with "incredible speed,"[33] and as early as April 1952, declared in a speech to the Chinese Chambers of Commerce that the government would only win "by enlisting the support of the Chinese villagers."[34] Templer wasted little time in cracking the whip. He developed a reputation for intimidating state and district-level officials by jabbing them with a cane when he addressed them.[35] Many officials were "awfully frightened of him."[36] Furthermore his effective if controversial method of resolving personality clashes in SWECs and DWECs was by threatening a mass sacking if those concerned failed to pull up their socks.[37] Templer was seen as a military dictator by some.[38] That being said, Templer seemed to know how to galvanize his team. One official recalled being overwhelmed by Templer's "electric personality" and "tremendous drive" and left the meeting "feeling like an electric torch" that had just been "filled with new batteries."[39]

Templer and the Strategic Rural Chinese Community

At the same time, as he was energizing the government machinery in general and the war committee system Briggs had set up, Templer never lost sight of what he understood to be his most critical objective: to close the dangerous affective gap between the government and the rural Chinese. Thus, in 1953, he fine-tuned and even abolished some of the unpopular Emergency Regulations, such as collective detention and deportation, as well as collective punishment—regulations that had hit the rural Chinese community the hardest since the Emergency had been declared in June 1948. The same year, he introduced so-called White Areas, in which all Emergency Regulations—including intrusive physical checks at village checkpoints, irksome curfews, and strict food rationing to deny rice from being smuggled out of villages to the MRLA insurgents—were removed, if the improving security situation warranted it. Furthermore, Templer further honed the food control policy introduced by Briggs, by introducing food denial operations targeting specific MRLA districts, identified based on good intelligence. Thanks to Templer, intelligence collection, analysis, and dissemination was also rapidly improving. For instance, to improve army-police intelligence processing, Templer set up a Special Military Intelligence Staff and integrated it with the Police Special Branch.[40] Intelligence-driven food denial operations became more sophisticated in targeting MRLA insurgent morale, and were designed to create "cumulative pressures, both mental and physical, over a period produced by privation, fear and hopelessness."[41] At the same time, such surgical and precise food denial operations spared the rural Chinese as a whole from the earlier large-scale "fire brigade operations" that had worried them previously. In essence, Templer was seeking to reassure and win the trust of the ordinary Chinese.[42]

To build such trust, Templer launched so-called Civics Courses: beginning in Malacca State in May 1952, up to thirty Chinese villagers were brought to government offices for a week each time, and exposed to a series of talks and tours of government installations. They also met other sections of the Malayan community and enjoyed entertainment and sketches put on by government staff.[43] While these ordinary Chinese were visibly moved by the experience, government servants for their part were able to "see their work in terms of human values and to appreciate the broader aims of policy, rather than carrying on their work in isolation."[44] The Civics Courses were extended to all states by 1953.[45] The most popular items of the Civics Courses were the "spectacular" or "practical items," such as army firing displays, Radio Malaya broadcast operations, and entertainment by British Commonwealth military units.[46]

Importantly, Civics Courses helped reduce the psychological distance between the Chinese and the police. For instance, it was found in some states that police sketches were far more useful than mere conducted tours of police stations. Moreover, in Pahang State, talks given at the Police Contingent Headquarters appeared to have "convinced" villagers of the need for encouraging and facilitating MRLA insurgent surrenders and information on their movements.[47] Civics Courses aside, closer government–rural Chinese ties were also forged within the increasingly better-defended, sited, and equipped New Villages—the name Templer had given to the old Resettlement Areas started by Briggs. Templer was fully aware that some New Villages were inadequately protected and served by insufficient amenities. He thus ensured that by March 1953, 218 of the New Villages that were known to have active MRLA supporters were given perimeter lighting.[48] He also formulated a checklist to measure the quality of life in the New Villages, which included criteria such as some agricultural land for full-time farmers, land titles for house plots and agricultural holdings, an adequate water supply, a school and teachers' quarters, a Village Community Centre, places of worship, good roads with side drains, and reasonable standards of sanitation and public health.[49] Village security was also enhanced through intensified training of Special Constables and the local village militia known as the Home Guard.[50]

Certainly, not all New Villages were able to meet Templer's high standards and thrive.[51] That was not the point, though. Although the rural Chinese had complaints, as one astute contemporary observer noted, "all administration is built on complaints" anyway,[52] and what was key was that the villagers were gradually bringing their problems, not to the Communists, but to the agents of government. As Datin Jean Marshall, a Red Cross administrator observed, the New Villagers "were glad to have people around who brought their needs to the notice of the authorities."[53]

Templer, Arthur Young, and the Reform of Malayan Policing

Templer had realized early on that the entire Malayan police force was geared toward "anti-bandit operations," not civil policing.[54] Worse, the Malay police rank and file and European lieutenants regarded all rural Chinese as potential Communists, and "adopted a hostile attitude" toward them.[55] Templer recognized that too many people considered the Malayan policeman a "bogey-man."[56] He thus brought in a new Police Commissioner, Colonel Arthur Edwin Young of the City of London Police, who arrived in February 1952. Young was a highly regarded officer who had served with distinction on the Gold Coast.[57] Young traveled all over Malaya, meeting all ranks, prompting a senior Malayan policeman to aver that Young exuded confidence and restored morale.[58] That said, improving police administration at all levels was only one aspect of what Young brought to Malayan policing.[59] Crucially, with Templer's backing, Young gradually introduced a philosophy of policing that was to enable the Malayan police to ultimately transform its relations with the public.

Declaring that "the police must be part of the people and the people part of the police," Young felt strongly that the police must avoid an overemphasis on force. He did not want a police force acting like a quasi-military body. He wanted Malayan policemen to act as individuals exercising sound judgment.[60] This, to Young, was the key difference between the policeman and the soldier. While the former sought to root out the individual offender from among the larger community, the latter tended to impact the community as a whole through curfews and other communal restrictions that fell on "friend and foe alike." The latter approach jeopardized the "public regard and public confidence upon which the Police essentially depend for their effectiveness."[61] To counter the MRLA threat, Young held that it was imperative to apply discriminate force so as to root out insurgents without harming the wider public, and this could only be done by first establishing sound relations with the rural Chinese community in particular. This would start an information flow that would expedite police intelligence-gathering that would lead to effective prosecutions.[62] To Young, while the soldier was taught to make up his mind fast, and a wrong decision was better than none at all, the policeman on the other hand had to take his time to make up his mind, "because the important thing wherever the law is involved is to be right from the start."[63] Furthermore, in order to be right from the start meant that the policeman had to possess sufficient training. Arguing that "instead of getting bigger the Malayan police must get better," Young embarked on an enormous retraining program with the aim of ensuring that by June 1953, every policeman in Malaya would be better trained.[64]

By July 1953, Young and his team had introduced a two-month recruit training course and a two-week refresher course for the auxiliary police known as Special Constables at new Federal Area Training Schools. He also formalized eight-month regular police recruit courses, as well as regular police refresher courses in August. Altogether 60,000 regular police and Special Constables were retrained.[65] A Federal Police College with a capacity of 140 was also established the same year to provide "comprehensive basic training" and promote esprit de corps among gazetted officers.[66] The bulk of the better-trained Special Constables were reorganized into 876 Area Security Units by the third quarter of 1953 to "dominate" the populated areas.[67] Templer and Young also tried to increase the proportion of Chinese police recruits in order to improve relations with the rural Chinese. Templer faced challenges in recruiting Chinese people to join the Malayan police, due to deep-rooted Chinese distrust of men in uniform.[68] At any rate, many of the 1,410 Chinese who did join the police rank and file in November 1953 were consciously put in uniform to be seen by the Chinese public.[69] Chinese-speaking European police numbers were also increased. In May 1952, there were forty-two European police officers who could speak Chinese, but enrollment continued apace.[70] In this context the Chinese language course at Cameron Highlands continued to be useful. European officers could learn operationally useful Chinese dialects such as Cantonese, Hokkien, Hakka, and Kuo Yu.[71] Another important reform Templer and Young oversaw related to police intelligence: Templer split the Special Branch from the Criminal Intelligence Department (CID), directing CID to focus on ordinary crime, while Special Branch officers specialized in "Emergency crime detection."[72] Importantly, Templer recognized that Asian officers should spearhead the Special Branch effort,[73] and before the end of 1952 more Chinese Special Branch officers were building close relationships with the rural Chinese and gleaning valuable information in the districts.[74]

The Impact of "Operation Service"

Although an intensive retraining program did increase police professionalism, Young felt that under the circumstances of the Emergency, this alone was insufficient to close the police-Chinese affective gap.[75] Like Templer, a bold, innovative, and creative thinker, Young drew inspiration from the *Wizard of Oz* in which a dejected lion was transformed into a brave one by being awarded a medal for courage. Young felt that a similar "symbolization" in the Malayan police context offered "the prospect of a successful public campaign."[76] Without consulting his senior officers, Young committed the entire force to a six-month campaign of seeking every opportunity, big or small, to demonstrate that they were friends of the common folk. Young went so far as to send a letter to every member of the force, informing them that their promotion prospects would henceforth depend not merely on the performance of routine tasks but also their "relationship with and attitude to the public."[77] Operation Service was thereby launched on December 15, 1952 via press and radio.[78] Like the lion in the *Wizard of Oz*, every policeman was issued a small oval badge showing clasped hands. The idea behind the "psychological label" of the badge was that rank-and-file police would be reminded that they were supposed to friends of the public.[79] Young also sourced other symbols to capture the public's imagination. Inspired by the Scout motto "Be Prepared" and the Rotary Club slogan "Service Above Self," he decided that the Operation Service equivalent should be "Ready to Serve."[80] In the first month of Operation Service, about 10,000 "deeds of service" were recorded by enthusiastic police officers and rank and file and subsequently the rate was 20,000 per month. These deeds included anything from summoning a doctor for a member of the public to giving information on the functions of government. Moreover, police constables visited schools more regularly, while Young hoped that the public would regard police stations as places not to "get <u>into</u> but to get <u>out</u> of trouble."[81] Backing Young, Templer himself broadcast in January 1953 that henceforth police stations would no longer be called *rumah pasong* (house of incarceration) but rather *balai polis* (house of the police). The same month, Operation Service was extended from the federal level to the states as well.[82]

Some contemporary critics dismissed Operation Service as a mere public relations exercise,[83] but this view was not widely shared. The British Colonial Secretary Oliver Lyttelton, although initially agreeing that it was a "gimmick," subsequently conceded the salience of Operation Service particularly in the context of Malay-Chinese relations.[84] To be sure, Operation Service was no magic bullet. As late as June 1954, a government study cautioned that Chinese confidence in the police still left much to be desired, because the scars of the detentions and deportations under the draconian Emergency Regulations in 1948 and 1949 still rankled.[85] Nevertheless, Operation Service came to be seen as a much-needed and positive step, because it gave formal expression to a year-long soul-searching within government, encouraged by Templer, over the need to win over the rural Chinese. In July 1952 for instance one observer had noted that not only the police but all government servants needed to engage in the "personal approach" toward "the people in the New Villages and the kampongs," so as to win their "confidence."[86] The following month, the incoming Director-General of Information Services Alec Peterson, had recommended that all government departments had to become more "propaganda-minded" in order to "win the confidence" of the public.[87] Subsequently, after Operation Service was launched by the police in December 1952, Templer extended it to other branches of government in January.[88] Hence the Post Office launched Operation Courtesy and the Medical Department followed suit.[89] Over time Operation Service became ingrained as the modus operandi of all government departments, and throughout the Templer period and that of his successors, the government was "fully aware that its policies and practices had to match its pronouncements."[90] In any case, the general contemporary assessment was that the Templer-Young tenure saw the Malayan police undergoing a much-needed "renaissance."[91]

Templer's Leadership in the Malayan Emergency: Its Enduring Relevance

General Sir Gerald Templer's leadership during the Malayan Emergency was pivotal in transforming the British response to the armed insurrection the MCP/MRLA. Three leadership accomplishments of his appear to stand out. First, the most fundamental challenge facing Templer on his arrival in February 1952 was rebuilding bridges with the strategically important rural Chinese constituency—the key source of material and moral sustenance for the MCP/MRLA. He had to overcome an affective gap that had arisen, as this community had borne the brunt of the harsh Emergency Regulations that had been imposed in June 1948. By abolishing the more draconian regulations by 1952, Templer contributed to the long and difficult process of closing the psychological distance with the rural Chinese. Second, Templer understood that closing the affective gap with this community was never a uniquely police problem but was something the entire governmental machinery had to contend with. In other words, building an effective police force was no magic bullet if the rest of the government apparatus remained moribund and disinterested. As seen above, Templer got the machinery to work well.

Third and perhaps most crucially, it required Templer's historic clear-sighted and forceful drive—and his selection of like-minded activist leaders such as Police Commissioner Young—to ensure the proper implementation of the Briggs Plan, as well as the gradual restoration of police morale and improved effectiveness. Templer, while a highly controversial figure, was always "more than just a soldier with full powers from Churchill."[92] One former British official, speaking decades later in 1998, opined that Templer was the most "effective and admirable leader" he had ever met.[93] Templer's drive was evident to all who worked with him. He never stayed in his office in Kuala Lumpur but set out on tours three days a week to "quiz those responsible, encourage the faint-hearted" and "congratulate the successful."[94] Templer consciously and deliberately sought to build the conviction among government officials, police, and army commanders that the Communists could and would be beaten. Templer's aide David Lloyd-Owen thus recalled that Templer communicated an "infectious and confident determination to win."[95]

Why is the above concise analysis of the role of General Sir Gerald Templer during the Malayan Emergency in the 1950s relevant for us today? This article does not wish to wade too deeply into the ongoing debate between historians that the Emergency was sui generis and one ought to not identify 'lessons' that could be applied elsewhere. Recent scholarship for example suggests that the US erred in seeking to apply the British "hearts and minds" approach developed in Malaya to South Vietnam a decade later.[96] It could be countered, actually, that the Americans actually misapplied the British model.[97] The 'lessons' strategy, in general, has to be approached with care. H. R. McMaster, a distinguished soldier-scholar who was also a former national security advisor in President Donald Trump's first administration, argues that "[i]gnorance or misuse of history often led to the neglect of hard-won lessons or the use of simplistic analogies that masked flaws in policy or strategy." McMaster asserts instead that "[u]nderstanding the history of how challenges developed would help us ask the right questions, avoid mistakes of the past, and anticipate how 'the other' might respond."[98] It is in this spirit of fostering inquiry along the lines McMaster suggests, that the leadership accomplishments of General Sir Gerald Templer during the Malayan Emergency are offered, for students, scholars, and practitioners alike to contemplate, in relation to the myriad conflicts of the current time.

Acknowledgements

The author is grateful for the feedback received when a version of this article was presented at the Conference for the Resolution of Intractable Conflict, Harris Manchester College, Oxford University, UK, September 23–25, 2024. The author would also like to thank Mr. Huzeir Ezekiel Dzulhisham for his invaluable research assistance as this article was being prepared.

Notes

[1] Jim Mattis and Bing West, *Call Sign Chaos: Learning to Lead* (Random House, 2019), 42.

[2] On the origins of the Emergency, see for example, Anthony Short, *In Pursuit of Mountain Rats: The Communist Insurrection in Malaya* (Cultured Lotus, 2000): 34–61; A. J. Stockwell, "'A Widespread and Long-Concocted Plot to Overthrow the Government in Malaya?' The Origins of the Malayan Emergency," *Journal of Imperial and Commonwealth History* 21, no. 3 (1993): 66–88, https://doi.org/10.1080/03086539308582907.

[3] One notable exception is Karl Hack, who has argued that Templer arrived in Malaya when the tide had already turned against the MCP. For instance, see Hack, "'Iron Claws on Malaya:' The Historiography of the Malayan Emergency," *Journal of Southeast Asian Studies* 30, no. 1 (1999): 99–125, https://www.jstor.org/stable/20072108. The current author took issue with Hack's analysis. See Kumar Ramakrishna, "'Transmogrifying Malaya': The Impact of Sir Gerald Templer (1952–54)," *Journal of Southeast Asian Studies* 32, no. 1 (2001): 79–92, https://www.jstor.org/stable/20072300. For another discussion of the Templer debate, see Simon Smith, "General Templer and Counter-Insurgency in Malaya: Hearts and Minds, Intelligence, and Propaganda," *Intelligence and National Security* 16, no. 3 (2001): 60–78, https://doi.org/10.1080/02684520412331306210.

[4] Richard L. Clutterbuck, *The Long, Long War: The Emergency in Malaya, 1948–1960* (Cassell, 1967), 3.

[5] This article draws upon and adapts the analysis in the following sources: Kumar Ramakrishna, "'The Police Must Be Part of the People and the People Part of the Police': Policing in the Malayan Emergency (1948–60)," in C. Christine Fair and Sumit Ganguly, eds., *Policing Insurgencies: Cops as Counterinsurgents* (Oxford University Press, 2014), 46–82; and Ramakrishna, "Making Malaya Safe for Decolonization: The Rural Chinese Factor in the Counterinsurgency Campaign," in *The Transformation of Southeast Asia: International Perspectives on Decolonization*, ed. Marc Frey, Ronald W. Pruessen, and Tan Tai Yong (M. E. Sharpe, 2003).

[6] Ramakrishna, "Making Malaya Safe for Decolonization."

[7] "The present day situation and duties of the Malayan Communist Party": note by Mr. Strachey for the Cabinet Malaya Committee commenting on a captured MCP document, PREM 8/1406/2, MAL C (50) May 12, 1950, in *British Documents on the End of Empire [BDEEP], Series B, Vol. 3, Malaya, Part II: The Communist Insurrection, 1948-1953*, ed. A. J. Stockwell (Her Majesty's Stationery Office [HMSO], 1995), Document 215.

8 Kumar Ramakrishna, "Anatomy of a Collapse: Explaining the Malayan Communist Mass Surrenders of 1958," *War and Society* 21, no. 2 (October 2003): 109–33, https://doi.org/10.1179/war.2003.21.2.109. Wartime British-MPAJA collaboration has been recounted in F. Spencer Chapman, *The Jungle is Neutral* (Times Books International, 1997).

9 *Communist Banditry in Malaya: the Emergency June 1948–Dec 1949* (Kuala Lumpur: Department of Public Relations, 1950), 59–60; "Talking Points for H. E.'s Farewell Visits on 29th and 30th April 1954," Templer Papers, 7410-29-1, National Army Museum [hereafter cited as NAM].

10 "Short History of the Emergency," October 21, 1952, MSS.Brit.Emp.s.486, A. E. Young Papers, Rhodes House Library, Oxford University [hereafter cited as RHO].

11 Judith Strauch, *Chinese Village Politics in the Malaysian State* (Harvard University Press, 1981), 65.

12 Kumar Ramakrishna, *Emergency Propaganda: The Winning of Malayan Hearts and Minds 1948–1958* (Curzon Press, 2002): 69–70.

13 Ibid., 62.

14 D. Gray to W. J. Watts, December 17, 1951, MSS.Ind.Ocn.s.320, W. J. Watts Papers, RHO; "Present Attitude of the Chinese Population," April 11, 1949, CO 537/4751, Public Record Office, UK [hereafter cited as PRO].

15 Gray to Watts, December 17, 1951, Watts Papers, RHO.

16 On December 12, 1948, troops from the Scots Guards shot dead twenty-four Chinese at Batang Kali village in Selangor in questionable circumstances. Firsthand accounts of the incident by two women, Ching Yoong and Wong Foo Moi, both interviewed by Granada Television in 1981, are found in The End of Empire Papers, MSS.Brit.Emp.s.527, RHO.

17 Rhoderick dhu Rhenick Jr., "The Emergency Regulations of Malaya: Causes and Effect," *Journal of Southeast Asian History* 6, no. 2 (1965): 1–39, https://doi.org/10.1017/S0217781100001861.

18 *Detention and Deportation During the Emergency in the Federation of Malaya* (Kuala Lumpur: Government Press, 1953), 14; W. A. Muller to H. Fraser, December 22, 1951, CO 1022/165, PRO.

19 Memorandum to the Right Honourable Oliver Lyttelton, Secretary of State for the Colonies, by an MCA Delegation headed by Dato Tan Cheng Lock at King's House, Kuala Lumpur, December 2, 1951, Tan Cheng Lock Papers, TCL.3.271, Institute of Southeast Asian Studies, Singapore [ISEAS].

20 F. A. Fielding, "The Malayan Police Service - Post War," n.d., MSS.Ind.Ocn.s.298, F. A. Fielding Papers, RHO.

21 Watts to Secretary of Chinese Affairs, Federation of Malaya, January 7, 1952, Watts Papers, RHO.

22 *Report of the Police Mission to Malaya, March 1950* (Kuala Lumpur: Government Printer, 1950): 15–16.

23 C. E. Howe, "A Few Memories of My 2 ½ years as DO in Jelebu, Negri Sembilan, Central Malaya, May 1948–Nov 1950," n.d., MSS. Brit.Emp.s.480, R. Heussler Papers, RHO.

24 Richard L. Clutterbuck, *Conflict and Violence in Singapore and Malaysia 1945–1983* (Graham Brash, 1985), 186.

25 John Cloake, *Templer: Tiger of Malaya* (Harrap, 1985), 326.

26 "Federation Plan for the Elimination of the Communist Organisation and Armed Forces in Malaya (the Briggs Plan)," report by COS for Cabinet Malaya Committee, CAB 21/1681, MAL C (50) 23, Appendix, May 24, 1950, in Stockwell, *BDEEP, Malaya: The Communist Insurrection*, Document 216.

[27] Ramakrishna, *Emergency Propaganda*, 103–4.
[28] "Organisation for Dealing with Emergency Matters," November 1951, CO 1022/7, PRO.
[29] "Summary of Meeting Between Prime Minister Attlee, Gurney and Briggs," November 27, 1950, CAB 130/65, PRO.
[30] Viscountess Davidson, letter to Oliver Lyttelton, November 1, 1951, CO 1022/1, PRO.
[31] Anthony Short, "Communism and the Emergency," in *Malaysia: A Survey*, ed. Wang Gungwu (Pall Mall Press, 1964), 155.
[32] H. Fraser, "Papers on the Emergency in Malaya," CO 1022/22, PRO; summary of a meeting between Prime Minister Attlee, Gurney, and Briggs, November 27, 1950, CAB 130/65, PRO.
[33] W. C. S. Corry interview transcript, n.d., MSS.Ind. Ocn.s.215, RHO.
[34] "Speech by H. E. the High Commissioner to F. M. S. Chamber of Commerce," April 25, 1952, 7410-29-1, NAM.
[35] Brian Lapping, *End of Empire* (Paladin, 1989), 220; Charles Allen, *The Savage Wars of Peace: Soldiers' Voices 1945–1989* (Futura, 1990), 37.
[36] Guy Madoc interview, August 1981, End of Empire Papers, RHO.
[37] A. Kirk-Greene's interview with Sir Kerr Bovell, June 12, 1972, MSS. Brit.Emp.s.397, RHO.
[38] Victor Purcell, *Malaya: Communist or Free?* (Victor Gollancz, 1954): 11–19.
[39] Cited in Cloake, *Templer*, 213.
[40] Hugh Stockwell, "Appreciation of the Situation in Malaya," October 15, 1953, Maj-General Dennis Edmund Blaquiere Talbot Papers, Liddell Hart Centre for Military Archives, King's College London [henceforth cited as LHCMA]; extract from "Malayan Bulletin No. 65," CO 1022/165, PRO.
[41] Ramakrishna, *Emergency Propaganda*, 140–42.
[42] Ibid., 136–39.
[43] K. J. Henderson, "Civics Courses and Community Development," November 25, 1953, Heussler Papers, RHO.; "HC's Speech at the Fifth Meeting of the Sixth Session, Legislative Council," November 25, 1953, Templer Papers, 7410-29-1, NAM.
[44] Henderson, "Civics Courses."
[45] "HC's Speech."
[46] "DGIS Impressions," n.d., Heussler Papers, RHO.
[47] Ramakrishna, *Emergency Propaganda*, 150–51.
[48] Extract from "Federation of Malaya Administrative Report for January 1953," CO 1022/30, PRO; "H. E.'s Speech Opening the Connaught Bridge Power Station," March 26, 1953, 7410-29-1, NAM.
[49] Extract from "Federation of Malaya Saving No. 470," March 16, 1953, CO 1022/29, PRO.
[50] "Progress Report Training: 1 June 1953 to 31 July 1953," CO 1022/168, PRO; Federal Government Press Statement, March 30, 1952, CO 1022/35, PRO.
[51] Richard Stubbs, *Hearts and Minds in Guerrilla Warfare: The Malayan Emergency 1948–1960* (Oxford University Press, 1993): 234–35.
[52] John Davis interview transcript, August 1981, End of Empire Papers, RHO.
[53] Author's interview with Datin Jean Marshall, Singapore, January 21, 1998.
[54] A. J. Stockwell, "Policing During the Malayan Emergency 1948–60: Communism, Communalism and Decolonization," in *Policing and Decolonisation: Nationalism, Politics and the Police 1917–65*, ed. David M. Anderson and David Killingray (Manchester University Press, 1992), 110–14.

55. D. Gray, "The Chinese Problem in the Federation of Malaya," Watts Papers, RHO. On European and Malay Police antipathy toward the Chinese, see Stockwell, "Policing During the Malayan Emergency," 117.
56. "Broadcast on Operation Service by H. E.," January 26, 1953, Templer Papers, 7410-29-1, NAM.
57. Arthur Young, "Malaya," May 1967, Young Papers, RHO; letter from Home Secretary to Lord Mayor, City of London, January 16, 1952, Young Papers, RHO.
58. A. Kirk-Greene's interview with Sir Kerr Bovell, June 12, 1972, MSS. Brit.Emp.s.397, RHO.
59. Separate departments were created to look after administration, operations, supplies, transport, and signals. Young also appointed two Deputy Police Commissioners, sixteen Senior Assistant Commissioners, eight Assistant Commissioners, and forty-five Superintendents. Locally recruited officers were brought in to fill permanent posts. A staff officer was also appointed to deal with resettlement issues while a supplies officer was stationed in London. Extract from "*Malayan Bulletin*, No. 65, 25 May 1952," CO 1022/165, PRO.
60. Arthur Young, "The Duties of the Police," n.d., Young Papers, RHO.
61. Arthur Young, "Malaya," n.d.,Young Papers, RHO.
62. Arthur Young, "The Duties of the Police," n.d., Young Papers, RHO.
63. Ibid.
64. *New York Herald Tribune*, June 3, 1953. See extract from "Federation of Malaya Savingram 1601, 19 September 1953," CO 1022/169, PRO; as well as extract from "Federation of Malaya Savingram 2455, 12 December 1952," PRO. See also Arthur Young, "The World Today," broadcast transcript, May 19, 1953, Young Papers, RHO; and Young, "The Federation Police in 1952," n.d., Young Papers, RHO.
65. *Straits Budget*, April 17, 1952.
66. Extract from "Federation of Malaya Savingram No. 1377, 10 July 1952," CO 1022/168, PRO; Young, "The Federation Police in 1952."
67. *Federation of Malaya Annual Report 1953* (London: HMSO, 1954), 227; *Federation of Malaya Annual Report 1954* (London: HMSO, 1955), 410.
68. Federal Government Press Statements, March 31, 1952, and April 13, 1952, CO 1022/149, PRO.
69. "Supplementary Memorandum from Secretary of Defence: Recruitment into the Rank and File of the Police Force, Supplement to Exco Paper No. 49/3/53," December 5, 1953, CO 1022/169, PRO.
70. Outward Savingram No. 1101 from Secretary of State for the Colonies to High Commissioner Federation of Malaya, May 1, 1952, CO 1022/343, PRO; Inward Savingram No. 1070 from High Commissioner Federation of Malaya to Secretary of State for the Colonies, May 28, 1952, CO 1022/343, PRO.
71. Ramakrishna, *Emergency Propaganda*, 133.
72. Extract from "Malayan Bulletin No. 65, May 25, 1952," CO 1022/165, PRO.
73. Madoc interview; extract from "Federation of Malaya Savingram No. 1377, July 10, 1952," CO 1022/168, PRO. See also Leon Comber, *Malaya's Secret Police: The Role of the Special Branch in the Malayan Emergency* (Institute of Southeast Asian Studies, 2008).
74. Paul Melshen, "Pseudo-Operations: The Use by British and American Armed Forces of Deception in Counterinsurgency 1945-1973" (PhD diss., Cambridge University, 1996), 64–65.
75. Young, "The World Today."
76. Young, "Malaya."

77 Ibid.
78 *Federation of Malaya Annual Report 1952* (London: HMSO, 1953), 6.
79 Young, "The World Today."
80 Young, "Malaya." See also Arthur Young, "Talk to Rotary Club, Kuala Lumpur," February 1953, RHO.
81 Draft of article for *New York Herald Tribune*, May 6, 1953, Young Papers, RHO.
82 "Broadcast on Operation Service," n.d., Templer Papers, NAM.
83 *orkshire Post*, May 19, 1953.
84 Professor Max Beloff's interview with Oliver Lyttelton, February 27, 1970, MSS.Brit.Emp.s.525, RHO.
85 P. B. Humphrey, "A Study of the Reasons for Entering the Jungle Within a Group of Surrendered Chinese Terrorists," ORS (PW) 8/54, June 17, 1954, WO 291/1781, PRO.
86 Lieutenant-Colonel Walter Walker, CO 1/6th Gurkha Rifles, to Colonel C. Graham, CO Gurkha Brigade, July 12, 1952, Stockwell Papers, LHCMA.
87 A. D. C. Peterson, "Report and Recommendations on the Organisation of Information Services in the Federation of Malaya," August 20, 1952, CO 967/181, PRO.
88 "A New Year Message from the HC to all Public Servants," January 1, 1953, Templer Papers, 7410-29-1, NAM.
89 "HC's Speech at the First Meeting of the 6th Session, Legislative Council, 18 March 1953," 7410-29-1, NAM.
90 Constance Mary Turnbull, correspondence with the author, July 31, 1997.
91 "An Appreciation of Police Affairs," February 5, 1953, Young Papers, RHO.
92 J. D. H. Neill to H. P. Bryson, June 11, 1969, Heussler Papers, RHO.
93 O. W. Wolters, personal correspondence, February 27, 1998.
94 David Lloyd-Owen to L. Hankins, April 15, 1969, Templer Papers, 8011-132, NAM.
95 Ibid.
96 Kate Imy, *Losing Hearts and Minds: Race, War, and Empire in Singapore and Malaya, 1915–1960* (Stanford University Press, 2024).
97 Robert Thompson, *Defeating Communist Insurgency: Experiences from Malaya and Vietnam* (Chatto and Windus, 1966); Douglas S. Blaufarb, *The Counterinsurgency Era: US Doctrine and Performance, 1950 to the Present* (Free Press, 1977).
98 H. R. McMaster, *Battlegrounds: The Fight to Defend the Free World* (Harper, 2020), 18.

SOLVING GLOBAL PROBLEMS REQUIRES GLOBAL COHESION

Harvey Whitehouse
Centre for the Study of Social Cohesion, University of Oxford

John, Lord Alderdice
Pembroke College, University of Oxford; Senator George J. Mitchell Institute for Global Peace, Security, and Justice at Queen's University, Belfast; Global Humanity for Peace Institute, University of Wales Trinity Saint David; House of Lords, UK Trade Envoy to Azerbaijan and Central Asia and Select Committee on International Relations and Defence; The Concord Foundation

Carlos Alvarado Quesada
Former President of Costa Rica; Fletcher School of Law and Diplomacy, Tufts University

Peter Gluckman
Koi Tū: the Centre for Informed Futures, University of Auckland, International Science Council

Hakima El Haité
Former Minister of Environment for the Kingdom of Morocco, Liberal International

Lukas Reinhardt
Global Cohesion Lab, Centre for the Study of Social Cohesion, University of Oxford

Harvey Whitehouse, a Statutory Professor of social anthropology at the University of Oxford, is the founding Director of Oxford's Centre for the Study of Social Cohesion and is a founding Director of Seshat: Global History Databank.

ABSTRACT

A growing body of evidence from evolutionary anthropology and social psychology suggests that group cohesion can be scaled up beyond the level of nations and even regional blocs and transnational religions to encompass humanity at large. This article brings together insights from globally renowned political leaders, activists, and academics by arguing that this scaling up is not only possible but necessary to address the most pressing collective action problems facing our planet today. Drawing on evidence from experiments, longitudinal studies, and multi-country surveys, along with extensive practical experience—from serving as a head of state to playing leading roles in climate diplomacy and peace processes—we seek to lay the foundations for a radically new roadmap for change in the management of global challenges.

For the first time in the history of our species, failure to establish effective forms of peaceful cooperation to address global problems poses an existential threat to humanity at large. In the past, humans have been able to plunder the world's resources; conquer each other's lands; enslave, exploit, and colonize the vanquished; and carry out mass killings as a way of consolidating wealth and power.[1] But the

---

John, Lord Alderdice is an Honorary Fellow of Pembroke College, Oxford and a professor of practice at the Senator George J. Mitchell Institute for Global Peace, Security and Justice at Queen's University, Belfast and at the Global Humanity for Peace Institute, University of Wales Trinity Saint David. A life member of the House of Lords, he is currently the UK Trade Envoy to Azerbaijan and Central Asia and a member of the House of Lords Select Committee on International Relations and Defence. He is the Founder and Chairman of The Concord Foundation, and as Leader of the Alliance Party of Northern Ireland, he was one of the negotiators of the 1998 Belfast/Good Friday Agreement.

Carlos Alvarado Quesada is a Professor of the Practice of Diplomacy at Tufts University. He served a full term as President of the Republic of Costa Rica (2018–2022).

Sir Peter Gluckman is a Distinguished University Professor at the University of Auckland where he heads Koi Tū: the Centre for Informed Futures. He is President of the International Science Council (ISC). From 2009 to 2018 he was the first Chief Science Advisor to the Prime Minister of New Zealand.

Hakima El Haité is the fourteenth President of Liberal International and a leader in the fields of environmental sustainability, development, and climate change. As the former Minister of Environment for the Kingdom of Morocco, she was a major actor in bringing COP22 to Morocco. She was vice president of COP 21, which resulted in the Paris Agreement.

Dr. Lukas Reinhardt leads the Global Cohesion Lab at the Centre for the Study of Social Cohesion at the University of Oxford. A behavioral economist by training, he has been a visiting scholar at Harvard University, the University of Pennsylvania, and the United Nations Research Institute for Social Development (UNRISD).

unintended consequences of human technological innovations particularly over the past two hundred years and the consequential threats to planetary and social ecosystems make it increasingly clear that there is a limit to these forms of extraction, oppression, and conflict as a basis for the advancement of human civilization.[2] The way we are using the Earth's resources is leading to a spiraling global climate crisis,[3] rapid changes in communications technologies are producing increasingly polarized and unstable societies,[4] and the lethality of weaponry—from cyber threats to nuclear warheads, some of them potentially hypersonic—now raises the specter of eventual breakdown in global systems and mutually assured destruction.[5]

Countering these threats clearly requires commitment from the world's richest and most powerful countries, effective operation of international institutions, and other forms of top-down and transnational cooperation. But what is far less widely appreciated is that our most powerful forms of political, economic, and military influence in world affairs are the outcomes of social cohesion and depend upon it to operate well. In turn this modus operandi relies on ensuring both social and institutional trust at every level of societal organization from local to global. To be maximally effective, global institutions must rely in part on the commitment of people worldwide—whether as leaders, citizens, consumers, producers, voters, educators, or industrialists—to foster peaceful and sustainable forms of human flourishing.

Such commitment to solving global challenges is not a given. All too often, good intentions expressed at international gatherings such as that of the UN General Assembly or G20 are later diluted to become more palatable to domestic audiences. Nations worldwide are currently becoming more internally divided and less able to cooperate internationally, owing in part to forms of populism that exploit this decline and forms of nationalism that amplify it. However, this state of affairs is by no means inevitable. Past leaders of conviction such as Nelson Mandela or Martin Luther King Jr. have often persuaded their followers to support visionary policies that were initially unpopular or seemingly impossible. New scientific research sheds light on the psychology behind forms of leadership and persuasion capable of generating and spreading support for collective action. Moreover, our collective concerns about the world around us and its future ultimately rely on group psychology that can be influenced in a great variety of ways, with the right forms of institutional support. Thus, it is not necessary to take as a given the parochial forms of cohesion that must be navigated by negotiated coordination and accommodation or appeasement of selfish interests. This article argues that strengthening global cohesion can help to address global challenges by establishing superordinate loyalties and commitments capable of driving public policy both domestically and internationally.

The key question posed in this article is whether we want our evolved group psychology to continue to be manipulated by ad agencies, mass media, populists, social media platforms, jihadis, right wing extremists, militant communists, dictators, and others bent on advancing parochial interests at the expense of everyone else, or whether we want to harness our potential for cohesion with humanity at large to solve global cooperation problems that matter for all of us. It is in our collective interests to choose the latter. But if that is our goal, how is it to be accomplished? The answer may lie in the science of social cohesion.

The Science of Cohesion Building

The human capacity to generate social cohesion and to use it to solve collective action problems has a complex evolutionary history. Like many other cooperative species, ranging from eusocial insects[6] to mammals,[7] humans have biologically evolved adaptations for cooperation in groups.[8] These include psychological mechanisms that lead us to favor cooperation with ingroups and to derogate outgroups,[9] to recognize ostracism threats and to adopt behaviors that mitigate the risk of exclusion,[10] and even under certain circumstances, to sacrifice oneself to protect other members of the group.[11] These panhuman psychological adaptations evolved over millions of years to enable humans to flourish in small foraging groups.[12] However, in a very short space of time in evolutionary terms, human groups have grown exponentially larger, from bands of hunter-gatherers comprising scores of individuals to complex states and empires unifying millions of citizens and even exceeding one billion in the cases of India and China. This rapid increase in the scale of human cooperation has its roots in the discovery of agriculture around ten thousand years ago and the emergence of the first states just a few thousand years after that, followed by a process of cultural group selection in which ever larger polities spread by means of political domination and military and economic exploitation.[13] The causal drivers of this process of socio-political evolution are becoming increasingly well understood as a result of the statistical analysis of patterns in global history, enabling scientists to test competing hypotheses against evidence gathered from large samples of past societies studied by archaeologists and historians.[14]

The science of cohesion building is also gradually unraveling the psychological processes involved in this expansion in the scale of human cooperation. In order for humans to live in larger and more complex societies, group psychology, which originally evolved for life in small face-to-face groups, had to be scaled up to solve collective action problems through the peaceful interaction of strangers living in much larger and denser urban settlements. At Oxford's Centre for the Study of Social Cohesion and elsewhere, researchers have established a global collaborative network of evolutionary theorists, data scientists, experimental psychologists, historians, archaeologists, and anthropologists who are collectively developing an integrated framework for explaining how this scaling up process came about.[15] The core features of the process as it is currently understood are as follows.

In ancient hunter-gather societies, the strongest forms of social cohesion were likely based on a form of group alignment known to psychology as 'identity fusion' whereby the personal self becomes fused with a group identity.[16] The fusion mechanism is rooted in feelings of shared essence—that is, the conviction that something essential to one's personal identity is also a defining characteristic of the group.[17] A particularly common example of this process at work is seen in psychological kinship rooted in phenotypic matching, the perception that people who look, sound, or smell like me are assumed to share some hidden biological essence (often conceptualized as being in the person's blood or bones) that is inherited from common ancestors. Kin selection can help to explain strong forms of cooperation in many other species, ranging from the high-risk predator distraction tactics of birds feigning broken wings to protect their fledglings to the willingness to forgo reproductive opportunities in favor of more dominant individuals in social species of canid.[18] In the case of humans, studies show that perceptions of shared biological essence underlie fusion in families and kin groups.[19]

Humans also associate their personal essence with unique autobiographical experiences, that is, self-defining events that make a person distinct from anyone else. When personally transformative events of this kind are shared with others—becoming group defining as well as personally defining—this can drive feelings of fusion in much the same way as perceptions of shared biological essence. Cross-cultural studies suggest that this pathway to fusion is similar in human populations the world over, even though it may be conceptualized and labeled in locally distinctive ways.[20] Moreover, studies with large samples of twins have shown that shared life experiences drive fusion with a sibling independently of the effects of shared biology.[21] Evolutionary modeling supported by evidence from psychological experiments suggests that fusion based on shared experiences evolved in conditions of strong intergroup competition associated with harsh environments (us versus nature contests) and local raiding and warfare (us versus them contests).[22] When people become fused together in this way, any attack on the group is taken personally and they will effectively stop at nothing to defend the group against perceived threats and insults, even being willing to fight and die to protect their fellows in extreme cases.[23]

In ancient foraging bands, fusion united small groups of people who knew each other personally. Psychologists refer to these groups based on ties between individuals interacting face-to-face as 'relational' groups. However, as societies grew in scale and complexity, interactions between relative strangers became increasingly important, for example for the purposes of trade and exchange or to implement centrally regulated norms and laws. In order for cooperation to operate successfully on such large scales, new forms of group alignment became increasingly important in human affairs, based on categorical rather than relational ties. An example of this is the extensively studied phenomenon of social identification.[24] When we identify with a group category, that is, with a generic identity such as a nation or a world religion, we are not aligning ourselves with people we know personally but with abstracted persons who are like us by virtue of merely sharing some traits (typically beliefs, dialects, norms, customs, and rituals). Because these kinds of traits are acquired socially from others rather than being rooted in personal autobiographies, identification is somewhat depersonalizing. Making the group salient for a highly identified person will make their personal identity less accessible. But this also means that when selfish interests conflict with those of the group, the former may trump the latter, making identification a less effective mechanism than fusion for motivating self-sacrifice.[25]

As groups became larger, identification became increasingly important as a basis for cooperation between strangers, but this also meant that cohesion became more diffuse. For example, whereas warrior bands would fight to the death to protect each other, wars between much larger armies were waged by increasingly professionalized militia whose cohesion was based on shared symbols more than personally shared experiences or ties of kinship. In the evolution of military cohesion, various solutions have been found to address this problem. For example, the division of armies into many smaller relational groups with high levels of identity fusion has allowed military tacticians to harness the most powerful forms of social cohesion among soldiers on the battlefield.

But another key development has been the evolution of extended fusion: a form of group alignment in which vast group categories have become associated with shared essence, capable of driving feelings of fusion. Examples of large-scale group bonding based on beliefs in shared ancestry, as in the case of beliefs about race, ethnicity, and nationality, extend feelings of psychological kinship to vast populations, leveraging shared physical traits and myths of descent from common origins. Indeed extreme nationalism and group-based identity thus come into conflict with the individualism exposed in liberal democratic thought and this tension is now playing out across the democratic world.[26] Extended fusion utilizes histories of oppression and intergroup conflict associated with categorical groups based on shared religious beliefs or national traits, to motivate feelings of patriotism and zealotry.[27] In recent decades the capacity for extremely large groups to fuse based on shared experiences has greatly increased as a result of new communications technologies that bring the sufferings of fellow group members into our computer screens and smartphones in ways that are more visceral and bonding than ever before.[28]

The evolution of cohesion-building gadgets brings with it many dangers, from organized crime and gangland violence to imperial expansionism, and from polarization and sectarianism to revolutions and genocides. But it also brings many opportunities for peaceful cooperation.[29]

Harnessing Cohesion with Humanity to Tackle Global Challenges

Although the fusion mechanism evolved to support strong forms of cooperation in small groups of closely related individuals and bands of fictive kin who had endured together the ordeals of tribal initiations and hand-to-hand combat in intergroup raiding parties, recent psychological experiments have shown that perceptions of both 'shared biology' and 'shared experience' can create feelings of fusion on a global scale. In one such experiment, participants were shown a video in which the journalist A.J. Jacobs explained in an intuitively compelling way that all of us are descended from common ancestors and therefore all human beings constitute a single family. By making our shared biology so salient, this video significantly increased levels of fusion with humanity at large among research subjects, compared with the control condition in which fusion was measured before rather than after watching the video.[30] The video had no negative effects on fusion with other groups such as the immediate family, the extended family, or the country, demonstrating that fusion with humanity does not need to weaken other identities. The same article also reported a study showing that globally shared transformative experiences can create fusion that transcends national, ethnic, and religious boundaries. It showed that mothers were more fused with other women around the world if they shared motherhood experiences with them, building on evidence that transformative experiences of childbirth provide a potent form of fusion.[31] In these studies, whether the key factor was shared ancestry or common experiences, feelings of shared essence and fusion with other human beings around the world was also shown to motivate action, in the form of money allocations to fellow world citizens.

Fusion rooted in shared experiences holds substantial potential in addressing global problems, such as the climate crisis. It may be possible to shift popular perceptions of this global threat in ways that lead to more urgent action by transforming the climate agenda into a citizen-centered narrative that encapsulates personal stories and lived experiences with climate change. Extreme weather events prompt efforts to strengthen infrastructure, improve emergency services, and tackle the root causes of climate change but these are all reactive and therefore typically short-term responses. By contrast, a collective narrative of climate experiences could empower collective action over the longer run. Such an approach would involve viewing each account of adaptation and resilience—whether in response to wildfires, floods, or droughts—not as isolated incidents but as integral chapters of a global story. By recognizing local and personal struggles as crucial components of a worldwide effort, we enhance this sense of fusion and invigorate a global collaboration aimed at safeguarding our shared planet. We can integrate these efforts into a cohesive, shared narrative, fostering more lasting forms of global cohesion and cooperation, aimed at protecting and sustaining our environment for future generations.

Another notable example of how these processes can unfold is the emergence of the Peace People in Northern Ireland in 1976. The Troubles had polarized the community, exacerbating deep divisions and violence between Protestant unionists and Catholic nationalists. On August 10, 1976, British soldiers opened fire on a car carrying two armed Irish Republican Army (IRA) men. The car went out of control and crashed into a mother and three of her children who were out shopping. The children died, two at the scene and the third the following day. Betty Williams, a Catholic woman who was passing, immediately began gathering signatures for a peace petition, and was joined in a march for peace by two hundred other women. When they passed the home of the children's aunt, Mairead Corrigan, she joined the march and the two women became the joint leaders of a movement that caught the imagination of other women, appalled by the death of the three children. The next march, to the place where the children were buried, brought 10,000 Protestant and Catholic women together and soon the Women for Peace movement included men and became the Community of the Peace People. In 1977 they received the Nobel Peace Prize and the change in community atmosphere was reflected in the growth of the cross-community Alliance Party in the May 1977 elections. This positive trajectory was not sustained or spread further but it demonstrated how, in the context of profound political division, women who felt a powerful sense of shared experiences as mothers, could find common cause and transcend their divisions.

Modern technologies and media provide ever more potent ways to facilitate fusion that could be used to motivate behavior change to address global challenges. For example, the killing of 'Cecil'—a wild lion illegally shot in Zimbabwe by an American dentist—that went viral, prompted worldwide condemnation and mass donations to support lion conservation. A survey of donors revealed that perceptions of shared experience with Cecil were driving fusion, which in turn motivated behaviors directed toward lion conservation.[32] Similar results have been achieved by presenting research participants with speeches that encourage listeners to donate to charities devoted to action on the climate crisis. Merely reminding people of our shared experiences and shared biology as a species may be just as important as persuasion based on scientific evidence when it comes to motivating climate action.[33]

Similar techniques may also contribute to a more peaceful world by supporting efforts to prevent or ameliorate seemingly intractable conflicts. For example, it has been shown that appeals to shared suffering on both sides can improve attitudes toward the outgroup in the context of the crisis in Gaza triggered by the Hamas attacks in Israel in October 2023 and the relentless Israeli bombardment of the region that followed.[34] These studies, and others, have shown that perceptions of shared essence (based on common ancestry and transformative experiences) can produce strong forms of cohesion and prosocial action on a global scale.

To apply this insight to real-world problems will require more effective institutional support and barrier-crossing leadership. We need our media and other organs of public information and communication to remind us continually of our shared humanity when it comes to tackling global problems, and we need trusted leaders to shape the public conversation on such topics. This is very different from leadership in which elected politicians seek to reflect public opinion and exploit it for selfish ends. Instead, we need leaders to actively shape public opinion in directions that harness our capacities for fusion, to support peaceful prosocial outcomes that transcend existing group boundaries. A thriving body of research on so-called barrier-crossing leadership shows that this is possible by harnessing shared experiences across groups. In one study, barrier-crossing leaders from three embattled minority groups (Muslims in London, Travellers in Omagh, and African Americans in Louisiana) were better able to recognize shared experiences with outgroups than their barrier-bound counterparts.[35]

A raft of new research along similar lines in sub-Saharan Africa and South Asia suggests that religious communities may provide particularly fertile soil for the cultivation of barrier-crossing leaders.[36] This may be in part because religious teachings, in theory if not always in practice, often emphasize universalizing principles. An often-neglected example of this is the imperative to take care of God's creation in the form of stewardship of the Earth. All of the world religions provide scriptural support for this idea and because the overwhelming majority of the world's population aligns with such religions, there is obvious potential to harness the cohesion of adherents and their more environmentally progressive beliefs to address the climate crisis more effectively on a global scale. Pope Francis's discourse, particularly in his encyclical *Laudato Si'*, emphasizes this call, highlighting the urgency of an ecological conversion. He urges everyone to "hear both the cry of the earth and the cry of the poor," reminding us that environmental destruction primarily affects the most vulnerable.[37] By insisting on our shared responsibility to protect the Earth, his message resonates deeply beyond religious borders, reaffirming that "everything is connected." Most of the world's religious adherents endorse similar teachings on the preservation of divine creation. When urgings to protect the Earth and all forms of life come from a spiritual leader, it likewise taps into feelings of extended fusion, capable of motivating unified global action.

Global unification can also bridge divides between religious adherents and nontheists. One memorable example of a movement that brought together people from many different religious and humanist backgrounds is the Campaign for Nuclear Disarmament (CND), which was formed at Methodist Central Hall, Westminster, in February 1958. Amid growing public anxiety about the possibility of nuclear war the CND organized (with others) the Aldermaston Marches, a series of demonstrations in the late 1950s and early 1960s from the Atomic Weapons Research Establishment at Aldermaston to London, with 100,000 participants at its height in 1963. One lesson from this initiative and the Peace People in Northern Ireland is that while a powerful unifying idea can quickly harness the power of shared experiences and change the public narrative, maintaining momentum requires organization and leadership.

What Next?

To realize the potential of social cohesion to address global challenges, we need to act fast. Increasing cohesion within existing global institutions, e.g., the United Nations (UN), the International Court of Justice (ICJ), the Group of Twenty (G20), the United Nations Educational, Scientific and Cultural Organization (UNESCO), the World Trade Organization (WTO), the World Health Organization (WHO), and the Organisation for Economic Co-operation and Development (OECD), and others, and commitment to core principles (e.g., human rights and sustainable development goals or SDGs) will be vital to improving global cooperation and governance. The recent Pact for the Future agreed upon at the last UN General Assembly in September 2024 makes vague statements in support of unity but invites skepticism as to whether it can lead to action.

We also need to find more ways to increase the salience of global citizenship and shared identity among the world's population, increasing the cohesion of humanity at large as part of a growing movement of worldwide support for global solutions to global problems. Research summarized in the previous section suggests that well-crafted speeches from politicians can have more transformative and lasting effects than may be generally appreciated but this will not be enough. The mass media and public figures of all kinds have an important role to play in changing the narratives we live by.

One of the main challenges will be to create a constructive information environment that reaches beyond the unholy alliance of platform companies and autocrats and their parochial objectives, media in which the sale of advertising space is also used to advance populist or narrow political agendas often fueled by disinformation. This will involve the creation and widespread dissemination of narratives and practices promoting global cohesion, drawing on state-of-the-art research in fields such as experimental psychology and evolutionary anthropology and building on existing cultural knowledge and traditions. Such narratives and practices should not only respect and celebrate human diversity but also emphasize the shared humanity of all individuals on the planet, recognizing them as part of a unified global family and community. Such a platform might seek to maximize diversity in terms of human experience, incorporating the perspectives of diverse cultures (including Indigenous peoples), independent thinkers, public intellectuals, artists, and young people, as well as senior politicians and academics. Achieving this will require the development and promotion of an ethical framework for global cohesion—a transparent agenda guided by clear and explicit objectives—along with the practical application of these concepts. This would entail the integration of scientific and cultural insights, translating both effectively into tangible political and social actions as part of the art of communication and implementation.

Such efforts to build global cohesion should naturally catalyze peace, foster collaboration on global challenges, and promote harmonious coexistence among people worldwide. It is crucial to avoid the divisive dichotomies prevalent in today's world, in all the "us versus them" forms, and ensure accessibility across diverse traditions using both digital and offline platforms. Previous attempts to develop international cooperation have generally focused on institutional links, rules, and regulations, without much attempt to address the quality of the relationships, or have been based on alliances formed to oppose other communities perceived as threats. While the latter are represented by bodies like NATO, as a defense alliance, the former are exemplified by the UN, which merely requires that a state is recognized by the international community and can therefore nominate its representatives to key positions. This results in states that are gross violators of human rights being elected to chair the human rights organs of the UN, bringing the notion of human rights into disrepute, and UN mediators being put in place without any of the skills or experience that are appropriate and necessary. Focusing less on institutions and more on relational imperatives would help move the global community toward more cohesive forms of engagement. It is not only the powerful who need to modify their aims and approaches to be less 'colonial' or dominant, but the less powerful must also recognize that they have a vital role to play beyond pointing out the historical and current faults of the more powerful states. All have their responsibilities in changing things for the better. The zeitgeist around leadership also needs to change. In the past, people like Mikhail Gorbachev, Nelson Mandela, F.W. de Klerk, and Bill Clinton appreciated that leadership was about resolving conflicts. In a globally divisive trend, most of today's political leaders believe that it is their role to conduct conflicts, not to resolve them.

Many leaders believe that their job is to identify and represent the perspectives of significant constituencies or combinations of groups. However, such people are not leaders but followers and representatives of increasingly polarized community sentiment. Leaders who are passionate about a cause, endeavor to persuade and inspire others to come with them and make change happen, but to be successful they must assemble support from across the boundaries of their communities and build a movement for change. This is why the most effective change-makers are trusted boundary-crossing leaders who understand the power of symbolism and the possibilities of shaping public opinion instead of merely representing or exploiting it for personal gain.

The problem of academic and cultural silos is also important to resolve. Instead of universities bringing together scholars with different approaches to knowledge—humanities, law, medicine, science, and technology—they ask for research proposals that tend to focus on single approaches while reinforcing the boundaries between departments and faculties, and with little understanding of the methods, theories, and findings of other disciplines. Consequently, as the collective stock of human knowledge accumulates, it becomes increasingly fragmented rather than cohesive. We need to bring people together, but we also need to bring ideas and perspectives together if we are to address these challenging and potentially existential problems. The International Science Council has taken the lead in promoting changed thinking in how transdisciplinary research should be funded and conducted.[38]

This article has brought together the diverse experiences of a loose network of leading academics, politicians, activists, and public servants from around the world who focus on how global identity and cohesion can be strengthened to foster international cooperation and mitigate conflict. We need others to join with us to further enrich this vision and shape the public conversation around it. To that end we invite readers of this article to contact lead author Harvey Whitehouse, with suggestions on how to strengthen a global identity.[39] Building on this feedback, we will post an evolving roadmap for change on the website of Oxford's <u>Centre for the Study of Social Cohesion along with those of our partners</u>.[40] This is one small step toward laying the groundwork for new forms of global cohesion and cooperation. Without such baby steps we will never progress. But with practice, and the support of others around us, giant strides become possible.

Notes

1. Peter Turchin, *Ultrasociety: How 10,000 Years of War Made Humans the Greatest Cooperators on Earth* (Beresta Books, 2015).
2. Peter Gluckman and Mark Hanson, *Ingenious: The Unintended Consequences of Human Innovation* (Harvard University Press, 2019).
3. Katherine Richardson, Will Steffen, Wolfgang Lucht, et al., "Earth Beyond Six of Nine Planetary Boundaries," *Science Advances* 9, no. 37 (2023): eadh2458, https://doi.org/10.1126/sciadv.adh2458.
4. Gluckman and Hanson, *Ingenious*.
5. Harvey Whitehouse, *Inheritance: The Evolutionary Origins of the Modern World* (Penguin Random House, 2024).
6. Edward O. Wilson and Bert Hölldobler, "Eusociality: Origin and Consequences," *Proceedings of the National Academy of Sciences* 102, no. 38 (2005): 13367–71, https://doi.org/10.1073/pnas.0505858102.
7. Jennifer E. Smith, "Hamilton's Legacy: Kinship, Cooperation and Social Tolerance in Mammalian Groups," *Animal Behaviour* 92 (2014): 291–304, https://doi.org/10.1016/j.anbehav.2014.02.029.
8. Coren L. Apicella and Joan B. Silk, "The Evolution of Human Cooperation," *Current Biology* 29, no. 11 (2019): R447–R450, https://doi.org/10.1016/j.cub.2019.03.036.
9. Henry Tajfel and John C. Turner, "The Social Identity Theory of Intergroup Behaviour," in *Psychology of Intergroup Relations*, ed. Stephen Worchel and William G. Austin (Nelson-Hall, 1986).
10. Rachel E. Watson-Jones, Cristine H. Legare, Harvey Whitehouse, and Jennifer M. Clegg, "Task-Specific Effects of Ostracism on Imitative Fidelity in Early Childhood," *Evolution and Human Behavior* 35, no. 3 (2014): 204–210, https://doi.org/10.1016/j.evolhumbehav.2014.01.004; Rachel E. Watson-Jones, Harvey Whitehouse, and Cristine H. Legare, "In-Group Ostracism Increases High-Fidelity Imitation in Early Childhood," *Psychological Science* 27, no. 1 (2016): 34–42, https://doi.org/10.1177/0956797615607205.
11. Harvey Whitehouse, "Dying for the Group: Towards a General Theory of Extreme Self-Sacrifice," *Behavioral and Brain Sciences* 41 (2018): e192, https://doi.org/10.1017/S0140525X18000249.
12. Peter J. Richerson and Robert Boyd, *Not by Genes Alone: How Culture Transformed Human Evolution* (University of Chicago Press, 2005).
13. Harvey Whitehouse, *Inheritance: The Evolutionary Origins of the Modern World* (Penguin Random House, 2024).
14. Peter Turchin, Harvey Whitehouse, Sergey Gavrilets, et al., "Disentangling the Evolutionary Drivers of Social Complexity: A Comprehensive Test of Hypotheses," *Science Advances* 8, no. 25 (2022): eabn3517, https://doi.org/10.1126/sciadv.abn3517.
15. Harvey Whitehouse, *The Ritual Animal: Imitation and Cohesion in the Evolution of Social Complexity* (Oxford University Press, 2021); Whitehouse, *Inheritance*.
16. William B. Swann Jr., Jolanda Jetten, Ángel Gómez, Harvey Whitehouse, and Brock Bastian, "When Group Membership Gets Personal: A Theory of Identity Fusion," *Psychological Review* 119, no. 3 (2012): 441–56, https://psycnet.apa.org/doi/10.1037/a0028589.
17. Harvey Whitehouse and Jonathan Lanman, "The Ties that Bind Us: Ritual, Fusion, and Identification," *Current Anthropology* 55, no. 6 (2014): 674–95, https://doi.org/10.1086/678698.

18. Tomas Kay, Laurent Lehmann, and Laurent Keller, "Kin Selection and Altruism," *Current Biology* 29, no. 11 (2019): PR438–R442, https://doi.org/10.1016/j.cub.2019.01.067. Kira A. Cassidy and Richard T. McIntyre, "Do Gray Wolves (*Canis lupus*) Support Pack Mates During Aggressive Inter-Pack Interactions?," *Animal Cognition* 19 (2016): 939–47, https://doi.org/10.1007/s10071-016-0994-1.
19. Harvey Whitehouse, Jonathan Jong, Michael D. Buhrmester, et al., "The Evolution of Extreme Cooperation via Intense Shared Experiences," *Nature: Scientific Reports* (2017): Article 44292, https://doi.org/10.1038/srep44292.
20. Whitehouse, *The Ritual Animal*.
21. Alexandra Vázquez, Juan R. Ordoñana, Harvey Whitehouse, and Ángel Gómez, "Why Die for My Sibling? The Positive Association Between Identity Fusion and Imagined Loss with Endorsement of Self-Sacrifice," *International Journal of Social Psychology* 34, no. 3 (2019): 413–38, https://doi.org/10.1080/02134748.2019.1639343.
22. Whitehouse et al., "The Evolution of Extreme Cooperation."
23. William B. Swann Jr., Ángel Gómez, J. Hart Dovidio, and Jolanda Jetten, "Dying and Killing for One's Group: Identity Fusion Moderates Responses to Intergroup Versions of the Trolley Problem," *Psychological Science* 21, no. 8 (2010): 1176–83, https://doi.org/10.1177/0956797610376656.
24. Whitehouse and Lanman, "The Ties That Bind Us."
25. William B. Swann and Michael D. Buhrmester, "Identity Fusion," *Current Directions in Psychological Science* 24, no. 1 (2015): 52–57, https://doi.org/10.1177/0963721414551363.
26. Francis Fukuyama, *Identity: Contemporary Identity Politics and the Struggle for Recognition* (Profile Books, 2019).
27. Christopher M. Kavanagh, Susilo Wibisono, Rohan Kapitány, et al., "Exploring the Role of Identity Fusion and Group Identification in Predicting Parochialism Amongst Indonesian Islamic Groups," preprint, PsyArXiv, May 24, 2019, https://doi.org/10.31234/osf.io/e8ytr.
28. Whitehouse, *Inheritance*.
29. Peter Gluckman and Hema Sridhar, "A Guide for Policy-Makers: Evaluating Rapidly Developing Technologies Including AI, Large Language Models and Beyond," International Science Council, 2024, https://council.science/wp-content/uploads/2024/04/A-guide-for-policy-makers_AI.pdf.
30. Lukas Reinhardt and Harvey Whitehouse, "Why Care for Humanity?," *Royal Society Open Science* 11, no. 4 (2024): Article 231632, https://doi.org/10.1098/rsos.231632.
31. Tara Tasuji, Elaine Reese, Valerie van Mulukom, and Harvey Whitehouse, "Band of Mothers: Childbirth as a Female Bonding Experience," *PLoS One* 15, no. 10 (2020): e0240175, https://doi.org/10.1371/journal.pone.0240175.
32. Michael D. Buhrmester, Dawn Burnham, Dominic D. Johnson, Oliver S. Curry, David W. Macdonald, and Harvey Whitehouse, "How Moments Become Movements: Shared Outrage, Group Cohesion, and the Lion That Went Viral," *Frontiers in Ecology and Evolution* 6 (2018): 54, https://doi.org/10.3389/fevo.2018.00054.
33. Lukas Reinhardt and Harvey Whitehouse, "What Kinds of Speeches Motivate Climate Action?," *Royal Society Open Science* 12, no. 4 (2025): Article 241563, https://doi.org/10.1098/rsos.241563.
34. Lukas Reinhardt and Harvey Whitehouse, "Can Appeals to Shared Suffering Provide a Recipe for Peace?," SSRN, March 18, 2024, https://ssrn.com/abstract=4763644.

35 Michael D. Buhrmester, Mike A. Cowan, and Harvey Whitehouse, "What Motivates Barrier-Crossing Leadership?," *New England Journal of Public Policy* 34, no. 2 (2022): Article 7, https://scholarworks.umb.edu/nejpp/vol34/iss2/7/.3

36 Christopher M. Kavanagh, Gagan Atreya, Jack W. Klein, et al., "The Role of Barrier Crossing Leadership in the Promotion of Religious Freedom," preprint, PsyArXiv, December 21, 2023, https://doi.org/10.31234/osf.io/csf6r.

37 Pope Francis, *Laudato Si': On Care for Our Common Home* (Our Sunday Visitor, 2015), 97.

38 Matthias Kaiser and Peter Gluckman, "Looking at the Future of Transdisciplinary Research," International Science Council, 2023, https://council.science/publications/future-transdisciplinary-research/.

39 harvey.whitehouse@anthro.ox.ac.uk

40 Centre for the Study of Social Cohesion, https://www.cssc.ox.ac.uk/.

EXAMINING SHIFTS IN GROUP-BASED MOTIVATIONS FOR CIVIL CONFLICTS IN LIBYA

Michael D. Buhrmester
University of Oxford

William B. Swann Jr.
University of Texas at Austin

Brian McQuinn
University of Regina

Alexis Everington
International Advisory Services

Layal Hafid
International Advisory Services

Harvey Whitehouse
Centre for the Study of Social Cohesion, University of Oxford

Dr. Michael Buhrmester is a senior researcher. He has published widely on topics that include the nature and function of self and identity, group cohesion, and extreme pro-group actions. Michael served as a postdoctoral researcher at the University of Oxford.

Dr. William B. Swann Jr. is a Professor of social-personality psychology at the University of Texas at Austin and developed the self-verification and identity fusion theories. He has served as President of the Society of Experimental Social Psychology and has received career awards from the Society of Personality and Social Psychology and the International Society for Self and Identity.

Alexis Everington is the founder and CEO of International Advisory Services. He has spent more than two decades working in and researching more than twenty conflict-affected countries, including Libya, Jordan, Syria, and Afghanistan. He worked in Libya during the 2010 revolution and for several years in collaboration with local and international political, civil society, and security-related groups.

ABSTRACT

This study examines shifting group alignments in Libya from 2011 to 2019, exploring their impact on continued conflict. Following up on our original research into group bonding among insurgents during the 2011 revolution, we conducted two surveys in Benghazi: first in 2015, during the aftermath of Operation Dignity, and again in 2019, as General Khalifa Haftar's forces waged war against Tripoli. Our results show that the previously very strong group bonds with 2011 revolutionary fighters had dissipated by 2015, replaced by allegiance to Haftar's militias. By 2019, this alignment extended to Haftar himself, reinforcing an "us versus them" mentality that fueled intrastate violence. Our findings highlight how shifts in strong forms of group alignment can both reflect and drive political fragmentation, with profound implications for Libya's governance and peace prospects. More broadly, our findings contribute to the study of how group loyalties shape and sustain civil conflicts, offering insight into the psychological mechanisms underlying failed state dynamics.

More than a decade after Libyans rose up against Muammar Gaddafi's forty-two year rule, the country was still struggling to form a national government. The country remained fragmented, built around cities and communities, each with specific grievances and contrasting visions for Libya's future.[1] During the popular uprising of 2011, opposition to Gaddafi's rule papered over many of these divisions, providing a common goal that united most Libyans.[2] The North African nation is among a growing number of postwar countries that are not in a state of war or peace.[3] Average Libyans must now navigate a dangerous and fluid security

---

Layal Hafid is the Counter-Disinformation Campaigns Lead at Innovation and Insight Global (IN2). She has more than fifteen years of experience working in and researching conflict-affected contexts such as Syria, Iraq, Libya, and Lebanon.

Dr. Brian McQuinn is an Associate Professor of international studies and the Co-Director of the Centre for Artificial Intelligence, Data, and Conflict at the University of Regina. He has spent more than two decades working in and researching more than thirty conflict-affected countries, including Libya, South Sudan, and Nepal.

Harvey Whitehouse is a Statutory Professor of social anthropology at the University of Oxford, the founding Director of Oxford's Centre for the Study of Social Cohesion and a founding Director of Seshat: Global History Databank. He has undertaken research in Africa, the Middle East, the Americas, Europe, Asia, and Oceania using methods including surveys, experiments, and ethnographic fieldwork.

and governance landscape that defies simple explanations or solutions.[4] At the heart of this complexity and instability is an evolving landscape of alliances among hundreds of armed groups.[5]

In this empirical report, we seek to shed light on the underlying psychological processes related to community alignment with armed groups in eastern Libya from 2011 to 2019. Guided by identity fusion theory, we propose that changes in eastern Libyans affinity ("fusion") to armed groups reflected and reinforced shifting political and security as the idea of Libya was replaced by more parochial realities of survival.[6] In particular, whereas in the western city of Misrata in 2011 we observed near universal fusion with the revolutionaries who hoped to create a unified state, by 2015 allegiances in eastern Benghazi had shifted to General Khalifa Haftar's militias during Operation Dignity. By 2019, eastern Libyans were aligned to Haftar himself. His ability to stoke "us versus them" rivalries (in part between eastern and western Libya) encouraged followers who were fused to embrace his advocacy of war. From this vantage point, tracking shifts in communities' fusion with armed factions serves as both a symptom and cause of the chronic violence and the factors that contribute to failed states.

To begin to unpack these dynamics, first we briefly introduce some of the key socio-political events and conflicts central to our analysis of Libya across the past decade. We then describe our empirical focus and aims, detailing the methods and results of two survey studies of Benghazians. We then discuss the implications of our findings for understanding both the future prospects for peace and conflict in Libya, and also the role of shifting group alignments during intra-state conflicts writ large.

Libyan Conflicts (2011–present)

Qaddafi's death marked the end of the armed uprising between the *thuwwar* (revolutionary fighters) and the regime's security brigades, but it did not conclude the revolution or the violence that followed.[7] The intense solidarity and shared purpose that had defined the February 17 Revolution soon gave way to divergent and competing visions for Libya's future. These conflicting interests have continued to vie for power and resources, further entrenching the country's localized political dynamics.[8]

In 2012, the National Transitional Council (NTC), which had led the political arm of the insurgency, fulfilled its promise to step down and clear the way for elections.[9] At the time, this decision was widely applauded by the international community. The

NTC's leaders hoped their withdrawal would empower Libyans by offering them political choices. However, this decision may ultimately be remembered as one of the most consequential missteps in Libya's post-revolution history. The dissolution of the NTC created a political vacuum that was quickly filled by hundreds of political parties and independents. Lacking a unifying authority with the legitimacy to consolidate power, Libyan politics and security reverted to a fragmented, city-by-city competition.

Nationally, Libyan politics remains tumultuous, marked by increasingly complex and polarized factions of political and military actors. However, this assumes the Libyan polity under Qaddafi was a coherent whole.[10] We would argue that Qaddafi's rule suppressed the expression of national and community divisions while simultaneously reinforcing them through a divide-and-rule strategy that entrenched Libya's localized political structures.[11] This has led some to argue that tribal or regional identities are the root cause of Libya's state-building challenges. Igor Cherstich, however, offers a compelling counterargument: Libya's reliance on local communities is not the cause of state failure but rather its consequence.[12] In the absence of a functioning central state and its services, Libyans have been forced to depend on localized social and political arrangements for survival.[13]

Since Qaddafi's death, the unity fostered by the February 17 Revolution has fragmented, giving way to subnational identities, many of which predate the creation of Libya itself.[14] Without institutional or charismatic leadership to unify the country, the question of who should determine Libya's future has become a point of contention, further exacerbated by international interference. The failure to establish a cohesive national government has resulted in a country divided among multiple power centers. Analyses often oversimplify this dynamic as a binary conflict between the UN-recognized Government of National Unity (GNU) in Tripoli and the eastern-based Government of National Stability (GNS), led by Haftar.[15] In reality, the situation is far more fluid and complex. Perhaps most concerning is the growing entrenchment of international actors—including Egypt, Turkey, Russia, Qatar, and the UAE—whose competing interests make domestic compromise increasingly elusive. Libyan elites, reliant on foreign support to maintain their positions of power, find themselves beholden to external agendas, further eroding Libyan agency in shaping the country's future.[16]

Having successfully prosecuted a revolution against Gaddafi, Libyans were in no mood to embrace a new government with prominent ties to the Gaddafi regime.[17] International pressure to foster democracy did little to counterbalance Libyan elites' reassertion of control, taking advantage of long-standing local and regional divisions. The new leadership knew that its legitimacy, strength, and even financial security required the support of fractionalized armed groups. But while Libyan fighters had initially been drawn to the perceived benefits of militia membership (including defending their communities, individual and social empowerment, and financial gain), politicians' promises of jobs, scholarships, and foreign placements ballooned the number of young men claiming military credentials.

By 2014, many who fought in the revolution had returned to civilian life. But for some, armed groups, whether newly created or preexisting, were an opportunity for employment, or worse. Some groups turned to criminality, where kidnappings and extortion became part of Libyan's reality as the government failed to provide security. Self-described Jihadists, including groups affiliated with the Islamic State of Iraq and Syria (ISIS), took root in the eastern city of Derna, long the home of Libya's most extreme political factions.[18] Opportunist militia leaders realized that although political leaders needed them, the converse might not be true. This was epitomized by the rise of General Haftar and his coalition of armed factions, which he named the Libyan National Army (LNA). Haftar had been a general under Gaddafi and quickly understood how international eagerness to tackle the new threat of ISIS could strengthen his legitimacy and access to international weapons and funding.[19] It did not take long for several other leaders across the Libya political and military spectra to announce their own battle against 'terrorists.' Unfortunately for the West, which had decided to follow the UN's lead in recognizing the government in Tripoli, General Haftar appeared to be the most effective at combating ISIS with his May 2014 launch of Operation Dignity in eastern Libya. More specifically, Western democracies found themselves in the unenviable position of supporting a weak and divided Tripoli government reliant on religiously-oriented political parties supported by Qatar and Turkey, while opposing the eastern government that was combating ISIS fighters.[20] To make matters worse, the Western decision gave countries such as Egypt, the UAE, and even Russia a chance to gain a foothold in Libya by supporting the LNA.[21]

Measuring Bonding in Libyan Armed Groups

As instructive and impactful as these changing political and financial considerations may have been in shaping the post-revolutionary landscape in Libya, it is just as important to understand the more visceral impulses that lead to changes of group alignment, including extreme forms of collective action of the kind that led thousands to lose their lives in intergroup violence. Understanding the psychology that inspires individuals' extraordinary acts of commitment to a cause must go beyond the rational pursuit of political and economic strategies. Despite the obviousness of this observation, however, no other systematic research has examined the group psychology underlying continued support and engagement in violent conflict over the past decade in Libya. This gap is all the more striking when one considers the range of ways in which extreme pro-group action was manifested in the Arab Spring and its aftermath.

Our research team was one of the first to measure the bonds among fighters during the 2011 uprising and how quickly these ties surpassed insurgents' bonds to their own families.[22] Recently, researchers have started to study the implication of insurgent victories for post-conflict rebuilding,[23] specifically in Africa.[24] Yet as described above, insurgent victory in Libya was never complete. A national government did not assert authority long enough to consolidate authority across the country. For this reason, the following research also draws upon the growing body of research on insurgent rule, as this better reflects governance in Libya.[25] A crucial finding also seen in Libya's experience is the wide variation in governance arrangements by armed groups, both politically and militarily.[26] This variation includes studies exploring how insurgents administer justice,[27] provide healthcare,[28] and establish education systems.[29]

Of particular interest in our study is community allegiance to insurgent rulers. Existing literature tends to portray insurgent groups as predatory to communities, ignoring the more delicate balance they must strike when communities have the power to shift their allegiance to competing groups.[30] The following research also builds on existing micro-level studies to test new methods for studying the extent to which community affinity to armed groups can and does change as circumstances and military power shift.[31] Specifically, the pictorial methodology described below is particularly useful in conflict settings (see Study 1, Methods section for additional details).

Our team's examination of the Libyan conflict began during the 2011 revolution in Libya that led to death of Gaddafi. Upon surveying armed revolutionaries from Misrata, we found ceiling levels of identity fusion among respondents.[32] Already a tight-knit urban community, Misratans saw intense fighting against Gaddafi's forces, likely contributing to the high levels of fusion.[33] Presented here, we conducted two additional studies in the eastern city of Benghazi, which like many cities in Libya has endured significant violence since the end of the revolution. For these studies, we had local Benghazi research assistants solicit the participation of residents of Benghazi for a small amount of monetary compensation.

To measure group bonds, in our surveys we utilized a construct known as identity fusion, in which personal and group identities operate synergistically, prompting very strong forms of pro-group action, including willingness to fight and die for other members of the group.[34] Fusion was measured using a pictorial scale in which a small circle (you) and a big circle (your group) are shown to overlap to varying degrees. At one end of the spectrum, the small circle and the big circles are separate (no fusion present) while at the other end the small circle is fully enclosed by the big circle (indicating high levels of identity fusion; see Figure 1).

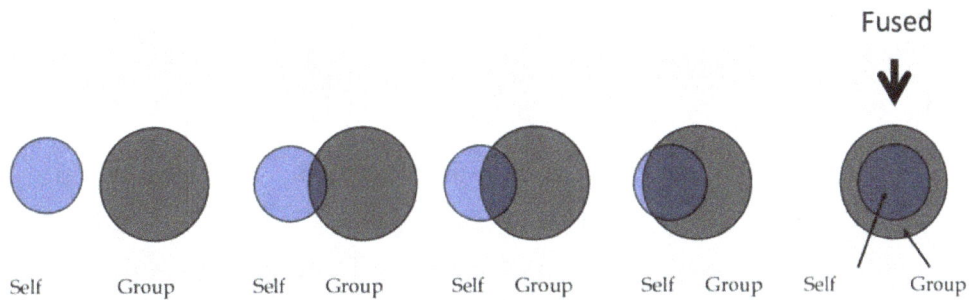

Figure 1. The Pictorial Identity Fusion Scale. Participants chose which of the five diagrams above best represented their relationship to the group, with "fused" represented by the right-most diagram.[35]

The fusion scale is particularly well suited for conflict areas as it is more visual and intuitive, reducing the time and attention required to complete. In the case of the 2011 survey involving active fighters, this was particularly useful as participants did not have the patience to answer text-based survey questions.[36] In the latter studies, we found that despite the politically tense circumstances in Benghazi, respondents varied their answers across groups. Again, the pictorial scale allows participants to distinguish between different levels of support. Additionally, the field researchers demonstrated to respondents that their responses were anonymized as they completed the surveys. Due to the potentially sensitive nature of the survey, the researchers tended to conduct surveys in their neighborhoods where they had some degree of familiarity with those being surveyed. All materials for both studies were approved by Oxford's research ethics board prior to data collection.

Study 1 took place in 2015 in the wake of Operation Dignity. In this conflict, which had substantial support from Libyans, an alliance of armed groups led by General Haftar repelled extremist factions from eastern Libya. Later, Haftar's alliance in eastern Libya attacked Tripoli, Libya's capital, in an effort to take over the country by force. This move, unlike Operation Dignity, was condemned by most Libyans and was repelled by militias from western cities like Misrata and Tripoli. Study 2 occurred in 2019 as that violence continued, with most of the fighting taking place around Tripoli and its southern highways.

The surveys addressed two major questions. First, did Operation Dignity and subsequent hostilities trigger shifts in identity fusion among those who experienced extremist violence? Second, did communities' alignment ('fusion') with eastern armed groups come at the expense of support for a unified Libya?

Study 1

Study 1 aimed to examine the relationships between Benghazi communities and political and military groups involved in violence in Libya in 2015. In addition, we studied how fusion to those conducting Operation Dignity, related to respondents' strength of support for continued conflict. Based on previous evidence that identity fusion is a predictor of extreme pro-group action, including fighting and dying for one's ingroup, we hypothesized that fusion to Operation Dignity fighters would be associated with high levels of support for continued conflict against adversaries. In addition, we hypothesized that the level of extremist violence experienced by Libyans living in Benghazi would shift their allegiance from revolutionary fighters to fighters and leaders involved in Operation Dignity.

Methods

A total of 236 males (average age = 36 years, with standard deviation [SD] = 11.52) living in Benghazi, Libya participated in Study 1. Due to cultural factors, females were not recruited as part of either study. Assistants approached males outside of public spaces (e.g., cafés) and asked if they wished to volunteer a small amount of their time to share their views about conflicts in Benghazi. Face-to-face research in fragile and conflict-affected situations requires unique considerations, including managing risk, considerations of 'do no harm,' and building rapport with respondents.[37] In this study, this was formalized through a Risk Register to help manage these risks and potential forms of bias.[38]

In eastern Libya, cultural norms (e.g., strong reticence to invite strangers into the home) prevented randomized door-to-door visits and interviews in respondents' residences. By contrast, cafés, gyms, restaurants, and shopping streets were well-known spots for social interaction and featured high levels of population flow (particularly of males, and especially at certain times of the day and week). After obtaining informed consent, assistants read questions to participants and recorded all responses, which was followed by debriefing. At no point were respondents asked their name, in an effort to elicit as truthful an answer as possible. After completing basic demographic questions, participants were asked the following.

Group Alignments

Participants were asked to look at the five pictorial scale options, each depicting two circles, one representing oneself, the other, the group target, Operation Dignity fighters.[39] They were then asked to choose which option best represented their relationship to the group target. Scores ranged from 1 = not at all fused, to 5 = totally fused. The mean response (M) was 3.48 (SD = 1.35). Identity fusion is defined as feeling a sense of shared essence with a group, in this case, with Operation Dignity fighters. Higher scores indicate a stronger sense of identity fusion with the group. The identity fusion measure was chosen because previous research has shown that it is a consistent predictor of extreme pro-group behaviors across many group contexts.[40] To minimize the amount of time participants needed to commit to completing the survey, we used the single-item, pictorial identity fusion measure instead of a longer, multi-item measure.[41] Participants next chose which pictorial option best represented their relationship to other group targets, including the 2011 revolutionary fighters, following the same format as the previous question (M = 1.81, SD = 1.06).

Views of Conflict

Participants then completed five questions concerning their views about conflict in Libya. These questions were developed to assess the extent to which participants supported a peaceful resolution versus continued conflict in Libya. In designing these questions, we were mindful of respondents' potential reluctance to explicitly state support for violence, so we crafted questions that were relevant and sensitive to the current state of affairs. The items were the following. Question 1: "Do you believe that the unity government will bring permanent peace to Libya?" with answer choices, 0 = yes, 1 = no (40% responded 'yes'; 60% 'no'). Question 2: "Do you believe that those Libyans who have supported the Tripoli government should be punished or forgiven?" with answer choices, 0 = forgiven, 1 = punished (47% responded 'forgiven'; 53% 'punished'). Question 3: "Do you support the formation of a military council headed by General Haftar?" with answer choices, 0 = no, 1 = yes (60% responded 'yes'; 40% 'no'). Question 4: "Do you agree that if a unity government is formed, armed conflict will continue?" with answer choices, 0 = no, 1 = yes (55% responded 'yes'; 45% 'no'). Question 5: "If the unity government makes compromises that you disagree with, would you support armed conflict as a way of dealing with the situation?" with answer choices, 0 = no, 1 = yes (46% responded 'yes'; 54% 'no').

Results and Discussion

Analyses of Study 1 revealed several key findings. First, fusion to revolutionary fighters devoted to a unified Libya was markedly lower in the Study 1 sample (collected in 2015; M = 1.81, SD = 1.06) than in our data collected in 2011 (M = 4.96, SD = .21).[42] We performed a t-test comparing the two datasets that resulted in a t-statistic of 38.95 with 410 degrees of freedom and a p-value less than .001, meaning the observed difference is statistically significant (t (410) = 38.95, p < .001).[43] Even allowing for the possibility that fusion in Benghazi was never as high as in Misrata in 2011, this difference suggests a decline in levels of fusion with revolutionaries across the country as a whole from 2011 to 2015. This finding was supported in interviews where support for the revolution, even among fighters, has declined as violence and insecurity has persisted.[44]

Additional analyses of findings from Study 1 revealed that mean fusion to Operation Dignity fighters was higher than fusion to 2011 revolutionary fighters, with M = 3.48 (SD = 1.35) in 2011 versus M = 1.81 (SD = 1.06) in 2015, and the percentage selecting the 'totally fused' option being 33% versus 3%, respectively (t (234) = 12.77, p < .001). Moreover, fusion to Operation Dignity fighters was negatively related to fusion to 2011 revolutionary fighters. A correlation analysis resulted in a Pearson correlation coefficient of −0.39 and p-value less than .001, meaning their negative relationship is statistically significant ($r(234) = -.39$, $p < .001$), further suggesting that bonds to Operation Dignity fighters were hydraulically related to bonds to past revolutionary fighters. This shift likely reflects Benghazi residents' lived reality as car bombings and assassinations spiked in the months prior to Operation Dignity.[45] Moreover, in interviews, residents expressed their frustration that the need for Operation Dignity reflected a failure of the revolution.

Following Operation Dignity, General Haftar set his sights on national power and attacked Tripoli, the capital of Libya. Haftar's followers shared his distrust of the internationally recognized government in Tripoli. Specifically, insofar as Benghazians were strongly fused to Operation Dignity fighters, they expressed doubt that the brewing conflict between east and western Libya could be peacefully resolved and supported General Haftar's efforts to take over Libya, with correlation coefficients ranging from .20 to .33 (r's = .20 to .33, p's < .01, df's > 232). Together with the foregoing results, these findings point to a shift in allegiances away from the 2011 revolution and those that advanced it, and toward Operation Dignity militias (whose mission had reduced violence in Benghazi, but then plunged the country back into conflict when they attacked Tripoli).

Study 2

Although the results of Study 1 were provocative, we sought to examine whether allegiances had shifted as Haftar's goals shifted from protecting Benghazi from self-described Jihadists to national domination. We therefore conducted a follow-up study in 2019. By this time, Libya was mired in a years-long battle to prevent Haftar's forces from taking control of Tripoli. Politically, no individual or government had demonstrated itself capable of uniting the country, reinforcing historic divisions between east and western Libya. International support was likewise polarized with regional countries like Turkey or Egypt, picking opposite sides.

Study 2 had several aims. First, we examined whether identity fusion among eastern Libyans to Operation Dignity fighters had changed from the preceding years. We hypothesized that fusion levels would decrease over time, as Haftar's legitimacy decreased after attacking Tripoli. We tested whether there were higher levels of fusion to the eastern Libyan government. We understood that this was a weak test as Haftar was seen as controlling the eastern Libyan government, but even a weak shift might indicate a change.

Second, we aimed to examine relationships between militia membership and fusion to Operation Dignity. We hypothesized that those who had remained highly fused to Operation Dignity fighters would be more motivated to become a member of an armed militia. Finally, we aimed to examine whether links between fusion to eastern Libya and involvement in its defense was rooted in part by one's experience of Operation Dignity itself. In line with previous work in another group context,[46] we hypothesized that fusion would be highest and militia membership likeliest for those Benghazians who had felt that Operation Dignity was a key, self-shaping event for them personally. To test our hypotheses, we conducted another survey study of Benghazians in collaboration with the researchers as in Study 1.

Methods

The same recruitment methods were used as in Study 1. We surveyed 265 male Benghazians in 2019 (age M = 32.28 years, SD = 7.13). Participants answered the following questions.

Group Alignment

Respondents were first asked to indicate their level of identity fusion to Operation Dignity fighters. The same instructions and protocol as in Study 1 were followed, resulting in a mean score (M) of 2.20 (SD = .98).[47] They were then asked to identify their level of identity fusion to the east Libyan government (M = 2.12, SD = .93).[48]

Memory of Operation Dignity

Participants were then asked two questions about their memories of Operation Dignity. They were instructed to recall their life during Operation Dignity. They were then asked two questions with possible answers on 5-point Likert scales (1 = not at all to 5 = totally): "To what extent did the event mark a key moment in defining who you are personally?" with results of M = 2.33 (SD = .96), and "To what extent did the event shape who you are as an individual?" with results of M = 2.03 (SD = .87). The two items were positively correlated (r (264) = .54, p < .001), and the mean of these two items, M = 2.33 (SD = .96), was computed to represent the extent to which Operation Dignity was a self-shaping event in participants' lives.[49]

Militia Membership

Participants were then asked, "Were you a member of an armed militia during Operation Dignity?" with answer choices 0 = no and 1 = yes. In total, 126 participants (48%) indicated they were part of an Operation Dignity militia. Next, participants responded to "Are you currently a member of an armed militia?" with answer choices 0 = no and 1 = yes. This time, 70 participants (26%) indicated they were currently part of a militia.

Willingness to Engage in Conflict

Participants then completed two questions about their willingness to fight and die for the eastern Libyan government, with answer choices on 5-point Likert scales ranging from 1 = not at all to 5 = totally. They answered, "To what extent are you willing to fight someone who physically threatens a supporter of the Tobruk government?" with results of M = 1.70 (SD = .77) and "To what extent would you be willing to kill others to protect supporters of the Tobruk government?" with results of M = 1.42 (SD = .60). These two items were positively correlated (r (264) = .39, p < 001), with M = 1.56 (SD = .57), and represent the extent to which participants were willing to fight and die for the eastern Libyan government. Current militia fighters scored higher on the mean of these two items (M = 1.81, SD = .49) than non-fighters (M = 1.47, SD = .57), t (263) = -4.36, p < .001. Participants last completed two questions about their willingness to sacrifice for Libya. Answer choices were on 5-point Likert scales ranging from 1 = not at all to 5 = totally. "To what extent would you be willing to sacrifice your life if it saved a Libyan that you don't personally know?" resulted in M = 2.58 (SD = 1.02) and "To what extent would you be willing to make personal sacrifices if it ensured lasting peace in Libya?" resulted in M = 3.03 (SD = .95). These two items were positively correlated (r (264) = .69, p < 001), with M = 2.80 (SD = .90), and represent the extent to which participants were willing to fight and die for Libya as a whole. Current militia fighters did not score higher on the mean of these two items (M = 2.77, SD = .95) than non-fighters (M = 2.81, SD = .89), t (263) = .33, not significant (*n.s.*).

Results and Discussion

We found that the mean level of fusion to the east Libyan government was not statistically significantly different from fusion to Operation Dignity fighters (Mean difference = .08, *n.s.*, with no respondents selecting option 5 'totally fused,' and similar percentages from each group selecting option 1 'not at all fused,' 28% versus 31%, respectively). The evidence demonstrated the public perception that Haftar dominated the eastern government and was for many the de facto leader of both. We found higher fusion among only those still involved in armed militias supporting east Libya—a possibility tested as part of the next hypothesis. In addition, although fusion to Operation Dignity fighters decreased from Study 1 (M = 3.48, SD = 1.35) to Study 2 (M = 2.20, SD = .98), t (498) = 12.22, $p < .001$, in Study 2 it still covaried with fusion to the eastern Libyan government, r (264) = .57, $p < .001$. This suggests that fusion to the two groups still moderately overlapped.

In testing the second hypothesis, we followed the steps of statistical mediation.[50] In an initial regression, fusion to Operation Dignity fighters was marginally related to whether one was a current armed militia member (total effect model), unstandardized regression (b = .24, standard error (SE) = .14, z = 1.73, p = .08) indicating that those who felt more fused to Operation Dignity fighters were more likely to be current armed militia members versus not. In a second regression, fusion to Operation Dignity was related to fusion to the east Libyan government (unstandardized b = .53, SE = .04, t (263) = 12.60, $p < .001$), indicating that those who felt more fused to Operation Dignity were more highly fused to the east Libyan government. In a third regression with both fusion scores set as predictors of current militia status, only fusion to east Libyan government was related to the outcome (b = .37, SE = .19, z = 1.98, $p < .05$), and fusion to Operation Dignity was no longer related (b = .04, SE = .17, z = .22, $n.s.$), respectively. A bootstrap analysis (N = 1000) showed that the indirect effect equals .20 (SE = .11, 95% confidence intervals (CI's): .002, .432), indicated that the impact of fusion to Operation Dignity fighters on milita status was mediated by fusion to the east Libyan government.

Furthermore, compared to non-fighters, current militia members were especially willing to fight and die for their eastern Libyan government (t (263) = -4.36, $p < .001$), but were not particularly willing to sacrifice for Libya as a whole, (t (263) < 1, $n.s.$). Together, these findings suggest that in contrast to the 2011 revolutionaries that fought for a unified Libya, armed militia members from Benghazi were aligned with and willing to sacrifice for only their brothers-in-arms in the east, not for Libya as a whole. This reflected how many leaders, including Haftar, framed the context for intergroup violence—protecting eastern Libya, initially from Islamic extremists and then western Libyan domination. The results highlight how group alignment can shift over time as the political and security landscape shift.

In a second mediation analysis, mean scores of the items concerning memories of Operation Dignity were related to whether one was a current armed militia member (total effect model), unstandardized regression ($b = .79$, $SE = .19$, $z (263) = 4.21$, $p < .001$), indicating that those who felt more self-shaped by Operation Dignity were more likely to be current armed militia members versus not. In a second regression, mean scores of the Operation Dignity items were related to fusion to the east Libyan government, unstandardized ($b = .20$, $SE = .07$, $t (263) = 2.87$, $p < .01$), indicating that those who felt more self-shaped by Operation Dignity were more highly fused to the east Libyan government. In a third regression with both mean scores of the Operation Dignity items and fusion to east Libyan government as predictors of current militia status, both predictors were related to the outcome: ($b = .75$, $SE = .19$, $z (262) = 3.93$, $p < .01$) and ($b = .32$, $SE = .16$, $z (262) = 2.04$, $p = .04$), respectively. A bootstrap analysis (N = 1000) showed that the indirect effect equals .07 ($SE = .04$, 95% CI's: .009, .179), indicating partial mediation. Thus, these results are consistent with previous studies that show that strong, personally meaningful memories of pivotal ingroup events may lead to especially high levels of ingroup fusion and extreme pro-group behavior.[51]

Conclusions

In 2011, the February 17 Revolution saw the majority of Libyans united by a vision of freedom from four decades of oppression. The failure of the 2012 elections to create a cohesive government or bring security to Libya has reinforced geographic and community interests. By 2014, Libya continued to be dominated by complex and fluid military alliances made up of hundreds of armed groups of varying size, ideology, and fighting history. For example, the Libyan National Army was often described as the overall military structure in the east of the country, but in reality it was a loose alliance of militias that included groups from Zintan (western Libya) as well as extremely devout Salafist groups from eastern Libya. The situation was no less complex in the west of the country. Understanding how communities navigate this complexity through their allegiance to armed groups is vital to understanding Libya's post-revolution prospects.

The research reported here builds on previous evidence that identity fusion is linked to willingness to fight and die for a group.[52] Here we show that shifts in the target of fusion can track psychological changes associated with the failure of a revolution to create a national government. We argue that communities shifted allegiance, particularly in the case of Operation Dignity fighters, through bonds of shared suffering in opposition to ideological extremists, and that these allegiances came at the cost of broader support for national unity.[53] However, the evidence suggests that these allegiances are not permanent, and could be influenced by future events and leaders.

It is important to note several methodological limitations of the two studies. First, due to the logistical challenges presented by collecting data during active fighting, we were not able to conduct panel interviews. This meant we could not analyze within-person changes in survey responses over time, a preferred approach in longitudinal research. Future research would benefit from developing a data collection method, likely online-based rather than in-person interview-based, to collect within-person level data. Second, given the political climate in Benghazi and the fear of dissent from Haftar, there would be some bias in favor of support of Operation Dignity. The pictorial instrument was, however, able to pick up on changes between studies, suggesting that while the baseline for support might be biased, it did change. Third, we were unable to obtain detailed data regarding participation in recent combat, as we judged the topic to be generally too sensitive for participants. Thus, we elicited participants' self-reported behavioral intentions regarding future conflict engagement, an outcome deemed less sensitive. Fourth, due to time constraints, we chose to measure group alignment with the single-item fusion measure. Though the measure's predictive validity is robust,[54] future research would benefit from a comparison of the measure's performance against similar measures of group alignment.

The implications of our findings are troubling. In particular, if persuasive leaders like General Haftar are capable of stoking civil war by redirecting identity fusion, then similar processes could potentially underlie parallel phenomena elsewhere. That said, it is also possible that so-called barrier-crossing leaders may actively extend fusion to larger imagined communities. In so doing, such leaders may embrace even long-standing enemies for the sake of mutual benefit or conflict resolution. The challenge, then, is to determine how to develop strategies for channeling shifts in identity fusion into more inclusive nonviolent outcomes rather than parochial, violent ones.

Notes

1. Wolfram Lacher, *Libya's Fragmentation: Structure and Process in Violent Conflict* (Bloomsbury Publishing, 2020).
2. Ian Martin, *All Necessary Measures? The United Nations and International Intervention in Libya* (Hurst Publishers, 2022).
3. Roger Mac Ginty, "No War, No Peace: Why So Many Peace Processes Fail to Deliver Peace," *International Politics* 47 (2010): 145–62, http://dx.doi.org/10.1057/ip.2010.4.
4. Jacob Mundy, *Libya* (John Wiley & Sons, 2018).
5. Tim Eaton, Abdul Rahman Alageli, Emadeddin Badi, Mohamed Eljarh, and Valerie Stocker, "The Development of Libyan Armed Groups Since 2014," Chatham House, 2017, 8–13, https://www.chathamhouse.org/sites/default/files/CHHJ8001-Libya-RP-WEB-200316.pdf.
6. William B. Swann Jr., Jolanda Jetten, Ángel Gómez, Harvey Whitehouse, and Brock Bastian, "When Group Membership Gets Personal: A Theory of Identity Fusion," *Psychological Review* 119, no. 3 (2012): 441, https://psycnet.apa.org/doi/10.1037/a0028589.
7. Dirk Vandewalle, "Libya's Uncertain Revolution," in *The Libyan Revolution and Its Aftermath*, ed. Peter Cole and Brian McQuinn (Hurst, 2015).
8. Lacher, *Libya's Fragmentation*.
9. Martin, *All Necessary Measures?*
10. John Wright, *Libya: A Modern History* (Routledge, 2022).
11. Dirk Vandewalle, *A History of Modern Libya*, 2nd ed. (Cambridge University Press, 2012).
12. Igor Cherstich,. "When Tribesmen Do Not Act Tribal: Libyan Tribalism as Ideology (Not as Schizophrenia)," *Middle East Critique* 23, no. 4 (2014): 405–21, https://doi.org/10.1080/19436149.2014.969890.
13. Peter Cole and Brian McQuinn, eds., *The Libyan Revolution and Its Aftermath* (Oxford University Press, 2015).
14. Dirk Vandewalle, *Libya Since Independence: Oil and State-Building* (Cornell University Press, 1998).
15. Kali Robinson, "What's at Stake in Libya's War?," Council on Foreign Relations, January 16, 2020, https://www.cfr.org/in-brief/whats-stake-libyas-war.
16. Wolfram Lacher, "Social Cleavages and Armed Group Consolidation: The Case of Khalifa Haftar's Libyan Arab Armed Forces," *Studies in Conflict & Terrorism* 47, no. 9 (2024): 1065–89, https://doi.org/10.1080/1057610X.2021.2013757.
17. Megan Doherty, "'Give Us Change We Can See': Citizen Views of Libya's Political Process," National Democratic Institute for International Affairs, 2012.
18. Mary Fitzgerald, "Finding Their Place: Libya's Islamists During and After the Revolution," in *The Libyan Revolution and Its Aftermath*, ed. Peter Cole and Brian McQuinn (Hurst, 2015).
19. Wolfram Lacher, "A Most Irregular Army: The Rise of Khalifa Haftar's Libyan Arab Armed Forces," German Institute for International and Security Affairs, 2020, https://www.swp-berlin.org/publications/products/arbeitspapiere/2020WP02_FG06_lac.pdf.
20. Eaton et al., "The Development of Libyan Armed Groups Since 2014," 8–13.
21. "*Who Supports Who in Libya's Complex Battlefield: Egypt, Russia, Turkey, Arab League*," Africanews, January 14, 2020, https://www.africanews.com/2020/01/14/who-supports-who-in-libya-s-complex-battlefield-egypt-us-russia-turkey-europe/.

22. Harvey Whitehouse, Brian McQuinn, Michael D. Buhrmester, and William B. Swann Jr., "Brothers in Arms: Libyan Revolutionaries Bond Like Family," *Proceedings of the National Academy of Sciences* 111, no. 50 (2014): 17783–85, https://doi.org/10.1073/pnas.1416284111.

23. Monica Toft, "Ending Civil Wars: A Case for Rebel Victory?," *International Security* 34, no. 4 (2010): 7–36, https://doi.org/10.1162/isec.2010.34.4.7.

24. Terrence Lyons, "From Victorious Rebels to Strong Authoritarian Parties: Prospects for Post-War Democratization," *Democratization* 23, no. 6 (2016): 1026–041, https://doi.org/10.1080/13510347.2016.1168404.

25. Ana Arjona, *Rebelocracy* (Cambridge University Press, 2016).

26. Zachariah Mampilly and Megan A. Stewart, "A Typology of Rebel Political Institutional Arrangements," *Journal of Conflict Resolution* 65, no. 1 (2021): 15–45, https://doi.org/10.1177/0022002720935642.

27. Cyanne E. Loyle, "Rebel Justice During Armed Conflict," *Journal of Conflict Resolution* 65, no. 1 (2021): 108–34, https://doi.org/10.1177/0022002720939299.

28. Megan A. Stewart, "Civil War as State-Making: Strategic Governance in Civil War," *International Organization* 72, no. 1 (2018): 205–26, https://doi.org/10.1017/S0020818317000418.

29. Reed M. Wood, "Rebel Capability and Strategic Violence Against Civilians," *Journal of Peace Research* 47, no. 5 (2023): 601–14, https://doi.org/10.1177/0022343310376473.

30. Zachariah Cherian Mampilly, *Rebel Rulers: Insurgent Governance and Civilian Life During War* (Cornell University Press, 2017).

31. Michael Weddegjerde Skjelderup, "Insurgent Engagement with Kinship Group Authorities: Production of Order and Governance in Somalia's Lower Jubba Province," *Third World Thematics: A TWQ Journal* 6, no. 1 (2021): 52–68, https://doi.org/10.1080/23802014.2022.2130968.

32. Whitehouse et al., "Brothers in Arms."

33. Harvey Whitehouse, Jonathan Jong, Michael D, Buhrmester, et al., "The Evolution of Extreme Cooperation via Shared Dysphoric Experiences," *Scientific Reports* 7, no. 1 (2017): 1, https://doi.org/10.1038/srep44292.

34. William B. Swann Jr., Michael D. Buhrmester, Ángel Gómez, et al., "What Makes a Group Worth Dying For? Identity Fusion Fosters Perception of Familial Ties, Promoting Self-Sacrifice," *Journal of Personality and Social Psychology* 106, no. 6 (2014): 912, https://psycnet.apa.org/doi/10.1037/a0036089.

35. William B. Swann Jr., Ángel Gómez, D. Conor Seyle, J. Francisco Morales, and Carmen Huici, "Identity Fusion: The Interplay of Personal and Social Identities in Extreme Group Behavior," Journal of Personality and Social Psychology 96, no. 5 (2009): 995–1011, https://doi.org/10.1037/a0013668.

36. Whitehouse et al., "Brothers in Arms."

37. Nathan Ford, Edward J. Mills, Rony Zachariah, and Ross Upshur, "Ethics of Conducting Research in Conflict Settings," *Conflict and Health* 3 (2009): Article 3, https://conflictandhealth.biomedcentral.com/articles/10.1186/1752-1505-3-7; Elizabeth J. Wood, "*The Ethical Challenges of Field Research in Conflict Zones*," *Qualitative Sociology* 29 (2006): 373–86, https://doi.org/10.1007/s11133-006-9027-8.

38. Fiona D. Patterson and Kevin Neailey, "A Risk Register Database System to Aid the Management of Project Risk," *International Journal of Project Management* 20, no. 5 (2002): 365–74, https://doi.org/10.1016/S0263-7863(01)00040-0.

[39] Swann et al., "Identity Fusion," 995.

[40] For a review, see Harvey Whitehouse, "Dying for the Group: Towards a General Theory of Extreme Self-Sacrifice," *Behavioral and Brain Sciences* 41 (2018): e192, https://doi.org/10.1017/S0140525X18000249.

[41] For further discussion regarding the relationship between identity fusion and other group identity constructs, such as group identification and group attachment, see Swann et al., "Identity Fusion."

[42] Note: The 2011 data was originally collected and reported in Whitehouse, "Dying for the Group," as part of a separate, prior, project.

[43] In past studies utilizing the pictorial measure of fusion, response distributions have been bimodal and interpreted as "fused versus non-fused"; for a discussion and review, see Ángel Gómez, Matthew L. Brooks, Michael D. Burhmester, Alexandra Vázquez, Jolanda Jetten, and William B. Swann, "On the Nature of Identity Fusion: Insights into the Construct and a New Measure," *Journal of Personality and Social Psychology* 100, no. 5 (2011): 920, https://doi.org/10.1037/a0022642.

In this dataset, we calculated Sarle's bimodality coefficient, a standard means of evaluating bimodality, and found a BC coefficient > .55, the cutoff value above which suggests presence of bimodality; for a discussion and review, see Nicolae Tarbă, Mihai-Lucian Voncilă, and Costin-Anton Boiangiu, "On Generalizing Sarle's Bimodality Coefficient as a Path Towards a Newly Composite Bimodality Coefficient," *Mathematics* 10, no. 7 (2022): Article 1042, https://doi.org/10.3390/math10071042. However, visual inspection of the distribution revealed a strong skew with just one, not two, clear peaks (55% selecting the 'not at all' fused option 1, 21% selecting 2, 17% selecting 3, 5% selecting 4, and 3% selecting 5). Nevertheless, we explored analyses treating this variable as dichotomous, and results were directionally consistent with treating it in its original units. In Study 1, 3% of respondents reported being fused, whereas 96% in the 2011 sample reported being fused. For the other fusion measure in Study 1 (fusion to Operation Dignity fighters) and both pictorial measures in Study 2, the bimodality coefficients were < .55, suggesting no bimodality. Thus, they were treated analytically in their original units rather than dichotomized.

[44] Borzou Daragahi, "Ten Years Ago, Libyans Staged a Revolution. Here's Why It Has Failed," *Atlantic Council*, February 17, 2021, https://www.atlanticcouncil.org/blogs/menasource/ten-years-ago-libyans-staged-a-revolution-heres-why-it-has-failed/.

[45] "Car Blast Hits Army Checkpoint in Banghazi," *Al Jazeera*, July 3, 2013, https://www.aljazeera.com/news/2013/7/3/car-blast-hits-army-checkpoint-in-banghazi.

[46] Whitehouse, "Dying for the Group."

[47] Of respondents, 28% chose 1 'not at all fused,' 38% chose 2, 21% chose 3, 13% chose 4, and 0% chose 5.

[48] Of respondents, 31% chose 1 'not at all fused,' 33% chose 2, 29% chose 3, 7% chose 4, and 0% chose 5.

[49] Martha Newson, Michael D. Buhrmester, and Harvey Whitehouse, "Explaining Lifelong Loyalty: The Role of Identity Fusion and Self-Shaping Group Events," *PloS One* 11, no. 8 (2016): e0160427, https://doi.org/10.1371/journal.pone.0160427.

[50] Andrew F. Hayes, *Introduction to Mediation, Moderation, and Conditional Process Analysis: A Regression-Based Approach* (Guilford Publications, 2017).

[51] For a review, see Whitehouse, "Dying for the Group."

[52] Swann et al., "What Makes a Group Worth Dying For?," 912.

[53] See Whitehouse, "Dying for the Group."

[54] For a review, see Swann et al., "When Group Membership Gets Personal," 441.

HOW GAZA SEES THE 2023–2025 WAR AND THE FUTURE OF THE ISRAEL-PALESTINE CONFLICT

Scott Atran
Artis International; Centre National de la Recherche Scientifique; Gerald Ford School of Public Policy, University of Michigan; Changing Character of War Centre

Laura Rodriguez-Gómez
Universidad Nacional de Educación a Distancia

Kamil Yilmaz
Artis International, Swansea University

Ángel Gómez
Artis International, Universidad Nacional de Educación a Distancia

---

Scott Atran is a co-founder of Artis International, Emeritus Research Director in anthropology at France's Centre National de la Recherche Scientifique (CNRS), Research Professor at the University of Michigan's Gerald Ford School of Public Policy, and Distinguished Research Fellow at Oxford University's Changing Character of War Centre. He is a member of the US National Academy of Sciences and an adviser to the UN Security Council on "Youth, Peace, and Security."

Laura Rodriguez-Gómez is a postdoctoral researcher at the Universidad Nacional de Educación a Distancia in Madrid. Her current research concerns processes of dehumanization and their association with uncivil and immoral behavior and violent conflict.

Kamil Yilmaz is a research fellow at Artis International and lecturer at Swansea University in Wales. His research focus is understanding international security and political violence, particularly violent extremists' exploitation of the internet and social media, using a variety of psychosocial measures and tools of computational social science.

Ángel Gómez is a senior fellow at Artis International and professor of social psychology at the Universidad Nacional de Educación a Distancia in Madrid. His research interest is to understand the nature of extremism and willingness to self-sacrifice, and he joins cross-cultural fieldwork with an interdisciplinary multi-theory and interactive multimethod approach.

ABSTRACT

In political science and international relations, as in foreign policy and military circles, a debate is ongoing between "realists" and "moralists" regarding the importance of material factors (territory, economy, security, etc.) versus value-laden factors (justice, ideals, identity, etc.) in motivating, sustaining, and ending wars. An early 2025 representative survey of Gaza's population considers both sets of factors in how Gazans perceive the present and future states of the Israel-Palestine conflict. Comparisons with our previous studies in the Middle East, North Africa, and Europe aim to extend this survey's relevance beyond the current Israel-Palestine theater. The survey suggests that after waging many months of 'total war,' Israel may be further from pacifying Gaza than ever before. The war has hardened Gazans' maximalist political goals for elimination of Israel, while offering virtually no backing for a binational democratic state "from the river to the sea" as advocated by Western pro-Palestinian activists. Although Hamas's popular support has declined significantly, political alternatives draw even less support, allowing Hamas to maintain outsize influence over Gaza. Perhaps most important for the long term, Gazans retain strong core values related to national and religious identity and attachment to the land, values they indicate their intention to uphold even at great personal sacrifice. However, the survey also reveals what movement toward peace might involve, such as humanizing an enemy as a predictor of willingness to sacrifice for peace in wartime. A final overview of historical developments within and between Hamas and Israel's Likud highlights their roles as peace spoilers.

A Wartime Survey: What Gazans Want

Following the collapse of Israel's January 2025 ceasefire and hostages-for-prisoners deal with Hamas, and after many months of pulverizing and pitiless war, the issue of what should happen to Gaza and its 2.1 million people seems to have become ever more intractable. Given that the region is suffused with fragile and failing states, and with competing powers seeking to play this anarchic situation for their profit, stabilization by outside forces appears remote. Donald Trump has floated chimerical ideas about an eventual US "takeover" of Gaza emptied of Palestinians, but the world community is set against it, except for Israel's far-right government.

Oddly missing from this debate have been Gazans themselves: what they want for their future, how they see their land, who they think should be their rulers, and what they consider to be the most plausible pathways to peace. Given the horrendous price paid for Hamas's actions on October 7, 2023, Gazans might be expected to reject the group for different leadership and to be more likely to compromise on larger political aspirations in favor of more urgent material needs.

In fact, a survey we conducted in Gaza in early January, shortly before the ceasefire came into effect, tells a more complicated story. The representative survey was formulated by the research group Artis International and Oxford University's Changing Character of War Centre and carried out by the Palestinian Center for Policy and Survey Research (PSR).[1] Using census data and sampling people in shelters based on the locations of their original homes, the survey comprised 500 face-to-face interviews with Gazans—248 women and 252 men—ranging in age from 18 to 83. Respondents were assured anonymity and interviewed outside others' earshot.

Interviewers were trained to recognize insincere responses, then courteously keep short the few interviews where insincerity was suspected and later discard them. The margin of error was plus or minus 4 percentage points. All correlations, interactions, and associations reported below are statistically significant, with no major gender differences.

This was not a general survey aimed at attitudes or opinions. Rather, the survey was designed to examine the interplay between the psycho-social components of 'will to fight.'[2] With support from the US Department of Defense Minerva Initiative and the European Research Council, the survey's integrative structure and interactive measures were developed through fieldwork and in prior surveys, and under experimental conditions manipulated to observe effects of particular variables. These studies were conducted in many countries and contexts (in North and Central America, Western and Eastern Europe, the Middle East and North Africa, and Southeast Asia). Basic research design and measures were validated previously through a standard science peer-review process.[3] These studies reveal a powerful common message: Thoughtful, well-informed people make fateful decisions based on moral grounds that entail great personal and community risks. They look for leaders who appear to embody those concerns. These profound commitments can empower them to prevail against opponents with far greater resources or suffer grievous losses in sacred struggles.

The survey found that although Hamas's appeal declined precipitously since the war's early months, political alternatives drew even less support, which has opened the way for Hamas to regain its influence over Gaza. The war has also hardened rather than softened Gazans' maximalist political goals, while eroding support for a negotiated solution and offering virtually no backing for the dissolution of Israel into a binational democratic state of Arabs and Jews "from the [Jordan] River to the [Mediterranean] Sea" of the sort advocated by Western pro-Palestinian activists. Perhaps most tellingly, the survey showed that the people of Gaza continue to retain strong core values related to their national and religious identity and their attachment to the land, values that they intend to uphold even at a cost of great personal sacrifice.

Profound commitments to core values can empower people to prevail against opponents with far greater resources or suffer grievous losses in sacred struggles. Gazans are no exception. What our survey reveals about their deep concerns may portend how the conflict will unfold and the options, if any, for peace, in the coming years and decades. The survey findings suggest that no movement toward peace with Israel is likely that fails to address Gazans' core values, at least to some mutually tolerable degree.

In the fields of political science and international relations, as in foreign policy and military circles, there is an ongoing dispute between "realists" and "moralists" regarding the relative importance of material factors (territory, economy, physical security, balance of power, etc.) versus value-laden factors (justice, ideals, principles of right and wrong, identity, etc.) in motivating, sustaining and ending wars.[4] This survey investigates contributions from both sets of factors in how Gazans perceive their present condition and the future end state of the Israel-Palestine conflict. The survey represents only one moment, however critical, in this long-standing dispute and seemingly intractable conflict. Nevertheless, comparisons with our previous studies elsewhere in the Middle East, North Africa, and Europe may help to extend this survey's relevance beyond the current Israel-Palestine theater.

What Does "Peace" Look Like?

In one of the primary questions in the survey, respondents were asked to select which of several possible resolutions to the Israel-Palestine conflict they viewed as both acceptable and realistic. Before the war in Gaza began, research showed that a clear majority of Palestinians in Gaza supported a two-state solution whereas just 20 percent supported a military solution that could result in the destruction of the state of Israel.[5]

In our January survey, less than half, or 48 percent, still preferred a two-state solution, while nearly as many, 47 percent, preferred the dissolution of Israel. A mere 5 percent viewed a democratic, binational state with equal rights for Arabs and Jews as acceptable and realistic.

Moreover, although partition was deemed acceptable and realistic by 48 percent, just 20 percent supported a two-state solution conforming to United Nations resolutions based on the 1967 borders. The rest of those supporting a partition favored two-state solutions that either required "right of return" of the descendants of Palestinian refugees to homes in Israel (17 percent) or reverting to the 1947 UN partition plan for Palestine (11 percent). Of the 47 percent who favored Israel's dissolution, a majority opted for a single state under sharia law that would tolerate a Jewish presence but allow Jews less than full rights (27 percent), followed by a smaller group that sought the transfer of Jewish immigrants and their descendants—but not Jews whose ancestors lived in the region before Zionism—from Israel proper and the Palestinian territories (20 percent).

To assess how Gazans now see the chances for peace in the future, the survey assessed their expectations about scenarios endorsed in the past by Palestinian leaders, including Hamas officials. Years before the October 7, 2023 attack, Scott Atran, one of the present authors, conducted several interviews with Hamas leaders: in 2006 then-Gaza Prime Minister Ismail Haniyeh, who later served as politburo chairman until his assassination by Israel last year; then-politburo chairman Khaled Meshaal in Damascus in 2009; and deputy chairman Mousa Abu Marzouk in Cairo in 2013. In each case, the leaders indicated an openness to a long-term truce or even peace with Israel.[6] Our January survey reminded respondents of these statements, noting that those leaders generally conditioned a truce or a longer peace on Israel's return to 1967 borders, an internationally backed "balance of power" with Israel, and the recognition of the right of return. The survey then asked which of three outcomes—truce (*hudna*), peace (*salaam*), or more war (*harb*)—seemed most likely for the next generation of Palestinians.

Recall that the public, when asked about its preference among outcomes, was almost evenly divided regarding the solution it views as the most realistic, one that Palestinians can accept, partition versus elimination. Here however, the question about the three possible outcomes is about expectation. About half of the respondents said they expected peace, 44 percent expected a long-term truce, and 7 percent expected more war (Fig. 1).

Of the roughly half that anticipated peace, however, two groups emerged, almost equal in size: those who expect peace as a negotiated outcome (24 percent) and those who expect peace to arise from Israel's dissolution (25 percent). Respondents who expected a provisional truce or war believe that Israelis and Palestinians will not reach a permanent peace, either because the concessions needed are spurned by the opposing side or are too painful to contemplate by one or both sides.

What do Gazans see as the most likely outcome of the conflict with Israel?

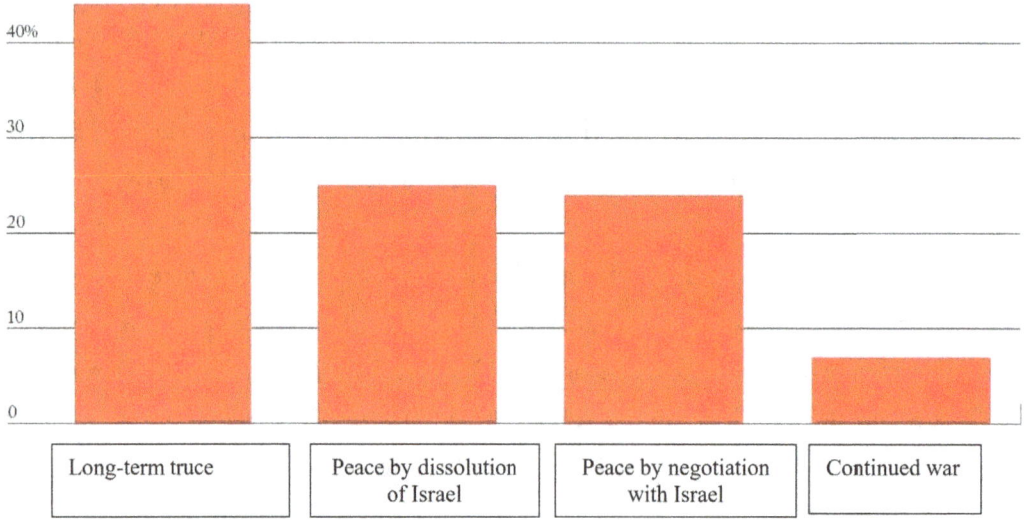

Figure 1. Comparison of Gazans' expectations of permanent peace, interim armistice, and continued war. Data source: January 2025 opinion survey in Gaza by Artis International, the Changing Character of War Centre, and the Palestinian Center for Policy and Survey Research.

In brief, only about one-fourth of Gaza's population anticipates a peace *between* a sovereign Palestine and Israel. Compared to those who expect Israel's elimination, two-state partition supporters judge themselves to be less religious; more likely to believe in a diplomatic end to the conflict and to humanize Israelis; less fused with Palestine and less willing to sacrifice for Palestine, right of return, national sovereignty, and sharia; and less considerate of balance of power, right of return, and sharia as "essential to the future of Palestine." This 'peace camp' is decidedly less committed to Palestinian nationalism and its core values than are most Gazans.

A Leadership Crisis

The survey also showed how Gazans' views of Hamas have changed. Before October 7, 2023, when the Gaza Strip was still intact, polls showed popular support for Hamas had been withering for some time. The decline resulted from a variety of factors, including stagnant living conditions and a lack of movement on Hamas's promise of armed resistance against Israel and toward the creation of a Palestinian state. As PSR's director, Khalil Shikaki, has argued, the October attack might be viewed as an attempt by Hamas to break out of a politically intolerable status quo.

During the initial months of war, Gazans' attitudes toward Hamas improved. In March 2024, a PSR poll of Gazans found that support for Hamas's control of the strip had increased to more than 50 percent, a 14-point rise from before the October 7, 2023, attack.[7] At the time, most Gazans believed that Hamas would continue to control the territory and that it was winning the war against Israel. By January 2025, however, after the decimation of the group's top leadership and further destruction of Gaza, that surge of support had eroded again.

Our January 2025 survey found that Hamas retained the support of only a fifth of Gaza's population—a steep decline from the March 2024 poll (Fig. 2). Yet support for other political groups was even lower. In fact, when asked to select from among the current options for Palestinian leadership, Gazans' most frequent response was that none of them truly represented the people. Indeed, Gazans believe that Israel's leadership does a much better job of representing Israelis than Palestinian leadership does representing Palestinians.

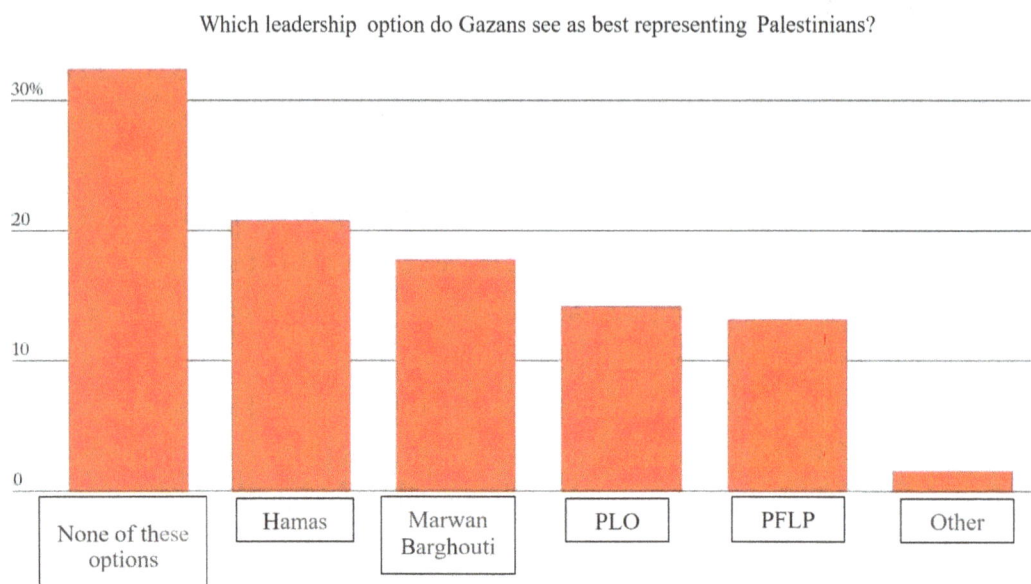

Figure 2. Ratings of forces that best represent Palestinians. None, Hamas, Marwan Barghouti (popular political personality, former PLO legislator, and peace negotiator imprisoned for life in Israel for authorizing terrorist bombings in the Second Intifada in 2000), the Palestine Liberation Organization (PLO, main component of the West Bank's Palestinian Authority), Popular Front for the Liberation of Palestine (PFLP, a secular Marxist-Leninist organization), and Other. Data source: January 2025 opinion survey in Gaza by Artis International, the Changing Character of War Centre, and the Palestinian Center for Policy and Survey Research.

In short, the survey reveals a Palestinian leadership vacuum that Hamas, as degraded as it is, is rapidly working to fill. As some analysts have observed, the organization's reassertion of power has been aided by the absence of a viable alternative plan for Palestinian governance from Israel or the United States and by the Trump administration's talk of a proposal long championed by the Israeli far right: population "transfer" (Hebrew: *ha'avarah*). According to Shikaki, most Gazans do not believe that Hamas has won the war. "Nonetheless," he adds, "they do not seem to find a better alternative." [8]

Devoted Actors and the Will to Fight

The lack of strong support for Hamas may obscure a larger reality about the role the group plays in Gaza. As our survey results indicate, despite Gazans' perceptions of a crisis in Palestinian political leadership, a majority of the population continues to be committed to Hamas's political ideals, such as sharia as the law of the land, the right of Palestinian refugees and their descendants to return to the homes they lost in Israel's creation in 1948, and the quest for national sovereignty for Palestinians. For each of these core values, the more that respondents are prepared to make costly sacrifices for them, the less willing they were to make peace with Israel.

The current situation with Hamas is reminiscent of what our research team found in camps for displaced persons in Iraq soon after the defeat of the Islamic State in Mosul.[9] Most Sunni Arabs interviewed had initially welcomed ISIS as the "revolution" (*thawra*) but judged ISIS rule as more brutal, corrupt, and hypocritical over time. Nevertheless, they remained committed to ISIS ideals of sharia rule in a transnational Islamic Caliphate, thoroughly rejecting democracy, as well as a unified Iraq as the tyranny of a Shia majority imposed on them by the US and Iran. Today, ISIS survives in the shadows because is still able to enlist such people.

We measure such commitment by first asking participants to drag a small circle ("Me") to a position that best affirms their relationship to a large circle representing a value or a group. They are considered "fused" with the value or group when they place themselves in the very center of the large circle. Findings from prior studies, from the battlefields of Libya and Ukraine to the US and Europe's culture wars, suggest that those who show total fusion see the value or group as a visceral and inseparable part of their identity.[10]

Fusion is one reliable predictor of willingness to make sacrifices for a group or greater cause. Another predictor of self-sacrifice is when the group cause becomes a nonnegotiable "sacred value." In real-world conflict and battlefield conditions, we find actual (not merely stated) willingness to fight, die, and sacrifice even family and friends for sacred values, whether religious or secular, like God or nation, holy land or right to arms.[11] Although much more is known about economic decision-making than value-driven behavior, the features of sacred values that we have validated are the following: immunity to material trade-offs, insensitivity to temporal and spatial discounting, blindness to exit strategies however reasonable or rewarding, privileged link to emotions, distinct brain signatures (in neural imaging), and actions dissociated from calculated risks, rewards, costs, or consequences.[12] Core cultural values can be sacralized or desacralized over time through major societal shifts, such as from war to peace (as with prewar vs. postwar Germany and Japan).

When fusion and sacred values operate in tandem they produce 'devoted actors' willing to sacrifice all, including their lives and loved ones: the totality of their self-interests. Between 2015 to 2017, for example, we conducted a series of studies in Iraq of groups—the Islamic State, or ISIS; the militant Kurdish separatists of the

Kurdistan Workers' Party (PKK); and the Kurdish peshmerga, or military forces of Iraqi Kurdistan—that kept fighting despite high numbers of casualties.[13] We found that members of these fused groups tended to show a high degree of willingness to sacrifice themselves for values they held sacred, a characteristic that gave these groups a spiritual strength that significantly outweighed their physical or material resources, such as firepower, manpower, logistical support, or training time.

In Gaza, this kind of interaction happens when individuals view Palestine as an inseparable part of their core identity (fusion) and regard sharia law as a sacred value. Gazans who show both qualities tend to have a greater willingness to make costly sacrifices for sharia than either fusion or belief in sharia could account for (Fig. 3A). The Gaza survey indicates that one-fifth (20 percent) of the population consists of devoted actors who fuse with Palestine, hold sharia to be sacred, and maximize costly sacrifices for their sacred value. The pattern closely parallels what we found in a 2016 study of jihadi sympathizers in urban neighborhoods in Morocco associated with previous terrorist bombing campaigns against the Moroccan state, attacks in Spain, and recruitment to the Islamic State in Syria and Iraq (Fig. 3B).[14] (It is also an evident pattern, albeit to a lesser degree, among the minority in Gaza who hold peace as a sacred value, as it was among a kin-like group of Spaniards devoted to democracy as their sacred value, Fig. 3C).

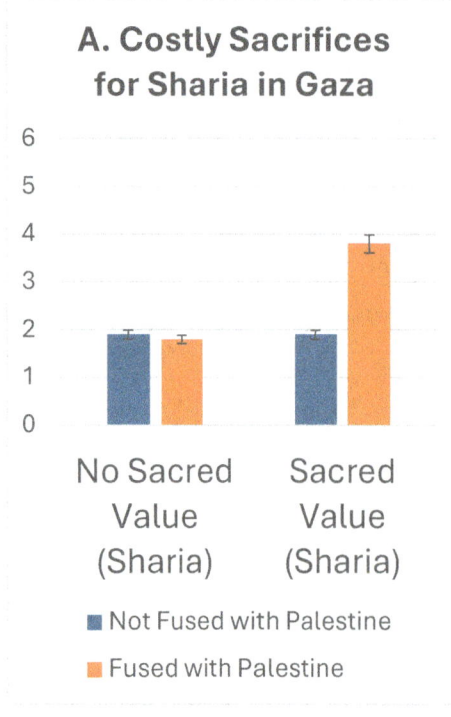
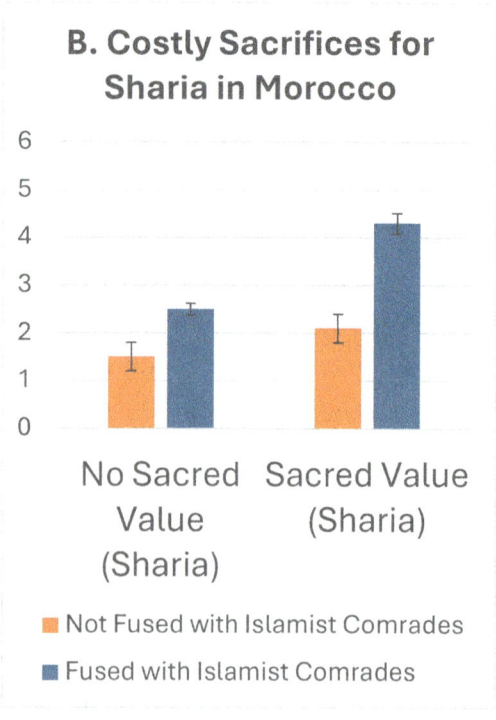

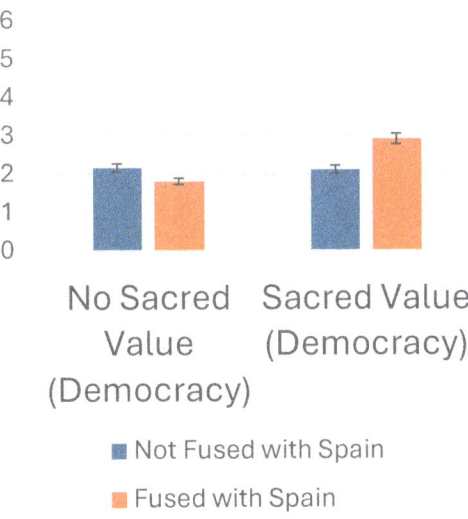

Figure 3. Costly sacrifices maximized via interaction of sacred values and identity fusion (self-reported on a Likert scale from 0 = not at all to 6 = completely).[15] (**A**) Among a representative sample of Gazans after fifteen months of war, those who considered sharia rule over the land to be a sacred value, and whose identities were fused with Palestine, expressed the most willingness to sacrifice, including fighting and dying. Only Gazans who considered sharia to be a sacred value and whose identities were fused with Palestine were above the midpoint in measures of willingness to make costly sacrifices. (**B**) In jihadi-supporting Moroccan neighborhoods, people who viewed strict imposition of Islamic law, or sharia, as a sacred value and who identified closely with a kin-like group (i.e., were fused with the group) expressed the most willingness to sacrifice for sharia, including fighting and dying. Only those who considered sharia to be a sacred value and were fused with a family-like group of comrades were above the midpoint (i.e., more willing than not to make costly sacrifices). (**C**) Spaniards reported a willingness to make costly sacrifices for democracy as a sacred value, but below midpoint and only under explicit threat priming.

To measure how Gazans view their physical and spiritual strength relative to other national groups, the survey used an approach that has previously been used in surveys of Iraqis, Ukrainians, and US armed forces, among others.[16] Respondents are shown a pair of semi-nude bodies side by side with national flags attached to their heads, which can be increased or decreased in size and musculature using a slider. They are then told to move the slider to assess the relative "physical" and "spiritual" strength of each national group. The measure of formidability was originally based on an evolutionary principle regarding perception of an intruder's body size and muscle power as a signal to fight or flee (or in the case of some primates, to negotiate).[17] But when we presented the measure to ISIS and PKK fighters, they literally threw their tablets down and declared that material strength is irrelevant and that only spiritual strength (in both Arabic and Kurdish, *ruhi bi ghiyrat*) was important. In our survey, Gazans were asked to compare themselves with Israelis, Americans, and Iranians. The respondents considered Palestinians to be far stronger spiritually than they are physically. This was the opposite of how they perceived Israel, the United States, and even their own putative ally Iran, which they viewed as much stronger physically than spiritually (Fig. 4).

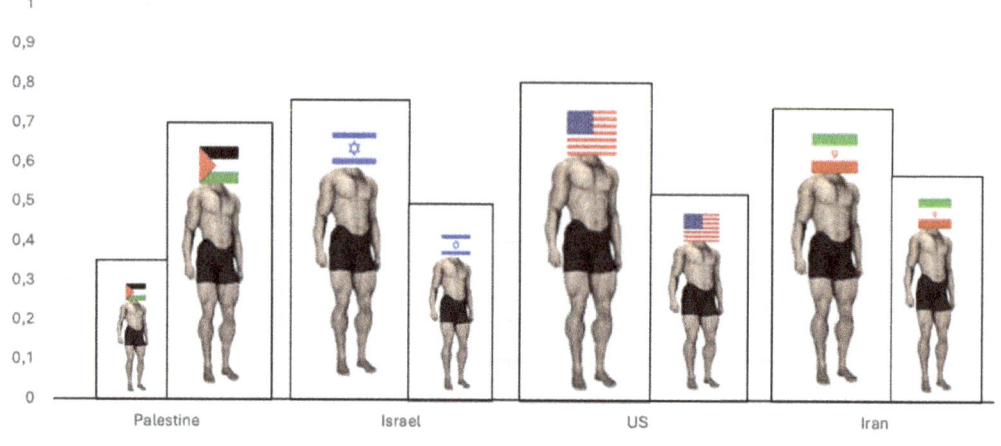

Figure 4. Gazans' mean ratings of relative physical vs. spiritual formidability of four national groups. Zero and one on the vertical axis represent the smallest and largest possible size to which participants could adjust the image. Data source: January 2025 opinion survey in Gaza by Artis International, the Changing Character of War Centre, and the Palestinian Center for Policy and Survey Research.

In similar studies conducted elsewhere, groups that perceive themselves as relatively weak physically but strong spiritually tend to be those that are more militant or radicalized and willing to continue fighting, even against a far more powerful foe. They perceive their readiness for self-sacrifice as an advantage over their adversaries. This is a common trait among extremist groups, such as fighters and supporters of ISIS or the Kurdish PKK (but also among others who may be just as devoted and willing to sacrifice themselves for democracy or peace).

Gazans also show a marked tendency to view the conflict with Israel in religious rather than political terms: as a conflict to liberate Muslims from Jewish oppression. But Palestinians' religious belief does not necessarily imply intolerance of other groups. For example, in a 2016 survey of Palestinian Muslim youths, we and colleagues found that many were disposed to place much greater value on the lives of Palestinians than on those of Jewish Israelis. Yet when they were asked to take the viewpoint of Allah (God), they valued the two more equally.[18] Their belief in God appeared to promote a more universal valuation of human life, attributing moral worthiness to Muslims and non-Muslims alike even amid prolonged conflict.

Nevertheless, when religion becomes identified with an assertive sociopolitical agenda ostensibly sanctified by God or a "party of God," opponents to that agenda and party become enemies of God who are easier to vilify and kill. In the January survey, barely 1 percent of Gazans considered themselves "not religious," whereas 67 percent identified themselves as "somewhat religious" and 31 percent as truly "religious." Those who considered themselves somewhat and truly religious generally considered Israelis significantly less "human" than Palestinians on a visual scale ranging from an ape-like figure through stages of semi-erectness to a fully upright human, with lower ratings indicating moral degeneracy and a violent nature. Studies from China, Europe, India, North America, and elsewhere indicate that the less human the chosen figure, the more respondents associate the adversary with moral degeneracy and violent threats and actions, and the greater their own impetus for violence against that adversary.[19] Respondents identifying themselves as truly religious were the most committed to Palestinian sovereignty and the right of return and the most willing to make major sacrifices, including fighting and dying, for those outcomes. This segment also was the most likely to support sharia and Hamas's leadership.

It is important to note that for most Gazans, religious and political commitments are not all-determining. Although most Gazans consider the core values associated with being Palestinian as central to their identity, only smaller minorities consider these to be 'sacred' and nonnegotiable: just 30 percent of Gazans view the right of return as immune to any trade-off for peace; 20 percent view sharia that way; and 15 percent, national sovereignty. Nonetheless, the great majority (82 percent) judged that even the cause of national sovereignty was significantly more important than family safety and security. This finding parallels our survey results from the most committed combatants for and against ISIS in Iraq in 2015–17, whereas in ongoing survey work in Taiwan, for example, we find much greater concern for family security than sovereignty.[20]

Failure to understand the commitment of devoted actors to exertions dissociated from material costs and consequences also results in failure to comprehend the outsize effect of devoted actors on an entire population's will to fight. As Darwin noted in *The Descent of Man*, there is an evolutionary logic to such commitment that enables low-power groups to survive the predations of the strong—a commitment to what he deemed "highly esteemed, even sacred" spiritual and moral values that "give an immense advantage" to one group over another when possessed by devoted actors who "by their example excite... in a high degree the spirit" in others to sacrifice for cause and comrades, for ill or good.[21]

Why Still War?

Paradoxically, the continued strength of Gazans' commitments to the Palestinian cause may point to forms of compromise that have until now been overlooked. For example, it is no secret that Hamas is committed to a sovereign Palestinian state, the right of return, and sharia law—all of which the elimination of Israel as a state would accomplish. Yet Hamas leaders have in the past suggested to us in public attribution for *The New York Times* that they do not consider a sovereign Palestine "from the river to the sea" and the dissolution of Israel as nonnegotiable, sacred values.[22]

Studies we conducted from 2006 to 2013 indicated that even the right of return, though held to be sacred, can be reframed so as to remain nonnegotiable in principle but negotiable in practice.[23] Such an accommodation might require, for example, meaningful symbolic gestures from the other side, such as a sincere Israeli apology for the expulsion of Palestinians from their homes and lands, Israel's acceptance of the return of a limited number of refugees and their descendants, and some form of *diya*, or financial compensation to victims or the heirs of victims of the Nakba, the mass displacement of Palestinians during Israel's founding in 1948, as a form of historic reparations. But our research also shows that material offers—whether proposed by Israelis, the US, or international actors—such as economic incentives or sanctions that aim to compel Palestinians (or Israelis) to forsake their core values only backfire, increasing resistance to peace deals and support for violence.[24]

Of course, Hamas leaders making such statements may have been engaging in insincere posturing aimed at relieving Israeli military pressure, as Israeli leaders have claimed. Nevertheless, there is evident willingness among Gaza's population as a whole to countenance an outcome that falls short of what they consider to be most acceptable and realistic should certain conditions be met, such as "balance of power" and "right of return." Balance of power, a negotiable material good, would ensure physical security. Right of return, a nonnegotiable but re-interpretable sacred value, would provide a measure of ontological security, that is, of having a place in the world: a respectful recognition of what Palestinians often cite as the conflict's central issue, *al-'Ard hiya al-Ard*, "Land is [family and community] Honor." To voluntarily cede the land, as US President Donald Trump proposes Gazans do, would mean they cease *to be* Palestinian, to exist in their own right. It would only add to generations of displaced Palestinians, unassimilated through a combination of willful choice and unwillingness of host nations to fully accept them, longing to return to the land much as diaspora Jews longed for Zion.

To be sure, public sentiments in the heat of war tend to be very militant. For example, there were marked differences between militancy levels during the second intifada (2000–2005) and the periods before and after.[25] But a failure to recognize the strength of commitment to values that Palestinians believe essential to *being* Palestinian, or even to recognize them at all—as when Israeli Finance Minister Bezalel Smotrich declared a few months before the Gaza war began that there is "no such thing" as a Palestinian people[26]—likely guarantees further extreme actions on their behalf whatever the costs. In fact, identity fusion with Palestine and belief in the sanctity of right of return, national sovereignty, and sharia are all associated with extreme actions to protect and defend Palestine but negatively correlated with sacrifices people are willing to make for peace between Palestine and Israel. Previous behavioral and brain studies with colleagues further indicate that continuing to threaten or marginalize people because of the group they belong to instigates sacralization of important but hitherto non-sacred values, generating wider willingness to make costly sacrifices for them.[27]

Even if there were an attempt to win over "hearts and minds" with offers of economic or social benefit, these likely would come to naught and may well backfire, as they have in the past, if there is disregard of the values that Palestinians hold dear and are willing to defend. This does not entail that Israel should accede to these values; however, even symbolic gestures of respect toward them that carry no initial promise of payoff, if considered sincere, appear to lessen will to violence and open possibilities for peace.[28]

Absent an Israeli willingness to make some concessions on Palestinian core values and absent the international community's willingness to enforce the terms of such an agreement, the survey suggests that Gazans will fight on—at least if the committed minority of devoted actors are still able to inspire people to take on unfathomable odds to seek to eliminate Israel. And Israelis would assuredly respond with incomparably greater destructive force.

After waging many months of 'total war' and achieving many of its declared (material) objectives, Israel may be further from pacifying Gaza than ever before. This is not just because Israel has offered nothing resembling a political strategy or plan for a Palestinian future, while further radicalizing Palestinians to seek revenge for relatives killed and homes lost. (Our survey shows a positive association between having experienced family displacement and preferring a military over a diplomatic end to the conflict.) It is also because Gazans, at least the most committed among them, believe that their identity and place in the world are more imperiled than ever: a sentiment not unlike the one that inspired the establishment of the Jewish state and fostered its people's intense will to fight.

Possible Pathways to Peace

What might the psycho-components of a change toward the path to peace look like? Experienced and successful negotiators in other once-seemingly-intractable conflicts, as between Catholic independentists and Protestant loyalists in Northern Ireland, suggest that genuine peacebuilding requires humanization or re-humanization of the adversary.[29] (Of course, developments in the 1990s that encouraged and facilitated humanization, including leadership committed to peace and the cooperative framework of the European Union, helped to improve prospects for peace in Northern Ireland. No such peace-nurturing framework or leadership presently exists in the Israel-Palestine context; however, there are ongoing efforts by several nations to help provide such a framework should an Israeli or Palestinian leadership emerge that sincerely is interested in peace between the two peoples.)

The Gaza survey allowed us to test whether humanizing an enemy in fact predicts willingness to make costly sacrifices for peace in times of war. It also enabled us to examine the role of three psychosocial factors that might help produce and predict the positive association between humanization of the enemy and sacrifices for peace. First, our previous work disentangling the transcultural pathways to the will to fight from populations as diverse as US military cadets, Ukrainian freedom fighters, and jihadis revealed that trust in a group, a leader, or a value is a potential mechanism that fosters costly sacrifices for the target of trust.[30] Second, the research has consistently shown that sacralization of a target is a potent predictor of willingness to fight, die, and make other costly sacrifices for the target. And third, more than a half-century of investigation has consistently demonstrated that sustained, positive contact between individuals in adversarial groups can significantly improve group relations.[31]

Our goal in formulating part of the survey design, then, was to test whether Gazans suffering brutal war are able to humanize their Israeli enemy and whether humanization might encourage willingness to make costly sacrifices for peace between the two parties. Statistical analyses reveal that 10 percent of Gazans humanize Israelis beyond the midpoint of the humanization scale (compared to 70 percent who humanize Palestinians beyond the midpoint). Although many proactive initiatives would be needed to increase the humanization profile of Israelis among Palestinians, perhaps through material and symbolic concessions of the sort described above, once the threshold of humanization is achieved (beyond midpoint on the ape-to-human scale), we find it to be positively associated with costly sacrifices to achieve peace. A mediation model generated from the survey results indicates that humanization of Israelis predicts willingness to make costly sacrifices for peace via specific pathways that could separately or (better) collectively involve: (1) increasing trust in Israelis, (2) desire for positive interaction with Israelis, and (3) sacralization of the value of peace between Israel and Palestine (Fig. 5). (This result was independent of fusion or sacralization of Palestine, right of return, national sovereignty, or sharia.)

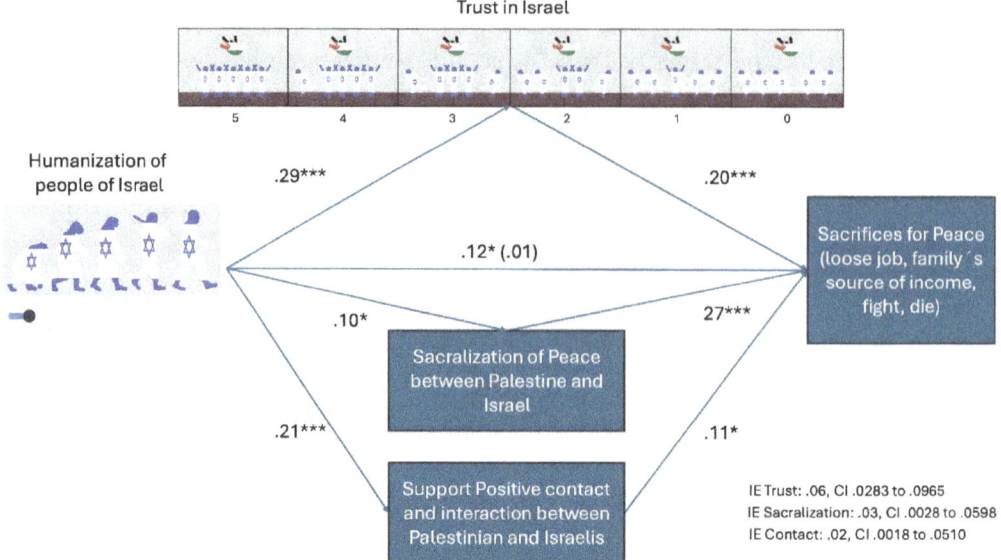

Figure 5. Mediation model showing that Gazans' humanization of Israelis predicts their willingness to make costly sacrifices for peace via increasing trust and desire for positive interaction with Israelis and sacralization of the value of peace between Israel and Palestine. Data source: January 2025 opinion survey in Gaza by Artis International, the Changing Character of War Centre, and the Palestinian Center for Policy and Survey Research.

In sum, the survey data suggest that initiatives toward reciprocal humanization through positive contacts, demonstrations of trust, and sanctifying peace as an ultimate value could help foster commitment to peace if accompanied by sincere symbolic concessions that open the way to material negotiation and mutual concession.[32] In the absence of such initiatives, either from a grassroots push or leadership pull, maximalist attempts to destroy one another will likely persist.

Conclusion: the Limits of Realism

According to realist bargaining theories, informational clarity about relative material force and credible commitment to a peace deal should lead to termination of conflict.[33] But when apparently indivisible and nonnegotiable 'sacred values' are in play, we find cross-cultural evidence from long-standing and seemingly intractable conflicts, such as the Israel-Palestine conflict, the nuclear standoff with Iran, and the fight with the Islamic State, that no deals are acceptable if they require abandoning such values (often perceived as wholly incompatible with the other side's core values).[34]

As Harvard's Stephen Walt acknowledges with respect to the recent war in Gaza: "framing this conflict in moral terms makes it harder to reach a peace settlement, because anything short of total victory inevitably invites a powerful backlash from critics fearing that these critical values are being sacrificed."[35] Yet rather than offering plausible approaches to deal with conflicting values in mutually tolerable ways, for example by creative conceptual reframing, Walt argues that conflicting sides should simply set aside disputes over "indivisible" moral values in favor of compromise over divisible goods (territory, resources, balance of power, etc.) based on realism and rationality. As our Gaza survey and other studies show, however, cherished moral values can become inextricably bound to personal and collective identity, to 'who I am, and what we are,' and inseparable from the very meaning of one's life and physical existence. Moreover, directly engaging instead of averting such cherished moral values could well open up, rather than block, realistic negotiations on material issues in this, and possibly other, hitherto intractable conflicts.

Epilogue: the Hamas-Likud Dialectic; a Brief History of Spoilers

Hamas's rhetoric and actions over the years arguably owe as much to the internal dynamics of political competition among Palestinian forces as to the struggle with Israel—a state of affairs made clear some years ago by then-Gaza Prime Minister Ismail Haniyeh, who asked in an interview with Atran: "Why has the United States and Israel insisted on dealing only with the PLO, when the people support us?" In response, Atran asked why Israel should deal with Hamas when its charter calls for the destruction of the Jewish state, which it justifies with antisemitic tropes like the Czarist forgery, *Protocols of the Elders of Zion*. Haniyeh responded, on the record, that should the United States and Israel begin political negotiations with Hamas, then they will find Hamas ready to deal: "We have no problem with a sovereign Palestinian state over all our lands within the 1967 borders, living in calm. But we need the West as a partner to help us through."[36] (Of all external powers, including Iran and members of the Arab League, Gazans indicate in our survey that the US "is most likely to help put an end to Palestinian suffering.")

Successive American and Israeli governments were well apprised of attempts at outreach from several quarters but shunned any form of political (as opposed to ceasefire and hostage) negotiations with Hamas so long as Hamas publicly insisted on the destruction of Israel. When in Damascus, Atran asked then-politburo chairman Khalid Meshaal why, on the one hand, Hamas signals it wants to deal but, on the other hand, continues to insist on Israel's destruction and the truth of the fake *Protocols* tract, Meshaal responded: "Why should Palestinians always be first to concede. Look at what it got [PLO Chairman Yasser] Arafat at Oslo, nothing. Let Israel make a first move for a change, then they will see that our actions are stronger than words today."[37]

Likud, the dominant party in Israel's ruling coalition today, emerged from a pre-state paramilitary movement whose objective was the establishment of a Jewish state on both banks of the Jordan River (including present day Jordan). The movement's founder, Ze'ev Jabotinsky (1880–1940), recognized that the Arabs of Palestine should have equal rights of life, liberty, and pursuit of happiness. The right to national self-determination, however, would be for the Jewish population alone because only a Jewish-governed homeland, with ample territory protected by a strong military, could offer world Jewry safety from the often deadly and spiritually debilitating scourge of antisemitism.[38] By contrast, many Arab nations could take in Arabs from Palestine.

Following the 1967 war, the parties of the left that had governed Israel since its inception, under the tenuous assumption that a socialist state led by a Jewish vanguard could sustain a worker's democracy with equal rights for Jews and Arabs alike, embarked on a program of "settlements as security." The program initially established some thirty scattered settlements, most originally army outposts. Likud, however, sought to colonize the Occupied Palestinian Territory from the Jordan River to the Mediterranean Sea in partial fulfillment of its pre-state ambition. The 1977 election of Likud and its leader Menachem Begin as prime minister instituted a program of accelerated settlement in an open effort to prevent establishment of a Palestinian state. A "magic number" of 100,000 settlers was proffered as a point of no return for permanent occupation. This was achieved during the second government of Yitzhak Shamir, Begin's successor (1986–1992).

Likud leadership has always considered the PLO (and the Palestinian Authority it dominates) to be a far more serious candidate than Hamas for international recognition and hence a grave threat to its project of (re)settling the biblical Greater Israel (*Erez Yisrael Hashleimah*). That is why successive Likud-dominated governments, including Benjamin Netanyahu's prior to October 2023, have selectively provided funds to Hamas to undercut the PLO, and then the Palestinian Authority that the PLO came to dominate. For example, in 1987, when Atran was researching the pre-state land system of Palestine as a visiting professor at the Hebrew University of Jerusalem's Harry S. Truman Research Institute for the Advancement of Peace, the assistants who the university helped him find included Muslim Brothers (*al-Ikhwan al-Muslimin*). They were then in the process of forming Hamas, welding together those rump parts of the Jordanian and Egyptian chapters of the Muslim Brotherhood resulting from Israel's conquest of the West Bank and Gaza. But Atran was still surprised when the assistants openly declared their intention to destroy the Israeli state funding them.

Ever since Hamas's creation, its bellicose rhetoric and actions against Israel have been tuned to its competition with the PLO and Palestinian Authority. Excluded from the Oslo Accords, Hamas's suicide bombing campaign following Yitzhak Rabin's assassination in 1995 by an Israeli ultranationalist helped scuttle the accords and sway Israeli voters to narrowly choose the first Netanyahu government, which then endeavored to further undermine the Oslo agreement. In 2005, Likud leader Ariel Sharon engineered Israel's withdrawal from the Gaza Strip to enhance Israeli security and its international status—a move Netanyahu opposed, forcing a vote for Likud leadership that Sharon only narrowly won. When Sharon suffered a massive stroke in 2006, Likud leadership passed to Netanyahu, who became opposition leader in parliament. In a bloody military takeover in 2007, Hamas wrested control of Gaza from the Palestinian Authority, which retained power in the West Bank. Upon return to power in 2009, the Netanyahu government's ploy to "divide and conquer" undercut attempts to reconcile the PLO and Hamas and prevent a unified Palestinian government from forming that might better make the case for statehood.

Hamas was left with three main options: build a successful mini-state in Gaza, reunify with the West Bank, and become the dominant force within the Palestinian Authority and the push for statehood or, failing these two options, re-engage in armed struggle with Israel to force a change in an intolerable status quo (stagnant living conditions in Gaza were eating away at Hamas's popular support). But the Netanyahu government sought to maintain the status quo by offering nominal economic incentives: providing Gazans some 20,000 permits to work in nearby Israeli towns and farms while allowing Qatar and Iran to fund Hamas's limited economic initiatives and administrative operations.

Israel's intelligence services were aware that some funds were earmarked for tunnels that could protect Hamas fighters and house light arms and primitive rockets filled with explosives made from agricultural fertilizer and sugar. But Israel's government and military were confident their tactics were working, and that the military threat from Hamas and its allies was minimal. This wishful assessment allowed Israel to shift military forces and intelligence gathering to the West Bank to support the strategic mission of plodding annexation through settlements. Hamas saw the blind spot as an opportunity to attack and rupture the status quo; however, Hamas was likely unprepared for the magnitude of the attack's initial success and gruesome horrors, much less the Israeli firestorm that would engulf Gaza, dubiously justified as a necessary defense against another Jewish Holocaust.

In Cairo, during the Muslim Brotherhood's short rule in Egypt in 2012, Marzouk (then-deputy politburo chairman of Hamas) said "no" to any trade-off for peace without granting a right of return. He became angry when the idea of substantial American aid for rebuilding was added: "We do not sell ourselves for any amount." But when offered a potential Israeli apology for 1948, he conceded: "Yes, an apology is important, as a beginning. It's not enough because our houses and land were taken from us and something has to be done about that."[39] A similar response came from Meshaal. "Words matter," he said, "but then there must be concrete actions." When asked what actions he meant, he offered to make a public pronouncement that he was willing to accept a settlement along the 1967 borders that could conceivably turn into true peace (*salaam*), not just a truce (*hudna*), should the Palestinian people so decide by referendum against Hamas's preference and steadfast opposition and preference for war (*harb*) from other members of the Hamas politburo and military wing. But there would have to be a "balance of forces," an international—especially American—commitment to guarantee compliance, and Israel's apology for "taking away our homes."[40] Shortly after start of the January 2025 ceasefire, Marzouk, still a top Hamas politburo leader, again attempted to reach out to the new US administration with an offer of dialogue on "achieving understanding of everything"—an offer more plaintive than practical.[41]

Until leaders and their peoples find the strength within, or outside forces compel them, to confront and reimagine spoiler attachments to a grievance-driven spirituality of opposed absolutes, there may be no realistic pathway to peace.

Notes

1. Palestinian Center for Policy and Survey Research (PSR), https://www.pcpsr.org/.
2. Scott Atran, "The Will to Fight," Science 373, no. 6559 (2021): 1063, https://www.science.org/doi/10.1126/science.abl9949.
3. Ángel Gómez, Alexandra Vázquez, and Scott Atran, "Transcultural Pathways to the Will to Fight," Proceedings of the National Academy of Sciences, USA 120, no. 24 (2023): e2303614120, https://doi.org/10.1073/pnas.2303614120.
4. John J. Mearsheimer, "Reckless States and Realism," International Relations 23 (2009): 241–56, https://www.mearsheimer.com/wp-content/uploads/2019/06/Reckless-States-and-Realism.pdf; Jonathan Leader Maynard, "What Is Political Moralism?," Topoi 44 (2024): 13–26, https://doi.org/10.1007/s11245-024-10060-9.
5. Amaney A. Jamal and Michael Robbins, "What Palestinians Really Think of Hamas," Foreign Affairs, October 25, 2023, https://www.foreignaffairs.com/israel/what-palestinians-really-think-hamas.
6. Scott Atran, "Is Hamas Ready to Deal?," New York Times, August 17, 2006, https://www.nytimes.com/2006/08/17/opinion/17atran.html; Atran, Talking to the Enemy: Violent Extremism, Sacred Values, and What It Means to Be Human (Penguin, 2010); Atran, "U.S. Must Help Deal Directly with Hamas," New York Times, August 5, 2014, https://www.nytimes.com/roomfordebate/2014/08/05/can-the-us-still-be-a-leader-in-the-middle-east/us-must-help-deal-directly-with-hamas.
7. PSR, Public Opinion Poll no. 91, March 5–10, 2024, https://pcpsr.org/en/node/973.
8. K. Shikaki to S. Atran, personal communication, February 6, 2025.
9. Scott Atran, Hoshang Waziri, Ángel Gómez, et al., "The Islamic State's Lingering Legacy Among Young Men in the Mosul Area," CTC Sentinel 11, no. 4 (2018): 15–22, https://ctc.westpoint.edu/islamic-states-lingering-legacy-among-young-men-mosul-area/.
10. Harvey Whitehouse, Brian McQuinn, Michael Buhrmester, and William B. Swann Jr., "Brothers in Arms: Libyan Revolutionaries Bond Like Families," Proceedings of the National Academy of Sciences, USA 111, no. 50 (2014): 17783–85, https://www.pnas.org/doi/10.1073/pnas.1416284111; Gómez et al., "Transcultural Pathways."
11. Jeremy Ginges, Scott Atran, Douglas Medin, and Khalil Shikaki, "Sacred Bounds on Rational Resolution of Violent Political Conflict," Proceedings of the National Academy of Sciences, USA 104, no. 18 (2007): 7357–60, https://www.pnas.org/doi/10.1073/pnas.0701768104; Scott Atran, "The Devoted Actor: Unconditional Cooperation and Intractable Conflict Across Cultures," Current Anthropology 57, no. S13 (2016): 192–203, https://www.journals.uchicago.edu/doi/full/10.1086/685495.
12. Scott Atran, "Psychology of Terrorism and Extreme Political Conflict," Annual Review of Psychology 72 (2021): 471–50, https://www.annualreviews.org/deliver/fulltext/psych/72/1/annurev-psych-010419-050800.pdf?itemId=/content/journals/10.1146/annurev-psych-010419-050800&mimeType=application/pdf.
13. Ángel Gómez, Lucía López-Rodríguez, Hammad Sheikh, et al., "The Devoted Actor's Will to Fight and the Spiritual Dimension of Human Conflict," Nature Human Behaviour 1 (2017): 673–79, https://www.nature.com/articles/s41562-017-0193-3.

14. Hammad Sheikh, Ángel Gómez, and Scott Atran, "Empirical Evidence for the Devoted Actor Model," *Current Anthropology* 57, no. S13 (2016): 204–9, https://www.journals.uchicago.edu/doi/full/10.1086/686221.
15. Sheikh, Gómez, and Atran, "Empirical Evidence"; Scott Atran and Ángel Gómez, "What Gazans Want," *Foreign Policy*, February 14, 2025, https://www.foreignaffairs.com/israel/what-gazans-want.
16. Chad C. Tossell, Ángel Gómez, Ewart J. de Visser, et al., "Spiritual over Physical Formidability Determines Willingness to Fight and Sacrifice Through Loyalty in Cross-Cultural Populations," *Proceedings of the National Academy of Sciences, USA*, 119, no. 6 (2022): e2113076119, https://www.pnas.org/doi/10.1073/pnas.2113076119.
17. D. M. Fessler, C. Holbrook, and M. M. Gervais, "Men's Physical Strength Moderates Conceptualizations of Prospective Foes in Two Disparate Societies," *Human Nature* 25, no. 3 (2014): 393–409, https://doi.org/10.1007/s12110-014-9205-4.
18. Jeremy Ginges, Hammad Sheikh, Scott Atran, and Nichole Argo, "Thinking from God's Perspective Decreases Biased Valuation of the Life of a Nonbeliever," *Proceedings of the National Academy of Sciences, USA* 113, no. 2 (2015): 316–19, https://www.pnas.org/doi/10.1073/pnas.1512120113.
19. Nick Haslam, "The Many Roles of Dehumanization in Genocide," in *Confronting Humanity at Its Worst*, ed. Leonard S. Newman (Oxford University Press, 2024); Shane P. Singh and Jaroslav Tir, "Less Human than Human: Threat, Language, and Relative Dehumanization," *British Journal of Political Science* 54, no. 3 (2024): 612–28, https://www.cambridge.org/core/journals/british-journal-of-political-science/article/less-human-than-human-threat-language-and-relative-dehumanization/01EE7ED5DD4B8704284D87E4703271BE.
20. Atran, "The Devoted Actor"; Gómez et al., "The Devoted Actor's Will to Fight."
21. Charles Darwin, *The Descent of Man* (John Murray, 1871), 167–71.
22. Atran, "U.S. Must Help Deal Directly with Hamas."
23. Scott Atran and Jeremy Ginges, "How Words Could End a War," *New York Times*, January 24, 2009, https://www.nytimes.com/2009/01/25/opinion/25atran.html; Scott Atran and Robert Axelrod, "Reframing Sacred Values," *Negotiation Journal* 24, no. 3 (2008): 221–46, https://direct.mit.edu/ngtn/article/24/3/221/122004/Reframing-Sacred-Values.
24. Ginges et al., "Sacred Bounds"; Scott Atran, Robert Axelrod, and Richard Davis, "Sacred Barriers to Conflict Resolution," *Science* 317, no. 5841 (2007): 1039–040, https://www.science.org/doi/10.1126/science.1144241.
25. Ariel Merari, *Driven to Death: Psychological and Social Aspects of Suicide Terrorism* (Oxford University Press, 2010).
26. Laurie Kellman, "'No Such Thing' as Palestinian People, Top Israeli Minister Says," *PBS News*, March 20, 2023, https://www.pbs.org/newshour/world/no-such-thing-as-palestinian-people-top-israeli-minister-says.
27. Clara Pretus, Nafees Hamid, Hammad Sheikh, et al., "Neural and Behavioral Correlates of Sacred Values and Vulnerability to Violent Extremism," *Frontiers in Psychology* 9 (2018), https://pubmed.ncbi.nlm.nih.gov/30627108/; Nafees Hamid, Clara Pretus, Scott Atran, et al., "Neuroimaging 'Will to Fight' for Sacred Values: An Empirical Case Study with Supporters of an Al Qaeda Associate," *Royal Society Open Science* 6, no. 6 (2019): 181585, https://royalsocietypublishing.org/doi/10.1098/rsos.181585.

28 Ginges et al., "Sacred Bounds"; Atran et al., "Sacred Barriers to Conflict Resolution."
29 "Civil Efforts Key to True Reconciliation, Says Lord Alderdice," *The Commonwealth News*, May 1, 2013, https://thecommonwealth.org/news/civil-efforts-key-true-reconciliation-says-lord-alderdice.
30 Gómez et al., "Transcultural Pathways."
31 Amit Goldenberg, Kinneret Endevelt, Shira Ran, Carol S. Dweck, James J. Gross, and Eran Halperin, "Making Intergroup Contact More Fruitful: Enhancing Cooperation Between Palestinian and Jewish-Israeli Adolescents by Fostering Beliefs About Group Malleability," *Social Psychological and Personality Science* 8, no. 1 (2016): 3–10, https://journals.sagepub.com/doi/abs/10.1177/1948550616672851.
32 Scott Atran and Jeremy Ginges, "Religious and Sacred Imperatives in Human Conflict," *Science* 336, no. 6083 (2012): 855–57, https://www.science.org/doi/10.1126/science.1216902.
33 James D. Fearon, "Rationalist Explanations for War," *International Organization* 49, no. 3 (1995): 379–414, https://www.jstor.org/stable/2706903; Dan Reiter, *How Wars End* (Princeton University Press, 2009).
34 Scott Atran, "Stones Against the Iron Fist, Terror Within the Nation: Alternating Structures of Violence and Cultural Identity in the Israeli-Palestinian Conflict," *Politics and Society* 18, no. 4 (1990): 481–526, https://journals.sagepub.com/doi/abs/10.1177/003232929001800404; Ginges et al., "Sacred Bounds"; Hammad Sheikh, Jeremy Ginges, and Scott Atran, "Sacred Values in the Israeli-Palestinian Conflict: Resistance to Social Influence, Temporal Discounting, and Exit Strategies," *Annals of the New York Academy of Sciences* 1299, no. 1 (2013): 11–24, https://nyaspubs.onlinelibrary.wiley.com/doi/abs/10.1111/nyas.12275; Morteza Dehghani, Scott Atran, Rumen Iliev, Sonya Sachdeva, Douglas Medin, and Jeremy Ginges, "Sacred Values and Conflict over Iran's Nuclear Program," *Judgment and Decision Making* 5, no. 7 (2010): 540–46, https://www.cambridge.org/core/journals/judgment-and-decision-making/article/sacred-values-and-conflict-over-irans-nuclear-program/46BB4FEA5A1B525413D6EC7F0F9384EC; Atran, "The Devoted Actor"; Atran et al., "The Islamic State's Lingering Legacy"; Sheikh et al., "Empirical Evidence."
35 Stephen M. Walt, "Morality Is the Enemy of Peace," *Foreign Policy*, June 13, 2024, https://foreignpolicy.com/2024/06/13/gaza-ukraine-ceasefire-war-peace-morality/.
36 Atran, "Is Hamas Ready to Deal?"
37 Interview with S. Atran, Damascus, December 16, 2009.
38 illel Halkin, *Jabotinsky: A Life* (Yale University Press, 2014).
39 Atran and Ginges, "How Words Could End a War."
40 Atran et al., "Sacred Barriers to Conflict Resolution," 1040.
41 Adam Rasgon, "Hamas Official Says Group Is Ready for 'Dialogue with America,'" *New York Times*, January 20, 2025, https://www.nytimes.com/2025/01/20/world/middleeast/hamas-trump-us.html.

UNDERSTANDING THE UNDERLYING MOTIVATIONS OF THE RUSSIA-UKRAINE WAR

John Bell
The Conciliators Guild

ABSTRACT

Conflict resolution often focuses on material interests or trust building rather than the core psychological needs of the sides. Mapping the key emotional red lines of parties and addressing them creatively may offer new opportunities for peace. This article examines such an approach for the Russia-Ukraine conflict, with reflection on the Middle East where such a mapping of needs has begun. This approach leads to the concept of mutual needs satisfaction, where all sides' critical red lines are addressed, if imperfectly. This is discussed regarding Russia, Ukraine, and the West today. As former Egyptian President Anwar Sadat demonstrated by going to the Israeli Knesset in 1977, symbolic steps that attend to core innate needs can pave the way to conflict resolution and peace.

John Bell is the director of The Conciliators Guild, an organization dedicated to emphasizing the importance of innate human needs and patterns of group behavior in politics as a critical way forward today. He is a mediator drawing on over thirty years of experience in Middle East conflict resolution. He served as a UN and Canadian diplomat in Beirut, Cairo, and Jerusalem and has worked with Search for Common Ground, the Toledo International Center for Peace, and the European Institute of Peace, among others.

The ideas in this article have been inspired by an approach to well-being called Human Givens that was pioneered in the UK. In 2021, this journal published an article by Ivan Tyrrell, one of the founders of Human Givens, "Psychological Dimensions of Peacemaking."[1] Since that time, Ivan Tyrrell has also published, in coordination with The Conciliators Guild, the Charter of Human Needs in Politics.[2] These documents lay out in greater depth and scope the importance of attending to basic human needs and motivations in the political sphere, and the risks of not doing so. It is with that same intention that these ideas have been applied to international relations in the article below.

Enemies are often former or potential friends who have been denied – or think they have been denied – something.

—Idries Shah

This phrase, expressed by Sufi scholar Idries Shah, contains much in a little space. It makes the link between opposites, 'enemies' and 'friends,' suggests that matters can evolve, 'former' or 'potential,' and goes to the heart of the matter: when humans are denied something, or believe that they have been, there will be conflict.

It is in that spirit that this article introduces an outlook to help us navigate between enmity and friendship, and deal with international conflict, specifically with regards to the Russia-Ukraine war. We start our journey in another region plagued by war and examine how events there elucidate the way forward.

In 1977, former Egyptian President Sadat flew to Israel and spoke to the Knesset of the need for peace. He did so after the 1973 war, and by doing so elicited the fury of many in Egypt and the rest of the Arab world who saw Israel as a permanent enemy. However, his symbolic move, tightly choreographed diplomatically beforehand, cut the Gordian knot of the Egyptian-Israeli conflict, and led to the Camp David peace agreements of 1978. Before that step, Israelis were in constant war with all Arab states, and felt ostracized by the region and denied a sense of belonging there. Sadat resolved this by going to the heart of the enemy, its capital and seat of government, to speak of a better future. The Camp David Accords have held from 1978 to this day.

Such a bold move is rare in politics, but it is also instructive. It attended to a basic core need in Israel, opening the path to successful negotiations. Much conflict resolution works in the opposite direction, with careful, confidence building steps that aim to accumulate the trust needed to dissolve enmity. Sadat circumvented this more peripheral process to boldly set up a new paradigm with Israel. It is not insignificant that he had fought a somewhat successful war before doing so.

The Middle East as a Tormented Example

The Middle East is a powerful example of a region torn apart by decades of war, much of it linked to ethnic and religious identity, powerful understandings of our place in history, and the future, that make negotiations seem intractable. Whether it is religious Zionists' links to the West Bank and Jerusalem, Iran's understanding of its geopolitical primacy in the Middle East, or the Muslim Brotherhood's many volleys into politics, all of these have played into war or peace in the region. Westerners sometimes diminish the importance of such factors in favor of material and economic interests. Although these are also key and cannot be ignored, talks based only on material interests often fail.

This is why former Iranian Foreign Minister Jawad Zarif stated at a conference in Doha, Qatar in 2019 that what is needed is a 'cognitive map of the Middle East,' a way of understanding how each country thinks about the region, their neighbors, and their enemies. This author would add that it is an emotional-cultural-cognitive map that is required.

We are all motivated by basic innate needs such as belonging, autonomy, status, attention, achievement, and meaning, among others, all of which operate often without our knowledge. If these needs are not met, we become anxious and conflictual; if they are, we are calmer and more open-minded. They are universal—enemies share them, even if their cultural or ideological expression differs from place to place, or across time.

The Conciliators Guild, an organization dedicated to addressing such core needs in politics, has done a mapping of the core interests of key countries in the Middle East as a reference for more effective management or resolution of conflict. This identifies where the red-hot points of inflammation are, and what needs to be addressed to settle the region down to some level of stability. From this arises the concept of mutual needs satisfaction: if we want to resolve conflicts in our complex world today, there is no way around addressing what enemies are—or think that they are—being denied, which is often their most basic, essential core needs.

With that in mind, we can turn to the Russia-Ukraine war. Given President Trump's foray into this issue since his election, this may be especially relevant and timely. We will first have a look at the basic needs of all sides before moving toward answers.

Mapping the Russia-Ukraine War

We start with Russia because it started the war and it is important to investigate why. From discussion with Russians, there are three main issues that motivated the invasion of Ukraine. The first is security concerns arising from NATO expansion into Eastern Europe that brought the Western alliance geographically very close to Russia and thus, the consistent Russian demand for a change in NATO's missile deployment in Eastern Europe. Furthermore, in its Bucharest summit of April, 2008, NATO welcomed Ukraine and Georgia's aspirations to join NATO. Russia believed NATO had crept up right to its doorstep, and in return, it invaded Georgia in August, 2008 and Ukraine in February, 2022.

As powerful as security in motivating Russian behavior is a besmirched sense of status vis-à-vis the West. NATO's expansion into former Warsaw Pact countries confirmed Russia's status as the loser of the Cold War. However, even more instructive is Russia's self-perception as a global power and protector of civilizational values that rivals the West. "Not just one country among many, but a pole in a multipolar world. A country destined to challenge the West," is what Russian diplomats are taught in their training academy.[3] A redemption of lost global status, a civilization as worthy as the West's, has intensely motivated Russia's leadership to pursue a disruptive anti-Western strategy. Importantly, the US is the Western power that matters for Russia, and no one else. The relevance of status is heightened by the fact that leaders pursue it at the personal level as well as in a confusing fusion with a nation's self-image.

Finally, and not unimportantly, there is the Russian-Ukrainian relationship based on historical and cultural identity. In the past, Ukrainians have had a sense of distinct nationalism. This was especially the case regarding the Soviet Union, driven by anti-communism. Yet, the two peoples are historically, socially, and culturally deeply intertwined. Nikolay Gogol, Anton Chekov, and Mikhail Bulgakov were all born in, or tied to, Ukraine; many Russians are of Ukrainian or mixed origin, and vice versa. In the eyes of Russians, a Ukrainian drift toward the West threatens this fundamental historical bond of identity and belonging. And this is without reference to the eastern regions of Ukraine whose populations are primarily of Russian ethnicity. From the Russian view, all of these basic needs: security, status, and belonging/identity cannot be ignored and, when unmet, or perceived to be unmet, they became the powerful drivers of conflict.

Ukraine also has basic needs and concerns. Having suffered a major attack from a large neighbor and continuing to suffer from war on its territory, it has a major security problem. Second, now more than ever, Ukrainians have a strong need for autonomy—they do not want to be absorbed into Russia and lose their independence. A sense of Ukrainian nationalism and independence has increased enormously as a result of the fight against Russia. This in turn affects the identity dynamic with Russia described in the previous paragraph. Third, they naturally wish for the return of land taken by force, i.e., Crimea and Eastern Ukraine. This is for every reason from integrity of the nation, to respect for Ukrainian sovereignty: a bundle of innate needs touching on security, status, and identity.

NATO countries have their own needs as well. With the memory of the Warsaw Pact still fresh, Eastern European countries continue to worry that their autonomy and separate identity from Russia will be threatened in the future—as Ukraine's has been. Security concerns pervade other NATO countries, no one knows what Russia's plans are, and there is already a hybrid war at play underwater in the Baltic Sea. Finally, the US, which was locked in a battle for global dominance with the Soviet Union for decades, does not perceive Russia today as an equal on the global stage. Statements that Russia is a "regional power that is threatening some of its immediate neighbors, not out of strength but out of weakness," as former President Obama made,[4] only deepen Russia's fixation on a return to a higher, global status that it believes it deserves.

Problematic Consequences

Once a group is inflamed and war kicks in, other ancillary but powerful emotions also join the fray. War reveals not only the desire for straight out victory, but also revenge for past wrongs, or turning the page on current failures. The heavy losses that have been incurred by both sides need to be justified through clear gains on the battlefield or through negotiations. For Ukraine, regaining lost territory is now a natural point of principle. Many Europeans also feel that Russia needs to be punished for having taken a neighbor's land by force, or to be deterred from further conquest.

These new dynamics complicate the search for resolution. A cycle of endless coercion ensues—neither side can be defeated, and the battle goes on. Furthermore, the leaders of both sides are locked into complex relationships with their domestic audiences. Having raised expectations of maximum victory, it is difficult for them to climb down. It is also to be noted that Western countries encouraged Ukraine to have such expectations.

Furthermore, political ideas do not exist as abstractions and are manifested and enacted by leaders who weave their personal agendas and outlooks into them. This can considerably complicate matters as we are all flawed creatures with vast capacity for deception, ignorance, and error. Therefore, a country's core interests can also become fodder for ever-expansive imperial agendas, or strengthening a leader's domestic position.

In the end, however, even tyrants need to somehow answer to their populations to maintain legitimacy. If the core needs identified above are real, then their fulfillment will resonate back to the citizens and their concerns, and satisfy national needs at all levels, that of both elites and citizens.

The reality remains that once the maelstrom of anger and emotional demands kicks in, including out of sheer resentment or for infinite redress, it becomes very difficult to return to a solution-oriented mind. Cures for this madness tend to be the very passage of time, a clear defeat of one side, or exhaustion. However, none of this negates the needs-based approach to identifying the underlying prime motivator of conflict that waits to be addressed, below the devil's intestines of emotional action and reaction. If indeed the fundamental causes of the war are the unmet needs of all the sides as described above, then answers lie there as well.

The concept that can help us move forward is "mutual needs satisfaction," where the core needs as described above are met to the degree possible, calming all and permitting new and more constructive perspectives. At the very least, if well understood, they can be put forward either as a reference for talks or as a prism for learning that can help us up our game in the future, a preventative outlook that thwarts the inevitability of war. The example of Sadat does speak to the power of addressing core needs in order to move toward peace. Indeed, Sadat explicitly remarked on the importance of understanding psychology. When negotiating with Israel after the 1973 war, he stated, "I want the [Israeli] Prime Minister to understand that the entire future of the agreement depends on psychological factors."[5]

What Can Be Done

It is difficult to attend to the array of needs presented above all at once. The key to the whole affair may not lie in Ukraine, despite its tragedy, but in global relations: the battle for status between Russia and the US, primarily driven by the former. All countries that feel mistreated, disrespected, and not dealt with at 'eye level' will seethe with the need for redress. Another key global example is the American-Chinese relationship. In our investigation, Russia perceives itself as a civilizational node and rival to the West. To regain that status, Russia needs strategic talks with the US, not with European countries, which it perceives as having lower global status. The other option, a multilateral format of talks involving, for example, the US, Russia, Ukraine, and key European countries all together would result in national competitions that logarithmically increase the complexity, and devolve into discussions pursuing a lowest common denominator.

Coincidentally, President Trump has delivered this gift of status to Russia. His direct, personal discussions with Vladimir Putin speak to an 'eye level' relationship. The Trump administration's intent to reset the American-Russian relationship and resolve Ukraine together opens up the possibility for a return to that special global status that Russia seeks (in stark contrast to how Barack Obama framed the relationship). However, this alone may not be enough. Although status is key, the substance of the talks also matters.

Trump is using the renewed relationship to discuss Ukraine. However, a frame premised on eye-level status between Russia and the US may be more powerfully used to address the security needs of all concerned. US-Russia strategic talks can focus on a bilateral reset and arms control and proliferation, as well as European security concerns, including maritime security in the Black Sea and, of course, Ukraine. The involvement of NATO's secretary general and close consultations between the US, Europe, and Ukraine will assuage concerns that the US would ignore European and Ukrainian security interests.

The question of identity and belonging identified above is more complex and will take time to disentangle. It draws back into history and culture and their connection to political aspirations on both sides. The current Western approach of focusing on the need to respect sovereignty is valid, but may be insufficient given Russian identity concerns.

A clearer understanding of what Russians mean by their identity links with Ukraine will be needed. Russian perceptions may be rooted in a distant past and insufficiently address Ukraine's need today for autonomy. Countries can have strong cultural and economic relations without one controlling the other. The reality that Gogol is a Russian author who hails from Ukraine, not a Ukrainian author, and part of the stream of Russian literary and cultural development is important, but these realities need to be translated into political understandings. These need not conflict with Ukrainian political independence. However, if Russia sees Ukraine slipping into the EU or NATO sphere of influence, then Russian understanding of history and relations with Ukraine become threatened and the spiral of conflict reemerges.

Healthy Russian-Ukrainian relations can ultimately be a rich combination of political independence mixed with economic and cultural integration. This can lead to future political arrangements very different from today's; however, they would have to be entered into voluntarily by all sides, not coerced. The drive for dominance, including through identity, is a tricky zone and it can be better understood through a properly constructed dialogue.

The above ideas on status, security, and belonging are not fixed. Countries evolve, which suggests an ever-evolving negotiation or discussion that requires the regular attention of governments. Such dialogues can be based on the concept of mutual needs satisfaction, i.e., that conflict is prevented or resolved by an attendance to the core needs of both sides. Given the preference for a top dog mentality, such a notion will take time to be absorbed. As the quote at the beginning of the article suggests, acknowledgment rather than denial of an enemy and their needs is the sine qua non for moving forward.

Behind all this lies an even more powerful yet elusive idea, that of mutual respect. Nations at war do not respect each other, despite instances of warriors doing so in battle. The road from enemy to friend, and to mutual respect, is not easy and requires courage but it is paved with mutual needs satisfaction.

Notes

[1] Ivan Tyrrell, "Psychological Dimensions of Peacemaking," *New England Journal of Public Policy* 33, no. 1 (2021): Article 7, https://scholarworks.umb.edu/nejpp/vol33/iss1/7/.

[2] Conciliators Guild, "Human Needs in Politics: The Charter," https://www.conciliators-guild.org/home-charter.

[3] Inna Bondarenko, "I Trained with Russian Diplomats. I Can Tell You How They Work," *Moscow Times*, April 14, 2025, https://www.themoscowtimes.com/2025/04/14/i-trained-with-russian-diplomats-i-can-tell-you-how-they-work-a88722.

[4] Steve Holland and Jeff Mason, "Obama, in Dig at Putin, Calls Russia 'Regional Power,'" *Reuters*, March 25, 2014, https://www.reuters.com/article/world/obama-in-dig-at-putin-calls-russia-regional-power-idUSBREA2O19J/.

[5] Henry Kissinger, *Leadership: Six Studies in World Strategy* (Penguin Random House UK, 2022), 249.

SUBNATIONAL DIPLOMACY AS 'POSITIVE FRAGMENTATION': OUR BEST HOPE FOR A PEACEFUL COLLAPSE OF THE NATION-STATE?

Alison R. Holmes
California State Polytechnic University, Humboldt

ABSTRACT

The current phase of globalization is one of fundamental erosion in the efficacy of the territorial nation-state and slow implosion of traditional sovereignty-based models of the state system. Combined with the breakdown of the rationalist-universalist 'consensus,' sub-state entities up and down the "vertical axis" of diplomacy are increasingly asserting mutually exclusive concepts of power and self-determination that could lead to a potential fragmentation of the basic structures of governance. Linear theories of state development and traditional definitions of sovereignty, with its consequent forms of recognition, urgently need to be revised or the likelihood of a continued disruption of international collaboration, more isolationist or secessionist activism, and even conflict will inevitably rise. Using the state of California as an illustrative case, this is a call for a "positive fragmentation" of the current state-centric system, thus opening space for a truly "global" or "relational" order that is more equitable and provides for the participation of multiple types of entity.

*Dr. Alison R. Holmes is a Professor of politics and international studies at California State Polytechnic University, Humboldt, where she chaired the International Studies program from 2011 to 2023, and Associate Editor of csu***global***. She is a member of the Yurok Tribal Bar and a consultant to the Karuk Tribe's Education Department. She worked for the UK Liberal Democrats as the national general election campaign manager in 1992 and 1997 and as a consultant in 2010, and has been Director of Strategic Communication for Burson-Marsteller, Deputy Head of Strategic Communication for the BBC, Managing Director of BritishAmerican Business Inc., and speechwriter and communications advisor to the US ambassador in London.*

> *California excites interest, envy, and longing throughout the world. It is a beacon for innumerable refugees, immigrants, and tourists from all quarters of the globe, seeking freedom, excitement, or improved economic opportunities. California is often compared to a lodestone, or a magnet, or the moon drawing tides. On occasion California is fancifully described as an enchantress - Circe, or one of the Sirens or the Lorelei…In the minds of some explorers, those island myths became fixed ideas. Out of them grew the obsession that California was an island. This notion persisted on and off for two centuries following California's discovery…California remains symbolically an enchanted isle.*[1]

—Dora Beale Polk, *The Island of California: A History of the Myth*

There are three reasons the myth of California and its 'island-ness' is a useful starting point for a discussion of what can be understood as both a reckoning for the modern nation-state and a paradigm shift toward a more holistic shape in the international system for what is now a global and relational world.

The first reason for 'why California' is one of timing in that the state's mythical origins also mark the beginning of a series of centennial milestones in the evolution of the international system. Dora Polk starts in the mid-1500s and offers an in-depth analysis of the facts around the fantasy of California from the earliest representations of the continent's western coast to stories of piracy and theft in an age of exploration and exploitation.[2] This buccaneering tale centers around Spanish power and the imagined Amazonian Queen Califia (from whence California's name) and the ways in which her presumed pearls haunted mapmakers and treasure-seeking sailors alike, even beyond the treaties of Westphalia more than one hundred years later.

In 1648, these three treaties were negotiated between the main European powers and brought an end to the Thirty Years' War and the Eighty Years' War. They also laid the foundation for a concept of sovereignty based on territory and, by codifying and privileging a specific set of rules for engagement, effectively enabled the domination of the 'New World' by the European powers.[3] Another century later in 1758, Emer de Vattel further consolidated the legal case for a system of formally equal sovereigns, by then more recognizable as 'states,' and asserting the idea that these actors should be the primary (if not the sole) actors in the international arena. This, in turn, arguably set the stage for the 'age of revolution' in the late 1700s that shifted power away from the crown and toward a new kind of citizen-based economic state-building. By the late 1800s, massive innovations in technology uprooted the term "global" from its French origins as something round or spherical, to become an expression of an awareness of the world in its entirety. This meaning morphed again at the end of the 1900s when the globalization debate, as we understand it today, began in earnest.

Each of these steps in the evolution in the system of states also had implications for California. European contact forced Indigenous peoples away from their 'spaces of meaning' and links to their environment, and into Western economic notions of 'place and property' within the US as California gradually became the digitized technology hub of the world it is today. As James Gregory points out, California operates "more on the plain of myth than fact" and that to understand California it may be necessary to first embrace that mythology.[4] It may also require the idea that, as Polk says, "myths are ultimately indestructible. Their spore lies dormant in the subsoil of the culture, awaiting only the proper combination of factors…[but]…As long as there are people to project on California all their dreams and expectations…there can be no ending of this story of California as an enchanted isle."[5] California's origins thus become useful here as a microcosm of the larger mythological pantheon that supports the current international system now in decline.

The second reason California is important here is more practical and refers to the idea of what is called here the "vertical axis of diplomacy." The state of California has recently become the fourth largest economy in the world, yet it remains enmeshed within a complex network of actors and entities, many with their own massive forms of political, economic, and cultural power. The most obvious is the fact that while California is a powerhouse in its own right, it is one state among many, constrained by the structure and Constitution of the United States. Unlike other entities in the world, California has not, to date, been secessionist, but remains a solid pillar of the national economy as well as an active leader of cultural and political change in American society. Less often recognized are the layers within the state that now seek more international influence.

The first among these would be major cities such as Los Angeles, San Francisco, and San Diego. Often identified as 'global cities,' the think tank Carnegie California has recently added six more, namely, Anaheim, Fresno, Long Beach, Oakland, Sacramento, and San José.⁶ Across these cities, there are plentiful examples of policy initiatives that take them deep into the international arena. From the creation of the Deputy Mayor of International Affairs for Los Angeles, one of the first in the country, to San Diego's negotiation of a free trade zone with Mexico, these places are increasingly taking the lead on issues they see as vital to their success. Other issues are also championed as a reaction to, or because of perceived inaction at the 'next level' of governance. Regardless of policy specifics and as then Deputy Mayor Hachigian points out, these cities make a strong case that they are 'closer' to the people affected and have more capacity to make change quickly.⁷ Further, and given the political reality that California mayors often seek higher state or national political office, these cities become proving grounds of political acumen and a would-be candidate's ability to assert their agenda. Yet California's cities are far from alone as cities and their mayors around the world have begun to demand more access to global platforms such as the European Union or the United Nations. Arguably in response, or at least in line with this trend toward urban or sub-state activism, the state of California has both led and mirrored the kinds of work taking place elsewhere by increasing its own efforts on issues that overlap or spill over any number of state, national, and international boundaries. This has included the building up of international infrastructure, a more overt global role for the Lieutenant Governor, as well as maintaining a more proactive international profile for the Governor.

However, mayors and cities are not the only entities operating along the vertical axis within and beyond the state. Counties in California and across the United States are also increasing their international capacity while major ports are beginning to look further afield not only for best practice but to improve both their defensive and offensive positions on specific issues. Another distinct group along this axis, but regularly overlooked even by the state, are the tribal Nations of California. For these groups, the forces of globalization have enabled more awareness of common issues and these "domestic dependent nations"⁸ are now seeking recognition if not redress and reparations from international bodies as well as the enforcement of global norms from their local and state entities.

There is a final group in California politics that may be outliers on the vertical axis now, but that cannot be ignored when considering subnational politics and prospects for conflict. This group has three distinct strands. The first includes people who, for some time, have argued for the creation of the 'State of Jefferson,' formed from rural areas currently in northern California and southern Oregon. Small membership groups pepper the area with flags and organize events supporting an independent state on the grounds they have been ignored by their respective urban, cosmopolitan capitals and starved of basic resources and development.[9] A second strand takes a broader approach, lobbying state government and promoting petitions calling for the breakup of California into what they view as more manageable pieces based on various metrics for economic sustainability.[10] The third group proposes secession for the state as a whole, with calls from Louis Marinelli for what he calls a "sovereign California" and arguing that his movement is not an "1860s breakaway," but a desire to ensure the state is "recognized as a nation within a nation, like Scotland in the United Kingdom."[11] More recently, and in light of a second Trump presidency, this secessionist strand may be gathering fellow travelers as sections on the left argue that the current Administration is dangerous to the vision of the state. Some believe that California is strong enough to go it alone and that it would be both more progressive and safer if it broke away. As of January 2025, a new petition has been put forward by Marcus Ruiz Evans that would require a vote on secession.[12] Clearly, despite differences in ideology, identity politics and demands for recognition by non-state or sub-state actors continues to rise on the agenda. In this space and place, the fault lines up and down California's vertical axis are sure to become more visible perhaps even to the point of conflict.

The third reason to start with California is a basic change in how we talk about the international or global space. It has become commonplace to talk about theories and institutions of governance as being 'post-' in some aspect or another, but if this is a period of massive systemic change, surely there is an urgent need to identify the features that define this phase rather than merely pointing out they are chronologically 'after' some previous stage. For California, issues such as migration and climate change have distinct sub-state implications and manifestations at the local, regional and national, and even inter- and trans-national levels. They are more accurately defined as "global" because they are so interrelated that the levels within the issue cannot be disconnected from each other. These issues are not isolated examples as more and more areas now require an understanding that to be "global" is not simply about state power and cannot be implemented only through recognition. To be global is now a feature of modern politics. States (and all entities) must recognize not only the global nature of today's problems, but also the impact of "globality" on their own status and capacity in the international arena. In short, any entity that would seek to change its fortunes must first learn how to operate on all levels simultaneously. As Kishan Rana points out, "'globality' is not anyone's property or monopoly. It is the objective fact of interdependence that lies at the root of this globalized world, and the choice of staying away altogether from external connections simply does not exist."[13]

There is, however, a crucial caveat to be made about the difference between what it now means to be global versus what it has meant to be universal in the past. Indeed, one could suggest that our growing sense and awareness of 'being global' has made possible a more critical view of the familiar or traditional understandings of the 'universal.' The line of reasoning is that, along with territorial identity, older ideas of the universal have been tainted with a false 'equality' and a 'same-ness' of peoples that tends to cast cultures to the side. Presumptions of universality effectively fail to reflect the lived reality of countries, or more relevant here, the nations now contained in most nation-states. Unfortunately, this Western idea of universality is also embedded in concepts such anarchy, hierarchy, and the linearity of time, as well as territory (discussed below) and so much a part of mainstream individualistic thinking that it is easy to forget their pervasive effects on policy proposals and options for implementation.

The processes of globalization have thus revealed and undermined the operating myths of the international state system. As the traditional models of state interaction continue to implode, entities up and down the vertical axis are asserting themselves in an effort to respond to this global 'turn,' or perhaps more accurately described as a global re-turn. California exemplifies this trend of sub-state entities seeking recognition and enough power to shape their destiny through an identity that is both connected to and separate from the rest of the world. The state of California is joined in this trend by entities both within and beyond its borders. Thus, California offers insight on the need for a theory of positive fragmentation and a more relational inter-entity system.

Myths, Assumptions, and Hypocrisy of Sovereignty

We joined the story of California in a 'pre-state' moment when its peoples were in a period of prehistory before written records and through its proto history as travelers began to write about and literally 'put California on the map.' However, the myth lingered long after the birth of more recognizable statehood and the traditional and current international state system formed in the wake of Westphalia. However, and much like California, the traditional international nation-state system is also premised on at least four myths or assumptions. These include anarchy, hierarchy, a linearity based on a specific way of seeing time, and a demarcation between domestic and foreign, all of which reflect and reinforce a fundamentally binary worldview. These myths have framed the current state models and privileged 'Western' ideas of statehood as well as the consequent definitions of recognition and identity. While these ideas have long been challenged, the entire system now appears to be in danger of collapse—due in no small measure to the collective impact of actors such as California.

The undisputed cornerstone of the international system is a specific form of sovereignty, a concept that has been adapted, merged, and expanded in multiple ways across time and culture. As Thomas Hansen and Finn Stepputat argue, interpretations of sovereignty range from the abstract idea of many "myths" to an "emergent form of authority grounded in violence that is performed and designed to generate loyalty, fear and legitimacy from the neighborhood to the summit of the state."[14] Jüri Lipping calls this a "vicious circle" in that the "territorial state…claims to be the bearer of sovereignty while sovereignty in turn is an essential attribute pertaining to the state."[15] Neil MacCormick identifies the same problem when he says, "Sometimes sovereignty is regarded as an attribute primarily of the state itself. A 'sovereign state' is one that is fully self-governing and independent of external control, and this condition is the sovereignty of the state."[16] Thus, he points out, sovereignty becomes the aggregate of the state's powers as well as a reference to the power-holder, be it king, president, dictator, or parliament. In light of this mercurial quality, it is hardly surprising that Hent Kalmo calls sovereignty a "liminal concept" that "inhabit[s] the frontier territories between law, ethics and political science."[17]

Despite or perhaps because of this conceptual soup, it is important to examine the ingredients of the system before being able to identify the factors that may precipitate its un-making. The most basic assumption of mainstream international relations is that the state, understood in a Vattel-ian sense as a territorially bounded entity that acts as an equal in a world of states, is the first, primary, and main actor in global affairs. Further, and more importantly for many traditional thinkers, this form of the state inevitably creates a system that is anarchic. In other words, states operate in an unregulated space where there is no higher power or authority. States strive to create place from space and answer only to themselves. As Stephen Bronner argues, the original underlying objective of sovereignty, at least in this territorial form, was to bring "stability" as expressed through a "balance of power, reciprocal recognition…[and] respect for international law."[18]

Closely linked here is the assumption that anarchy leads to hierarchy. In pursuit of the order and balance Bronner identifies, smaller or weaker states are willing to submit themselves to those with perceived power. Hierarchy becomes a logical consequence in a system that reifies military might and where entities are ranked on the basis of their hard power capacity and/or ability to coerce others, creating a world in which violence or the threat of violence underpins the entire system.

The third assumption is a linear development or progression in the development of the political entities that govern our societies. Our 'common sense' tells us that societies move through stages of less developed/advanced systems to higher or more 'civilized' forms of organization and governance. As a result, this highly Westernized idea of 'band-tribe-chiefdom-state model of social complexity'[19] has pervaded our understanding of identity, recognition, and statehood with entities 'lower' on this scale being deemed unworthy of a voice on the stage of states. There is a presumption that 'too many' (a number entirely unspecified) entities would endanger the system's order and balance. As these are seen as core needs to the system, smaller nations and nation-like entities have regularly been frozen out of the world of recognition.

Interestingly, these notions of linear development also require a very specific sense of time. Both Carol Greenhouse and Mary Dudziak argue that asserting a linearity to time (rather than what they call "cyclical" or "social time" based on seasons, harvest, and the essential relations between a people and a specific place) has allowed time to control both the purpose and direction of individual lives within entities, as well as the overall direction of the modern nation-state.[20] Staying with concepts of time, and not unlike the vertical axis, Stewart Brand worked with Brian Eno to lay out what he called "pace layering," identifying the different speeds at which the various parts of a system are able to adapt, change, and absorb shock, a feature he considered essential to a system's survival. Their diagram has six layers including nature, culture, governance, infrastructure, commerce, and fashion and recognizes that while our attention is focused on the fast, it is often the slow that has more power.[21] Crucially, and with Dudziak and Greenhouse, these authors also argue that time has been organized and periodized by the state in support of a narrative reliance on hierarchy and power.

The fourth myth is that there is a clear distinction between the domestic and the foreign. This binary identification has created an 'us' and a 'them'; a 'People' and an 'Other' and crucially, by granting the state the power to define fundamental belonging, it is able to assert control from a distance. The creation of a delineated place with a clear inside group inevitably leaves any individual, group, or political entity beyond that territory as estranged, and outsiders become a danger to internal peace and order. Moreover, this assumption, like all the core assumptions of the traditional nation-state, are designed to serve and reinforce the state's supremacy and block the route to recognition of other entities who may seek a role in the international system.

From the late 1990s, globalization has been identified by Anthony Giddens, David Held, and others as the compression of time, space, and distance, creating a force that has undermined the foundational assumptions of the traditional nation-state.[22] Meanwhile, the speed of technology and the shock of "global" events, used here in a more total sense, such as COVID-19, have disrupted the system, compressed the pace layers, and forced basic change on states and sub-state actors alike. The answer to the question at the heart of the late 1990s debate of whether globalization was forcing homogenization or fragmentation seems to be 'both at the same time.' As different layers of the system have been conflated while change is taking place at different rates, the layers have become more linked and intertwined. This "globality" presents both the possibility and the need to create a three-dimensional concept to better understand nation-state dynamics. All states may exist in a condition of anarchy, but even if they share that perception of reality, some are organized by a strict hierarchy while others are governed via heterarchy or connected networks, some operate on strictly linear time while others have a keen sense of cycles and movement. For some, boundaries are proxies for power, order, and control while others look to a kind of collective center for a sense of belonging and identity. Actors up and down the vertical axis are bisected and intersected by their understanding and acceptance of these assumptions in a world that has, to date, conflated sovereignty with recognition and asserted a universality of culture and identity. Multiple actors now take issue, sometimes violently, with those enforced ideas. We turn now to the models built on these assumptions before exploring the opportunities and the dangers offered by an activist subnational-ism.

State Models: Rise, Decline, or Parallel?

If individual actors such as California operate along a vertical axis, there is a question as to what is along the horizontal axis or the models in which these actors function? Robert Cooper, a former British diplomat and official in the European Union, does not dismiss the idea of a linear pattern of state development, but complicates it by suggesting that their progression through different types of political and economic forms (resulting in different behaviors in the international arena) does not happen simultaneously. This seems an obvious suggestion, but the consequence, he believes, is that today's biggest challenge to international affairs is understanding that states must operate in a world where 'pre-modern' and 'post-modern' states share the same time, space, and place.[23] Building on Cooper, it is therefore helpful to examine both the evolution of the state and the models they have created.

International relations often reads as if it assumes history has brought the world to the modern nation-state in its current form and then stopped, forgetting that the process continues. Cooper reminds us that both actors and the systems of operation evolve while engaging with each other in real time. In effect, they co-create each other, thus the modern nation-state is not an end-state, but as suggested by Stephen Krasner, a "staging post." Further, and unlike many international relations theorists, it is assumed here that the 'European/Westphalian' system did not entirely overwhelm, let alone destroy, alternative entities or systems but that they developed in parallel and along connected tangents. There was, of course, a significant influence by the more 'Western' ideas, but core features of other systems remain vital in the search for a model that may be better able to accommodate and respond to this moment. A 'system of fragments' may be necessary as we come to the end of the Westphalian era.

Bilateral to Transatlantic Model

Within the European/Westphalian or Vattel-ian states system there are arguably two main models. The first we will call 'Bilateral' or 'Transatlantic' as it remains firmly organized around the assumptions laid out above. As one might assume, Bilateral is the most classic form of state engagement. Actors tend to be clearly defined and long recognized. Not only do they negotiate freely with other individual states, but they take an active role in multi-lateral alliances and organizations. They are territorially settled and have a full set of policies focused on their individual and separate national interest(s).

The Transatlantic model is also based on the primacy of state action, but it creates a different kind of relationship between actors as these states are usually democratic, more advanced economically, and certainly enmeshed politically and culturally while still remaining separate. This second, 'evolved' form of the Bilateral model is perhaps best illustrated by, and thus named for, a classic 'special relationship.' The United Kingdom and the United States are two separate, but intimately and mutually involved states acting in their own interests while also regularly acting in concert at the transatlantic and even global level. One could suggest that this quality of 'specialness' is based only on some sentimental sense of shared history or language. However, and while these factors are important in this specific dyad, enough 'pairs' exist elsewhere to suggest that it is their common stage of state development that produces a shared approach to both domestic and global issues that is pursued separately or in combination. Thus positioned, it is possible to expand the concept of 'specialness' to better understand not only UK/US relations, but a number of other non-European, bilateral relations. These might include Canada and the United States,[24] Ireland and the United States, Canada and Australia, or the United Kingdom and Australia. From this wider list, again it could be countered that these relationships are still not special but merely by-products of a regional hegemon or former colonial power. However, that assessment would leave out other pairs such as Cuba and Brazil or countries recently free of the shadow of Soviet Russia where claims to 'specialness' are possible on the basis of region, specific issues, or personal and ideological links.

Community Model

There is a second 'post-Westphalian' model that is even more formally embedded and networked. Called 'Community' here, this model includes advanced, democratic states seeking to 'share' their power in essential ways. Rather than the more rigid traditional ideas of power and coercion, so-called Community states have created a vision of sovereignty that recognizes, but is not hindered by, their cultural and political separateness.

The European Union has agreed to a set of shared norms, values, and behaviors that might be found in any 'society' of states. However, the EU has gone much further by linking key aspects of state agency to build a structure based on the 'pooling' of sovereignty. Not only do they share economic or political ideas and ideals, they have an expectation of joint, or at least agreed, action in all areas of statecraft—including the military which remains at the core of any sovereign identity. Thus, the Community model represents a form of interpenetrating states overcoming divisions to create a union that is both wide and deep, forging habits of consensus and cooperation, but at the same time retaining clear lines of separation. Each state of the union has both a domestic and an inner-national sphere that is still distinct from their own separate inter-national relations with the world beyond Europe or the relations of the EU as an institution to the world.

Relational Model

While the Bilateral or Transatlantic and Community models have become and remain dominant since the Westphalian 'settlement,' the history of India and China and much of Southeast Asia as well as some parts of Central and South America suggests the possibility of another option. While overlooked or at least not generally seen as part of 'mainstream' or at least 'Eurocentric' international relations, this model, called here 'Relational,' is proposed as a more 'realistic realism' in that it recognizes power but does so in a specific place and context. A Relational state is one that remains aware of the complicated connections between different sources of power and is able to prepare for, and defend against, multiple forms of encroachment. This model carries many of the traditional assumptions, but retains its own horizontal identity that has persisted and continued to evolve, albeit in the shadows of more dominant structures that have colonized (in a literal sense) most global governance institutions.

In contrast, this model is based on an idea of sovereignty where power is not delineated by territories and external borders but is based on centers of power and overlapping areas of influence with different forms of control.[25] Rather than using binary juxtapositions between anarchy and order, hierarchy and chaos, inside and outside, this model understands that hierarchy and heterarchy can coexist. The image is not a series of dyads and triads of bilateral or special relationships, or even a slightly more egalitarian structure of community. This model recognizes there are multiple hubs and spaces where states of different capacities interact. The more 'powerful' states may form a center (or centers) of influence, while other states can operate through spokes of a wheel that radiate out to the 'rim' or even participate in more than one 'wheel.' This is not a structure that commands power through coercion or threat of violence, but a complex system of communication, balance, and awareness of interrelated and layered interests.

Finally, and bringing these nation-state models back to the issue of rising sub-state activism, it seems clear that examples of the Relational model, arguably such as California, currently exist. This kind of behavior can be seen in certain nation-state relationships, and it certainly reflects many models of domestic politics that understand the importance of issue-by-issue partnerships, multiple and relative power bases, and networks of relations between people and place. Thus, it seems logical that, as nation-states have become more "porous" or what James Der Derian and Costas Constantinou call "perforated,"[26] their constituent nations, sub-state or subnational units, as well as non-state actors have begun to operate on a more international or global level, at least on issues that affect them directly. Globalization may have finally produced the fragmentation so feared in the late 1990s in as much as sub-state actions have effectively dissolved the core myths and assumptions of the traditional nation-state. The question will be, as the Bilateral, Transatlantic, and even the Community models implode, whether that process will produce conflict, or force a paradigm shift that allows space for a Relational and "global" system to evolve.

Subnational-ism as Critique

States have been relentlessly changed by the processes of globalization, but perhaps the most important question is not by how much but where to begin that story? Mainstream international relations literature often starts with the age of exploration and stories about (mainly) European powers forcing place on spaces (such as California) in a march toward statehood. However, by focusing on the unit of the nation-state rather than power dynamics, political entities, systems, and their relations, much has been lost. The horizontal axis of the governance of peoples across space and time began long before the treaties of Westphalia and one should expect more change along that axis into the future. As Rebecca Adler-Nissen points out, "states are not born into this world as fully developed states that then 'exist'; states are made in continuous relations with other states and non-state actors. The development, consolidation, weakening (or even disappearance) of states can only be understood in terms of continuous processes that play out in relation to other social processes."[27] Further, by starting 'inter-national history' at the point of the nation privileges the link between sovereignty and the power of recognition that is granted primarily to 'founding' participants and generally denied to assimilated entities and wishful latecomers. Stephen Krasner therefore suggests we must stop thinking of the Westphalian model (and here we mean the various forms discussed above) as "some ideal or historical reality,"[28] while Michael Keating argues that his goal is to "present the territorial state as historically contingent" while indicating that the process of integration is "at least potentially reversible."[29]

Where does that leave sub-state actors in the current reckoning and paradigm shift? By accepting the importance of social processes and the nature of relations involved in state creation and re-creation, the imposition of place has been eroded and vital space (re)opened for other sub-state and non-state actors. The increasingly porous and perforated nature of the international system is now encouraging (or driving) more and more actors to the global arena. Those without territory in a traditional sense as well as territories unable to assert their authority consistently within their territorial boundaries or abroad are all seeking a voice to deal with the global issues they face while the system itself is being changed by the entities that engage. Iver Neumann identifies this breakdown in representation as a "cascading of sites" in which traditional points of state contact are either disappearing or becoming less important while new sites are being created by other forms of social interaction.[30] More importantly, by taking seriously the assertion that sovereignty is a social construct, it is possible to understand it as an integral part of a cultural identity that is, according to Amanda Cobb, fundamental to "cultural continuance" in an "inter-sovereign relationship."[31] Actors may not have formal sovereign claims but they do have what Denis Baranger calls its "manifestations" and "marks" that are readily understood by their people.[32]

These deeper, relational definitions of sovereignty also fatally undermine the foundational concept of recognition, once considered the primary aspiration of any political entity seeking to navigate the international stage. This breaking of the link between sovereignty and recognition is particularly relevant not only for California but all sub-state entities as the focus shifts toward what is called inherent sovereignty, more commonly identified with Indigenous studies. This idea is laid out by Kirke Kickingbird et al. who say "Sovereignty is a difficult word to define because it is intangible, it cannot be seen or touched…What can be seen…is the *exercise* of sovereign powers…Sovereignty is inherent; it comes from within a people or culture. It cannot be given to one group by another."[33]

Motivations and Types of Subnational Activity

Brian Hocking identifies this growing sub-state space as a new "frontier" where domestic and foreign policy have become a "seamless web" and where, once an entity has established their "actor-ness," they can make claims to jurisdiction and authority. In what he calls "frontierland," Hocking concludes that "the local is not the antithesis of the global" but rather there is a relatively unexamined and less understood "global-local dialectic."[34]

This dialectic space is important for the study of sub-state and subnational activity and while, as Francisco Aldecoa and Michael Keating point out, paradiplomacy and the activities of subnationals are not new, the increasingly rapid erosion of the boundaries between foreign and domestic presents a pressing need to broaden the scope of the actors studied and the sites involved.[35] They suggest these kinds of interactions will be a "crucial factor" in our understanding of the problems related to the ongoing "processes of centralization/decentralization"[36] that is globalization.

Interestingly, though probably not surprising given the state-centric nature of the field, much of the early work on paradiplomacy focused on secessionist states and regularly presented these entities as endangering the peaceable order of the state system. Later, as an increasing number of entities took a more collaborative approach to their central government, a differentiation between entities seeking to break away and those simply seeking to operate globally became more apparent. As result, a distinction particularly relevant to the state of California as a firmly sub-state or subnational actor, the term "protodiplomacy" came to imply a narrower, secessionist motivation,[37] while "paradiplomacy" covered a broader and quickly growing group.

For the wider sub-state or subnational actors, Panayotis Soldatos identified four broad patterns of engagement between a state and its sub-state entities. The first he calls cooperative-coordinated to indicate that the subnational and the national are able to coordinate and cooperate in areas where the subnational seeks international action. The second is cooperative-joint behavior and includes the formal or informal inclusion of regions or subnationals in the creation and implementation of national policy. The third is parallel-harmony for situations in which the subnational acts on its own, but remains largely in harmony with the overarching government. The fourth pattern is parallel-disharmony, where the subnational is actively pursuing its own goals, regardless of whether it is out of sync or in outright opposition to the federal or national structure.[38]

Ivo Duchacek and others focused more on the efforts of the subnational entities themselves as their efforts crossed international borders. These authors came up with three different, though broadly similar, types. The first is cross-border regionalism, commonly found between adjacent regions who come together on shared interests and issues. The second is transregional paradiplomacy, where non-central and not geographically neighboring governments come together but still on specific issues of concern or promotion (e.g., Quebec and Louisiana). The third is what they call global paradiplomacy and presents the biggest 'reach' for non-central governments in that they engage with both non-central and central governments in other countries.[39]

Taken together, the conclusion being drawn here is that sub-state or subnational activism is a 'local' answer to 'global' issues. In their practice of sovereignty and their relations with others at their own 'level' and at levels across the international system, they form and an increasingly sharp critique of the governance of traditional state systems. Collectively, they are an existential challenge to the current paradigm of the territorial nation-state. Thus, it becomes possible and necessary to talk about sovereignties plural, in the context of time and of location.

Sub-States and Subnationals in Action

It may be helpful here to briefly discuss two specific examples of state and sub-state actors and their approach to their own international activities. The first example, where this discussion began, is California, a powerful player in the Bilateral or Transatlantic model. The second is the United Kingdom and its sub-state entities of Scotland and Wales, engaged as a Bilateral, Transatlantic and, until recently, a Community state.

As mentioned above there are several distinct strands of thought about California's international role and profile. Many people would immediately think of Governor Jerry Brown, a global activist on climate change (terms: 1975–1983, 2011–2019), as embodying this idea. However, California governors have used the language of the state and specifically the nation-state for the last thirty years. Governor Gray Davis (term: 1999–2003) was the first to assert the idea as fact when he welcomed Mexican President Ernesto Zedillo in 1999,[40] but that was already nearly a decade after James Strock, California's founding Secretary of the California Environmental Protection Agency under Governor Pete Wilson (term: 1991–1999) observed that "California is, in many respects, best understood as a nation-state."[41] However, it was Governor Arnold Schwarzenegger (term: 2003–2011) who argued that California not only had the power but almost a duty to provide leadership to the country and the world on climate change if not a host of other issues. During his tenure the rhetoric of nation-state status became a regular feature of speeches and the basis of his entire approach to the international arena as evidenced in the places, platforms, and venues in which he chose to assert California's policy objectives.[42]

As mentioned, many would have assumed that Governor Brown was a nation-state champion, but interestingly and perhaps by way of evidence of the local/global dialectic, he argued that his focus was not on the world per se and that his activism was not born of a global sensibility or a desire for nation-state status but on what he called a "laser focus" on the state, its interests, and its people.[43] Yet given the rise of sub-state activism around the world and particularly in California in recent years, it is only logical that it is Governor Gavin Newsom who has built the strongest policy platform around California as nation-state. Some of his initial steps as governor included the creation of an international committee led by his Lieutenant Governor and an international 'fact-finding' trip to El Salvador in his first one hundred days to explore the issues around immigration. He ultimately found that, as governor, his ability to deal with the factors driving immigrants to the California border was limited, but the die was cast in terms of his global positioning. He has continued in that vein throughout his tenure, making trips, negotiating, and dealing with other sub-state entities as well as national governments around the world. The global disruption of COVID-19 offered him ample opportunity to demonstrate both his nation-state power and his political prowess,[44] while more recently, he has flexed his international connections by declaring peace in President Donald Trump's trade war and calling on other countries to exempt California from their retaliatory measures.[45] It remains to be seen if his actions, both local and global, will be enough to move him to the national level.

The sub-state or subnational challenge may be even more obvious and more complicated in the case of the United Kingdom. As suggested above, the UK is a Bilateral and Transatlantic state but it has also been, until recently, a Community state. The UK's leadership of an empire, the Commonwealth, and within the European Union has shaped their understanding of their sub-state entities as well as their relationship with the world. Perhaps it was their unique love/hate relationship with the European Union that encouraged and allowed both Scotland and Wales the space to further develop their national identities, but their different paths are very much two stories of intensely local context. Scotland clearly fits into the protodiplomacy or secessionist motivation and their efforts to leave the UK have been as checkered as they have been persistent. The European Union adds another dimension to this ongoing struggle offering, as Fintan O'Toole points out, a "buffer from London" and "an international body in which they could advocate for their own interests and remain connected to bigger powers without being dominated by them."⁴⁶ Wales, on the other hand, retains a passionate sense of national identity but has not overtly sought a split with the rest of the UK. As John Loughlin writes, "Wales in Europe" also conveys the meaning that Wales might be present in Europe in a way that is different from being simply a "region" of the UK. He also wonders if Wales, as a "stateless nation," would have a higher profile on the European scene.⁴⁷

The differing levels of devolution between these two nations arguably speaks to the ability of the UK as a whole to address and possibly de-escalate pressures created by sub-state entities. A point of particular interest and a skill perhaps in evidence as the new Labour Prime Minister, Keir Starmer made it a highlight of his first days in government to visit not only the devolved nations but the UK's major cities.⁴⁸ One can speculate whether this was, at least in part, driven by a recognition of the rising tide of sub-state actors and a need for change to the national system of governance if the state as a whole is to overcome the dangers of fragmentation—a concern understood all too well by Northern Ireland, a partially devolved entity precariously sitting atop another country at the edge of a less than united kingdom in these post-Brexit times.

The shock of Brexit on the UK also rippled across the other states of the Community model and may even have created an awareness of a need for change lest they suffer the damage and dangers of continuing fragmentation. As recently as April 2024 President Emmanuel Macron of France made a dramatic speech, not only claiming a more pronounced role for his country in a Europe without the UK, but also outlining what he called the European neighborhood and a need for a "more united, more sovereign and more democratic Europe." He went on to express an urgent call for Europe to embrace its power both as separate states and as a collective, including its military might, but argued that the core, the real bedrock of Europe, "wasn't institutional" but in its "multiple geography."⁴⁹ In the frame being proposed here, his point suggests that state power is moving away from the top and shifting to the peoples and spaces that make up the Union.

Effects of the Models

There is every possibility that this breakdown of regional bodies and the erosion of the traditional assumptions of the sovereign nation-state, combined with a welling up of local power, and claims by sub and separate entities, will bring unrest and even conflict. Looking at the world today, the denial of recognition and the blurring of boundaries with claims and counterclaims are at the center of at least two wars and a number of other lower-level conflicts.

The question here is what would be required to allow for a more equitable model of entity interaction, a more representative system of governance and a new form of recognition that gives voice to more peoples but without creating disorder or chaos? The response to that question is that while the dangers of fragmentation are ever-present, existing features of the system also have the potential to create a "positive fragmentation" of the traditional nation-state model, and further, that the roots of this idea can already be found in both the United States (specifically California) and Europe.

David Vogel, as early as 1995 identified a counterintuitive trend as regulation (often environmental) created in California had the power to influence other entities, other states in the US, and even other countries. This finding ran counter to the expectation of what is often called the 'Delaware effect' or the idea that, given the opportunity, policy will flow to the lowest common denominator in what becomes literally a race to the bottom. Instead, Vogel found that, given the size of the economy, number of consumers, and perhaps a feeling of moral suasion, California was able to create new norms and to blaze what they felt was a more progressive agenda not only for the state but for other entities as well.[50]

In Europe, there was a similar fear that the widening (versus deepening) of the number of member states would open the possibility of lower standards. Again, this proved not to be the case. Anu Bradford, following Vogel's work, called this the 'Brussels Effect' after its American cousin and argued that two or three powerful anchor states could set the agenda not only for the region but for the world. Further, that smaller states and entities were effectively protected by this 'shell' as they could up-grade their own regulation safe in the knowledge they would not be undercut by their neighbors.[51] In the US, subnational change and in Europe supranational change could leverage their separate and collective power to support policy initiatives that were then re-created by fellow states, constituent nations, and beyond.

Taking the rise of subnational activism and the impact of separate and collective leadership together, there is a strong case for what is called here "positive fragmentation" as a basis for new norms and a collaborative relational community. This 'Effect' would be focused not only on regulation, but the importance of identity and space. Voluntary alliances and soft power could be the foundation for a peaceful transition from a globalization/globalist order to a multi-polar, postmodern world.

Conclusion

Michael Keating argues that the history of the state, writ large is often presented as "universal" and as the only narrative with a claim to legitimacy. He contrasts this with what he calls the "peripheral historiography" in which there is often a "myth of primordial innocence and primitive democracy before the alien intrusion of the modern states."[52] Thus, we return to the world of myths and universalist assumptions, to the frontiers and boundaries of sovereignty, the struggle between space and place, and ideas of the individual versus collective governance.

Georg Jellinek originated the phrase "fragments of state" in the nineteenth century to argue against what he believed was a growing tendency to see states as the only unit of value or importance.[53] Today, we find ourselves living in a world in which states and fragments of states are interacting on a daily basis. Globalization has created both fragmentation and homogenization among a vast range of entities through a process that has brought many worlds together while at the same time forcing single worlds apart. If we accept the idea that sovereignty is a social construct and historically contingent, we must also accept that the myths and assumptions of the territorial nation-state with its traditional claims to recognition have been irreparably broken. If the power of sovereignty is in its practice, what first appears as an anarchic system that inevitably creates strict hierarchies is, in fact, a heterarchy in which both hierarchies and heterarchies can coexist.[54] Horizontal and vertical connections can create social power networks that can be arranged and rearranged depending on the social context.[55] Finally, and evidenced by the rise of sub-state, subnational, and non-state activity, non-linear and asymmetrical structures can exist in which power can be ranked in a number of different ways or even "counterpoised" while still retaining what we would recognize as order.[56]

Underlying this entire discussion is the idea of what it now means to be "global." In a fascinating discussion, Jan Art Scholte explores Manuel Castell's "network society" where a "new 'space of flows' exists alongside the old 'space of places.'" He argues that today's world is both territorial and supraterritorial, or in the terms used here, sub-state and subnational as well as international and supranational, but that none of these have completely overwhelmed the others. His point, and a lesson we can take from subnational activity, is that relations are always located in a place or a domain, but "a social condition is not positive or negative because it is local or global, since the situation is generally both local and global at the same time. It is the particular blend of local and global that matters." His overarching conclusion is simply that "space matters."[57]

As quickly as international relations scholars such as Barry Buzan, Amitav Acharya, and Iver Neumann feverishly work to de-center the state and disentangle the system from its European/Westphalian roots;[58] cities, countries, tribes, nations, and others are pushing further into the international and global space. A paradigm shift is underway in what has been called "late modernity" and where, Henrik Bang argues, many of our certainties have come to an end. Hierarchy has been replaced by networks and there has been a general hollowing out of the state and an increase in the fluidity of identity.[59] John Gray calls this "the gap between late modern thought and emerging postmodern realities" in what has "become a culture of endings…amid the ruins of the projects of the modern age we are leaving."[60]

More hopefully, amid those ruins, there is an inherent form of sovereignty that is not granted by others and that does not require external recognition. There is a basis for legitimacy that allows for a form of identity located within the culture of a people and that retains a vital link between its power and its expression. Taking a longer timeline of governance can equally support the idea that the state's current form is only one of a huge range of choices. People have managed to create countless entities that have been born, decayed, or been destroyed for centuries. Keating concludes that we should begin to view the nation-state as an "exception or interlude rather than an end point" as we move toward a "postsovereign order" in which states must learn to share. So while the rise of sub-state and subnational entities may precipitate the end of the Westphalian model of sovereignty, it may also be the foundation of something new: a world that recognizes entities not because of their size or military power but because they respect identity and the connectedness of all peoples. California, as one sub-state actor among so many, is not in the vanguard of this change, but it is a significant actor and remains a leader at the 'intermestic' level. The size and diversity of this specific subnational entity puts it on the edge of the simultaneity of the local/global realm of world politics where, we hope, it will become a force for peace as we set course, not toward some mythical enchanted isle, but a form of positive fragmentation, rooted in the relations between peoples and their cultures of governance.

Notes

1. Dora Beale Polk, *The Island of California: A History of the Myth* (Arthur H. Clarke Co., 1991), 13–14.
2. Polk, *The Island of California*.
3. Costas M. Constantinou and James Der Derian, eds., *Sustainable Diplomacies* (Palgrave Macmillan, 2010).
4. James Gregory, "The Shaping of California History," in *The Encyclopedia of American Social History* (Scribners, 1993), https://faculty.washington.edu/gregoryj/California%20History.htm.
5. Polk, *The Island of California*, 332.
6. Wyatt Frank and Marissa Jordan, "California's Global Cities," Carnegie California, September 5, 2024, https://carnegieendowment.org/research/2024/09/californias-global-cities.
7. See, for example, Nina Hachigian, "Cities Will Determine the Future of Diplomacy," *Foreign Policy*, April 16, 2019, https://foreignpolicy.com/2019/04/16/cities-will-determine-the-future-of-diplomacy/.
8. Vine Deloria Jr. and Clifford M. Lytle, *The Nations Within: The Past and Future of American Indian Sovereignty* (University of Texas Press, 1998).
9. For background on the State of Jefferson see Rheegan King, "State of Jefferson: Rural California's Struggle for Representation," *Berkeley Political Review*, November 14, 2023, https://bpr.studentorg.berkeley.edu/2023/11/14/state-of-jefferson-rural-californias-struggle-for-representation/; Jonathan Vankin, "State of the State of Jefferson: How This Secessionist Movement Started and Where It Stands Today," *California Local*, March 24, 2023, https://californialocal.com/localnews/statewide/ca/article/show/31200-state-of-jefferson-california-north-counties-sisikiyou-oregon/.
10. For background on various plans to split California see "History of Proposals to Divide California," https://phrelin.com/3Cals/History.htm, accessed April 3, 2025; Christopher Cadelago, "'Risk Master' Tim Draper Soliciting Ideas for Next Ballot Proposal," *Sacramento Bee*, April 29, 2015, https://www.sacbee.com/news/politics-government/capitol-alert/article19881507.html.
11. Patt Morrison, "Meet the Man Who Wants to Make California a Sovereign Entity," *Los Angeles Times*, August 26, 2015, https://www.latimes.com/opinion/op-ed/la-oe-morrison-marinelli-20150826-column.html.
12. California Secretary of State, "Proposed Initiative Enters Circulation: Requires Future Vote on Whether California Should Become Independent Country. Initiative Statute," January 23, 2025, https://www.sos.ca.gov/administration/news-releases-and-advisories/2025-news-releases-and-advisories/Proposed-Initiative-Enters-Circulation-Requires-Future-Vote-on-Whether-California-Should-Become-Independent-Country.
13. Kishan S. Rana, *Inside Diplomacy* (Manas Publications, 2014), 440.
14. Thomas Blom Hansen and Finn Stepputat, "Sovereignty Revisited," *The Annual Review of Anthropology* 35 (2006): 16.3, https://doi.org/10.1146/annurev.anthro.35.081705.123317.
15. Jüri Lipping, "Sovereignty Beyond the State," in *Sovereignty in Fragments: The Past, Present and Future of a Contested Concept*, ed. Hent Kalmo and Quentin Skinner (Cambridge University Press, 2010), 153.
16. Neil MacCormick, "Sovereignty and After," in *Sovereignty in Fragments: The Past, Present and Future of a Contested Concept*, ed. Hent Kalmo and Quentin Skinner (Cambridge University Press, 2010).

17 Hent Kalmo, "Sovereignty in Pieces," in *Sovereignty in Fragments: The Past, Present and Future of a Contested Concept*, ed. Hent Kalmo and Quentin Skinner (Cambridge University Press, 2010), 114.

18 Stephen Eric Bronner, "Trump the Sovereign," *Jacobin Magazine*, November 2, 2017, https://www.jacobinmag.com/2017/11/trump-foreign-policy-un-sovereignty-america-first.

19 Carole L. Crumley, "Heterarchy and the Analysis of Complex Societies," *Archaeological Papers of the American Anthropological Association* 6, no. 1 (1995): 1–5, https://doi.org/10.1525/ap3a.1995.6.1.1.

20 Mary L. Dudziak, "Law, War, and the History of Time," *California Law Review* 98, no. 5 (2010): 1669–1709, https://www.jstor.org/stable/25799950; Carol J. Greenhouse, *A Moment's Notice: Time Politics Across Cultures* (Cornell University Press, 1996).

21 Stewart Brand, *The Clock of the Long Now: Time and Responsibility* (Basic Books, 1999).

22 nthony Giddens, *The Third Way* (Polity Press, 1998); David Held, *Political Theory and the Modern State* (Polity Press, 1989); Anthony McGrew, "Making Sense of Globalisation," in *The Globalisation of World Politics: Introduction to International Relations*, ed. John Baylis and Steve Smith (Oxford University Press, 1990).

23 Robert Cooper, *The Breaking of Nations: Order and Chaos in the Twenty-First Century* (Atlantic Books, 2003).

24 John Dumbrell and Axel Schafer, eds., *America's "Special Relationships": Foreign and Domestic Aspects of the Politics of Alliance* (Routledge, 2009).

25 Alison Holmes, ed., *Global Diplomacy: Theories, Types and Models* (Westview Press, 2016).

26 Constantinou and Der Derian, *Sustainable Diplomacy*.

27 Rebecca Adler-Nissen, "Conclusion: Relationalism or Why Diplomats Find International Relations Theory Strange," in *Diplomacy and the Making of World Politics*, ed. Ole Jacob Sending, Vincent Pouliot, and Iver B. Neumann (Cambridge University Press, 2015), 286.

28 Stephen D. Krasner, "Compromising Westphalia," *International Security* 20, no. 3 (1995/6): 115–51, https://doi.org/10.2307/2539141.

29 Michael Keating, *Plurinational Democracy: Stateless Nations in a Post-Sovereignty Era* (Oxford University Press, 2004), 30.

30 Iver B. Neumann, *Diplomatic Sites: A Critical Enquiry* (C. Hurst & Co. Ltd., 2013).

31 Amanda J. Cobb, "Understanding Tribal Sovereignty: Definitions, Conceptualizations, and Interpretations," *American Studies* 46, no. 3/4 (2005): 115–32, https://www.jstor.org/stable/40643893.

32 Denis Baranger, "The Apparition of Sovereignty," in *Sovereignty in Fragments: The Past, Present and Future of a Contested Concept*, ed. Hent Kalmo, and Quentin Skinner (Cambridge University Press, 2010).

33 Kirke Kickingbird, Lynn Kickingbird, Charles J. Chibitty, and Curtis Berkey, "Indian Sovereignty," in *Native American Sovereignty*, ed. John R. Wunder (Garland Publishing Inc, 1999), 1.

34 Brian Hocking, "Patrolling the 'Frontier': Globalization, Localization and the 'Actorness' of Non-Central Governments," in *Paradiplomacy in Action: The Foreign Relations of Subnational Governments*, ed. Francisco Aldecoa and Michael Keating (Frank Cass Publishers, 1999), 19–20.

35 Francisco Aldecoa and Michael Keating, eds., *Paradiplomacy in Action: The Foreign Relations of Subnational Governments*, (Frank Cass Publishers, 1999).

36 Alexander S. Kuznetsov, *Theory and Practice of Paradiplomacy: Subnational Governments in International Affairs* (Routledge, 2015), 4.

37 Rodrigo Tavares, *Paradiplomacy: Cities and States as Global Players* (Oxford University Press, 2016); Noé Cornago, "On the Normalization of Sub-State Diplomacy," *The Hague Journal of Diplomacy* 5, no. 1–2 (2010): 11–36, https://doi.org/10.1163/1871191x-05010102.

38 Kuznetsov, *Theory and Practice*.

39 Ivo D. Duchacek, Daniel Latouche, and Garth Stevenson, eds., *Perforated Sovereignties and International Relations: Trans-Sovereign Contacts of Subnational Governments* (Greenwood Press, 1988).

40 Dave Lesher, "Zedillo Begins Historic Tour of State," *Los Angeles Times*, May 18, 1999, https://www.latimes.com/archives/la-xpm-1999-may-18-mn-38328-story.html.

41 "James M. Strock: An Interview by Bob Morris," bobmorris.biz, September 8, 2011, https://bobmorris.biz/james-m-strock-an-interview-by-bob-morris.

42 Arnold Schwarzenegger, Second Inaugural Address, January 5, 2007, https://governors.library.ca.gov/addresses/38-schwarzenegger01.html.

43 Jerry Brown, interview with author, April 6, 2019.

44 Joe Garofoli, "Gavin Newsom Wants California to Be Its Own Nation-State in the Trump Era," *San Francisco Chronicle*, February 12, 2019, https://www.sfchronicle.com/politics/article/Gavin-Newsom-wants-California-to-be-its-own-13611747.php; Francis Wilkinson, "Gavin Newsom Declares California a 'Nation-State,'" *Bloomberg*, April 9, 2020, https://www.bloomberg.com/opinion/articles/2020-04-09/california-declares-independence-from-trump-s-coronavirus-plans.

45 "Governor Newsom Directs State to Pursue Strategic Relationships with International Trading Partners; Urges Exemptions of California-Made Products from Tariffs," April 4, 2025, https://www.gov.ca.gov/2025/04/04/governor-newsom-directs-state-to-pursue-strategic-relationships-with-international-trading-partners-urges-exemptions-of-california-made-products-from-tariffs/.

46 Fintan O'Toole, "Disunited Kingdom: Will Nationalism Break Britain?," *Foreign Affairs*, March/April 2023.

47 John Loughlin, "Wales in Europe: Welsh Regional Actors and European Integration," Papers in Planning Research, Department of City and Regional Planning, University of Wales, 1997.

48 Tom Scotson, "Keir Starmer Will Visit All Four Nations After Election Landslide," *PoliticsHome*, July 6, 2024, https://www.politicshome.com/news/article/keir-starmer-visit-four-nations-election-landslide.

49 Emmanuel Macron, "Europe Speech," April 24, 2024, https://www.elysee.fr/en/emmanuel-macron/2024/04/24/europe-speech.

50 David Vogel, *Trading Up: Consumer and Environmental Regulation in a Global Economy* (Harvard University Press, 1995).

51 Anu Bradford, *The Brussels Effect: How the European Union Rules the World* (Oxford University Press, 2020).

52 Keating, *Plurinational Democracy*, 32.

53 Keating, *Plurinational Democracy*, 21.

54 Crumley, "Heterarchy."

55 Chureekamol Onsuwan Eyre, "Social Variation and Dynamics in Metal Age and Protohistoric Central Thailand: A Regional Perspective," *Asian Perspectives* 49, no. 1 (2010): 43–84, at 47, https://www.jstor.org/stable/42928772.

56 Crumley, "Heterarchy"; Carole L. Crumley, "Pattern Recognition in Social Science," *Social Science Newsletter* 70, no. 3 (1985): 176–79.

57 Jan Art Scholte, "Globalization and the Rise of Super Territoriality," in *Mastering Globalization: New Sub-states' Governance and Strategies*, ed. Guy Lachapelle and Stéphane Paquin (Routledge, 2005), 20–30.

58 See Amitav Acharya, "Global International Relations and Regional Worlds," *International Studies Quarterly* 58 (2014): 647–59; Barry Buzan, "The Inaugural Kenneth N. Waltz Annual Lecture: A World Order Without Superpowers: Decentred Globalism," *International Relations* 25, no. 1 (2011): 3–25, https://doi.org/10.1177/0047117810396999; Iver B. Neumann, "Euro-centric Diplomacy: Challenging but Manageable," *European Journal of International Relations* 18, no. 2 (2012): 299–321, https://doi.org/10.1177/1354066110389831.

59 David Marsh, Paul 't Hart, and Karen Tindall, "Celebrity Politics: The Politics of the Late Modernity?," *Political Studies Review* 8, no. 3 (2010): 322–40, at 326, https://doi.org/10.1111/j.1478-9302.2010.00215.x.

60 John Gray, *Endgames: Questions in Late Modern Political Thought* (Polity Press, 1997), xi, 156.

POLITICAL AND PSYCHOLOGICAL EFFECTS OF POLITICAL PUBLIC ART IN CONFLICT ZONES

Leora Sotto
Art Psychotherapist

Caryl Sibbett
Art Psychotherapist, Kairos Consultancy

ABSTRACT

This article will explore the topic of conflict-related visual-political media displayed in public in Israel and Northern Ireland, such as posters, banners, and murals. We will discuss examples of such political public art, looking at graphic characteristics as well as several multi-faceted topics that tend to appear: first, the topic of victim / victimizer, art expressing feelings of aggression, blaming, injustice, or pain; second, cross-cultural similarities and differences in the art expression; third, art promoting peace. We will reflect on these from a psychotherapy perspective, noting themes of trauma and dis/empowerment. We will discuss visual art and war, their interaction, and their influence on society, the individual, and the collective, and question to what extent such art forms are helpful or not.

Leora Sotto is an art psychotherapist and senior accredited supervisor in Israel. She lectured at Seminar Hakibuzim College on the MA art therapist course. She is a peace activist working with the Palestinian-Jewish community regarding conflict and with other minorities, and is a member of Psychoactive - Mental Health Professionals for Human Rights.

Dr. Caryl Sibbett is an art psychotherapist, senior accredited supervisor, psychotherapist, trainer, and founder of Kairos Consultancy in Northern Ireland. She founded master's level art psychotherapy training in Northern Ireland at Queen's University Belfast, the Belfast Health and Social Care Trust, and Ulster University and led it as a Senior Lecturer until her retirement in 2019. She co-leads several post-qualifying psychotherapy courses. Her therapy practice has included working with people affected by conflict-related trauma and people imprisoned during the Troubles.

This article was developed from a presentation given at the annual conference of the Centre for the Resolution of Intractable Conflict at Harris Manchester College, University of Oxford, in September 2024.

This article will try to shine a light on the topics of visual art, war, psychotherapy, and how they interact and the influence they have on society, the individual, and the collective. It was originally presented at the Conference on the Resolution of Intractable Conflict (CRIC) in 2024 in the University of Oxford. The goddess Minerva was chosen by CRIC as a symbol of the conference. She was the Roman goddess of war, but also of wisdom, art, justice, and commerce. Regarding bringing *wisdom* to bear on the problem of war—we will do our best. But, we will also explore *art*, and how art and *war* influence each other, noting also how *injustice* can evoke the expression of both art and conflict.

We will try to demonstrate a sample of the conflict-related visual-political media displayed in Israel and Northern Ireland—posters, banners, and murals—the visual (art and the written word) rather than what is spoken. This is to question: To what extent do they release political tensions, or do they create the opposite? Do they create awareness, positive changes, and peace in the world, or do they create more hostility and upheaval? Do they have any impact?

We will reflect on this from our perspective and experience and from literature showing what influence this media has on the public and why societies create it. The authors have personal and professional experience of living and practicing in conflict zones and have been exposed to the posters and murals in real life, one author in Israel and one in Northern Ireland.

Art psychotherapists think from a psychological point of view, but they also work with the visual, the non-verbal, which is a more primal language than the verbal.[1] In the origins of our species, we made art on cave walls, in order to create an inner dialogue, to process our needs, and to communicate with others.

In relation to psychotherapy, we will also draw some similarities between how the psyche operates at individual and large group levels.[2] Often people see themselves as individuals yet they can underestimate the influence of their norms and culture that shape them.[3] Understanding the subjectivity of a person or a large group includes understanding the core needs, values and beliefs, and 'sacred values' of the identity and culture of the client or society.[4]

This article will focus only on graphic political public media in conflict zones, rather than on wider issues. We will not be focusing on political art in galleries, on costumes, or on flags, badges, etc. It will investigate a number of needs and influences, whether conscious or unconscious, that the individual and the group have, and which are reflected in the posters, banners, and murals that we will depict. When a country experiences conflict within or with other countries, multi-faceted topics tend to emerge in the political public art, such as victim / victimizer, aggression, blaming, and making peace. We will also demonstrate how such art is expressed similarly or differently in each country because of different cultures and narratives.

Victim / Victimizer

From a psychological perspective, psychotherapy attempts to give a voice to and clarify a person's position of being a victim and/or a victimizer, meaning a subjective and/or objective state. These states relate to being threatened/ing, harmed/ing, blamed/ing, accused/ing, invaded/ing, disadvantaged/ing, and other positions. The positions of victim or victimizer as a mental or physical state may be experienced as an individual and collectively as a country, society, or nation.

When working with a client, as well as communicating empathy for whichever position, victim or victimizer, that the client feels they are in, at times it is important to help them explore other more constructive, beneficial positions that they can adopt, such as assertive rather than aggressive.

In transactional analysis theory, the 'drama triangle' proposed by Stephen Karpman is a model of social interaction depicting how a person can experience positions of feeling that they are a victim, persecutor, or rescuer.[5] Karpman proposes that any of these positions is problematic and a person can be in more than one position. It is a disempowering, complex interaction that can also occur among people embroiled in conflict. The 'empowerment dynamic' was proposed by David Emerald as a constructive alternative to drama triangle dynamics, and it offers the more positive roles of creator (rather than victim), challenger (rather than persecutor), and coach (rather than rescuer).[6]

Israeli Jews in Israel often see themselves as victims as a collective group and country, being surrounded by enemies (Lebanon, Syria, Jordan, Egypt, Gaza, and the West Bank) and having lost many soldiers and civilians over the years. Jews in Israel justify that the land belongs to them by citing historical facts, that it is the only country that the Jews have, and that it is a very small country. Yet some say they feel they are "the chosen" (taken from the Bible) or "have the best army in the world," which is a superior position, but not necessarily victim or victimizer. There is a small number of Israeli Jews who would say they, as a group, are the victimizer, but they are a very small parentage of the population. When one feels one is a victimizer, one should feel guilt and shame, which is a positive reaction that expresses empathy.[7]

A person may feel they are a victim, or they may be recognized as a 'victim and survivor' by official organizations or country states, for example as outlined in The Victims and Survivors (Northern Ireland) Order 2006.[8] Or they may be recognized as a victimizer by a country state. In a war or conflict situation, people are faced with an ongoing trauma. This situation of power relations often creates feelings of being a victim or victimizer. Psychologically a person can be in both roles simultaneously.[9] It is not always clear when we are in one or the other role, and they can overlap. The position of a victim or victimizer can be subjective. A person or country can see itself as one of these positions, while the other person or country may see them as the other. Research indicates that there can be a symbiotic relationship between the two positions.[10] In both cases, whether they overlap or not, it is unhealthy to be in either position.

Any of these can result from and create physical and/or psychological trauma. Trauma has been categorized using many different terms, e.g., trauma, post-traumatic stress disorder (PTSD), complex PTSD, collective trauma, secondary trauma, re-traumatization, and trans-generational trauma. In psychotherapy when working with people affected by trauma, it is vital that the practice is trauma-informed, which means it promotes mutuality and constructive empowerment.[11]

Figure 1 shows some examples of Israeli public graphic art relating to the topic of victim / victimizer. The images are of blaming, directly and indirectly.

Figure 1. Photographs of Israeli public graphic art relating to blaming. The center and right billboards read "You are the head. You are to be blamed" in Hebrew. These three are displayed in 20–30 different towns in Israel (2024–2025).

Figure 1 shows how, during 2023–2025, citizens in Israel bought advertising spaces on billboards all over the country and put up enormous banners of Prime Minister Benjamin

Netanyahu. They are mass groups of private people who feel he is a danger to the survival of Israel. Most Israelis are less concerned about what has been happening in Gaza to the Palestinians, especially since October 7, 2023. Rather, they are concerned with matters such as Israel's stability and democracy that they feel is at stake, the return of hostages, and the safety of Israeli citizens and soldiers—all in regard to conflict or war with Palestinians or other Arab nations. The groups of people behind the initiative to put up these banners feel that the political decisions made by the prime minister will harm Israel, that Israel will not be safe as a democracy, extremists will take over, and fighting the enemy will not be done effectively. The posters are designed to show him in a very bad light, and are an example of expressing feelings in order to tarnish and blame a political figure. Only half of his face is shown or it is partly covered, which psychologically we understand is an aggressive position graphically. The posters use colors—red, black, white—that can be identified with primal states such as aggression and fear, and what's written also boldly blames him: "you are the head, you are to be blamed." The font used is bold with sharp edges.

Like any language, the graphic language in each culture has created a vocabulary of shapes, lines, and colors that express different feelings and thoughts. This evokes a response in the viewer, whether they are conscious of it or not. Whether it is the color of a wall in a hospital, a banner wishing to show aggression, or a sweet soft toy for sale, the color, shape, and wording is deliberate. The world of advertising uses this with the intent to influence.[12] There are examples from different countries, e.g., the Nazi flag using red, black, and white, or a poster of Che Guevara mainly using red, black, and white.

We question what impact such banners have on individuals or on society.

Does it help in any way to change a leader's decisions, or will it create the opposite effect? In other words, if a banner is trying to say something, can it create change on political decisions, is it a 'conversation,' or is it just an expression?

Again questions to consider include the following: What function do these visual expressions serve, what effect do they have, and on who? Do such examples of banners and murals create resolution or further opposition, do they evoke feelings of anger or reconciliation, in one or other side of society? Does it create an active act of violence or conflict between people, or unite them? Does it clarify the situation? Does it create a more extreme division between people, or does it reinforce a sense of connectedness and mutual understanding within one's community?

We consulted an Israeli senior graphic designer who is the head of a large graphic design office and was the head of a school of graphic design in Israel.[13] We asked him whether the posters of Benjamin Netanyahu help or damage, convince, or clarify anything to the viewer. Did he think it would help Israel in the long run, or not? Do posters against a leader have an effect on him, or not?

The graphic designer's answer was, "to begin with it is very difficult to know what will influence what. There have been times when a certain slogan\image seemed to have generated a movement, but often it is very unclear."[14] Maybe even more fascinating to us was that he said, "People have the need to create, to express themselves, and that in itself is very important. Yes, a poster or mural or banner can be damaging in that it creates anger or tension, but not expressing oneself as a private person or as a group might be even more damaging because people have the need to express themselves and release emotion." We found it fascinating because this is exactly what we understand as therapists, that the most important thing that we should help a client do is to express themselves in a professional, physically and emotionally safe environment. Psychotherapy uses terms for this function such as 'containing' or 'holding,' and the art psychotherapist is needed to provide this function when a person expresses themselves creatively in art therapy.[15] Yet, when a person does this in public art, it is very different; there are no safe boundaries present as there would be for client and therapist, therefore, such art might be damaging for the creator or viewer, or both. This may be damaging not only in a direct way, but it could evoke an equal and opposite reaction, or an even more extreme response. Then it could escalate and lead to a negative snowball effect.

Figure 2 is an example from Israel. In this case these posters of hostages initially had no intent to blame, but were more of a cry for help.

Figure 2. Photograph of Israeli posters of hostages abducted on October 7, 2023.

This shows posters from an initiative of an Israeli graphic designer who lives in the US, who took all of the photos of the hostages and made a poster of each one with their name, age, and the slogan "bring them home," in a clear factual design. They have been displayed in public places in Israel and have been distributed all over the world, usually by private people, and have been put up in public internationally. This has had a dramatic impact in Israel and in some other places in the world. In Israel they are regarded as sacred, yet internationally they have also created controversy and some have been torn down by pro-Hamas or pro-Palestinian individuals around the world. These images, while still political and public, are not designed to provoke the other side, between two countries or between sides in a country. Initially, this was more a cry for help to get the hostages home. Later, it is also blaming the Israeli prime minister who is not doing enough to get them released.

We are questioning again: How helpful are such posters? Do the posters of the hostages help bring them home earlier or not?

Technically, in Israel over the past year and a half there have been weekly organized public protests with the banners and posters to try to influence the government to get the hostages back. Some of the hostages have been returned, yet by Israeli standards we cannot say that the poster initiative has created an amazing success.

We asked the senior graphic designer about the posters. His answer was, "It has given the people involved actively or passively the feeling that they are not indifferent to the subject. It has given people a feeling that they are united on the subject and given them a sense of agency, that they are doing something to try to help the situation. Yet again, it is not necessarily achieving a practical outcome."

The images in Figure 3 are from Northern Ireland. More than 2000 political murals have been created in Northern Ireland over many decades, mostly in working class areas in Belfast and Derry. Loyalist murals have been painted since the early 1900s and republican murals since 1981.[16] Murals on both 'sides' reflect dearly held values of the community making them, indicate feelings of insecurity, and were intended to reinforce identity or a cause, or to highlight injustice, and were generally positioned within one's own locality to be seen primarily by one's own community.[17]

Therefore, the purpose of the murals portrayed below is perhaps less about direct blaming or for the other 'side' to see. Figure 3, from left to right, shows a republican mural and a loyalist mural. These images depict expressions of not only a cry for help, for rights and justice, but also indirectly they are expressions of blaming the other 'side' for imprisoning them or killing them.

Figure 3. Photographs of a republican mural in Derry (1994) and a loyalist mural in Belfast (2007).

The left mural is about seeking the release of Derry prisoners who are described here as "Irish Political Hostages." The image has two fists, one holding barbed wire and another morphing into a dove. The right mural is loyalist and shows various bombings in which members of their community were killed or injured by "violent Republicans" and "IRA INLA PIRA" and is an expression of one's rights and of commemoration of those killed.[18] Such murals express feelings of being wronged, of injustice, and of that community's loss and suffering.

In relation to psychotherapy, it can be understood that expression about loss gives people the feeling that they have not forgotten the lost ones, or it can be an expression of anger or hope for the return of lost ones or for justice.

Figure 4 is a 2010 mural about an incident in 1971 known as the "Ballymurphy massacre" in which civilians in West Belfast, Northern Ireland were killed by the British Army. At the time, the army reported this as a gun battle with terrorists. The mural is a cry for acknowledgment of truth and justice. This incident was determined later by a coroner in 2021 to be killings of "innocent" civilians that were "a violation of Article 2" of the European Convention on Human Rights.[19] We include this mural to show how over time a proposed public narrative can change: persons portrayed as victimizers were actually later acknowledged as victims.

Figure 4. Photograph of a Belfast mural (2010) about the Ballymurphy massacre.

In psychology, we note how there is a strong link between victim and victimizer; often they think about the mutual experience. It is also the case that a person who is described as a victimizer may in fact be a victim, or vice versa. The victimizer, let's say the murderer, is carrying within them the awareness that they have killed someone, and this trauma can make them also a victim. The psychological distress of perpetration has been noted in literature on war, such as the Asia-Pacific War.[20]

> Though its origins are controversial, the trauma of the victimizer, many researchers believe, is related to identification with the victim. The victimizer imagines himself in the place of the victim and experiences in his imagination the latter's suffering and terror of annihilation. As is the case with trauma generally, not all victimizers experience trauma and its occurrence seems related to factors of conscience, that is, to cognitive factors. However this may be, clearly, the emotional relations between victims and victimizers are complex and the resulting identifications go in both directions - the victims identify with their victimizer and the other way around.[21]

We are questioning the following: How do such images relate to a theme of victim / victimizer? Does the need to create posters, murals, or banners of the pain of a community help to express pain? To what extent are they also created to mask or acknowledge the pain of the other community?

Maybe, in such situations, each 'side' in general (Israeli right or left wing, religious or non-religious, Palestinian, republican, loyalist), no matter which, can be busy being consumed by their own pain and loss and switches off from seeing the other. In psychological terms, not necessarily of an individual but rather of each 'side,' we would use the phrases traumatized, defense mechanisms, blind spots, compartmentalization, self-centered, or even more extreme mental reactions such as narcissism, or loss of empathy or morality.

We can also understand a victim / victimizer mental state in terms of subjectivity and intersubjectivity. In her book *Politics – Therapy – Love*, Leora Sotto cites Jessica Benjamin's and Georg Wilhelm Friedrich Hegel's work on relationships where one party is dominant over another, and these authors note that both parties are harmed by their respective roles.[22] Further citing Benjamin's and Hegel's work, Sotto notes that the relationship does not allow either to draw strength and respect from one another, and ultimately, in a dominant-submissive constellation, both sides lose. Both must take responsibility and adopt a new, mutual model. Achieving this moral stance is, according to Benjamin, related to moral values such as humility, acceptance of uncertainty, and compassion, and according to Benjamin, "One of the most important insights of intersubjective theory is that identity and difference exist simultaneously through mutual recognition."[23]

Cultural Similarities and Differences in Political Public Art

As art therapists we know, and it has been researched, that children all over the world draw similar compositions and images such as houses, trees, flowers, the sun, etc., and they are generally analogous in style.[24]

Therefore, we understand that the human species shares common cultural similarities, yet we also have cultural and individual differences. We will begin to explore this topic by looking at some similarities in political public art.

The depiction of a fist is an example of a commonly used symbol all over the world, and in all cases it is connected to power. It is important to understand that this symbol also has different narratives unique to each culture.

Figure 5, from left to right, shows an Israeli poster, a republican mural with a fist in the colors of the Irish flag, and a loyalist mural depicting a red fist symbol used by the Ulster Freedom Fighters, a loyalist paramilitary group. A red fist symbol was also used by the Loyalist Prisoners Aid group.[25]

Figure 5. Photographs of the symbol of a fist in Israeli art (left), a republican mural (center), and a loyalist mural (right).

There are other examples from other cultures and causes from all over the world, where the fist symbol represents strength, resistance, and solidarity, such its use in the context of Black Lives Matter.

These Israeli and Northern Ireland examples have similarities: the fist symbol is in the center of the composition; whether it is painted, drawn, or designed graphically, it is clear and prominent; it often presented in primal colors or colors associated with the nation or 'side.'[26]

The human species is known to copy from one another and, in relation to the subject of our article, certain symbols seem to resonate cross-culturally. The symbol of a fist relates to expressing power and, in psychotherapy, the subject of power and feeling disempowered or empowered is analyzed at length. A therapist tries to help a client be in touch with their feelings about disempowerment and also with their empowerment in socially constructive ways. When working with those imprisoned due to their involvement in armed conflict, an art psychotherapist aims to share power safely with clients and help them to find more socially constructive ways forward.[27] Hopefully a country can reach that point, to resolve their conflict by themselves or with the help of others.

In Israeli political public art the symbol of a yellow ribbon has been adopted from its American use. In Israel, it symbolizes the wish for the return by Hamas of the hostages taken on October 7, 2023, and it is often accompanied with the slogan "Bring Them Home NOW." Figure 6 shows three examples of yellow ribbons in Israel.

Figure 6. Photographs of yellow ribbon images in Israel (2025). The image in the center reads "together" in Hebrew.

Both in Northern Ireland and in Israel, sometimes the political public art makes a link to a higher power. Figure 7 is a Belfast mural of a hunger striker in an H Block in the Maze prison. It suggests that the cause is "Blessed" as it includes symbols of the rosary, an image of the Virgin Mary, and a quotation from the Bible.

Figure 7. Photograph of a republican mural in Belfast of a hunger striker (circa 1982).

Psychologically, attachment research and theory shows that humans have a need to attach themselves to another, which can help our basic need for security and validation.[28]

As for differences in political public art, the following are some examples from recent Israeli posters and banners and Northern Irish murals over the past forty years. It is interesting to note that there are no political murals in Israel and never have been, and there are hardly any that are not political. There is not a word for 'mural' in Hebrew. In Israel, the political public art is posters or banners that are word-based, pictorial, or photographic.

Most of the Israeli political art is the written word, slogans, a sentence that has irony or sarcasm in it, a clear picture, an image, or a photo. But it is not a painting; it does not usually have shades of color or other features of a painting. It is more graphic, rather than being like a painting from the art world. Northern Ireland murals tend to be paintings with shading, composition, perspective, etc. One must note that we are comparing the political art of the two areas that was generally made decades apart, yet each culture has its uniqueness over many centuries.

Figure 8, from left to right, shows examples of this in a Northern Ireland mural, an Israeli poster, and an Israeli banner.

Figure 8. Photographs of a Northern Ireland mural (1960s), an Israeli poster (2024), and an Israeli banner (2024–2025).

It is worth mentioning this artistic difference, because we need to be able to understand a culture, its language, its symbolism, and all its aspects, to be able to help it solve its conflict.

In psychotherapy, a therapist pays attention to a client's demeanor and style, not only to what they are saying, and helps them to be in touch with all their ways of being and expressing. A client needs to feel first that they are understood, but also to see where and how they interact with the world around them. Similarly, countries should feel that they are understood but also understand the enemy. Both with a client and countries, we are addressing the issue of relationships—relationships with the self and with other.

Another phenomenon that occurs in political public art is linking one's suffering or cause to that of another nation's cause. In Northern Ireland, some loyalists feel a link to

Israel and some republicans feel a link to Palestine and the African National Congress (ANC) in South Africa. This phenomenon appears also in murals. Figure 9 on the left shows a republican mural in Belfast identifying with Palestine and using the colors of the Irish and Palestinian flags, and the right shows a loyalist mural in Belfast identifying with Israel and showing the Israeli flag colors.

Figure 9. Photographs of a republican mural identifying with Palestine (left) and a loyalist mural identifying with Israel (right).

In Israel, public political art does not link to the cause of another country.

There are many other cultural differences in the political public art in terms of the unique meanings within them that mostly only people from the respective communities will understand.

The theme of the CRIC conference was "ending wars." In conflict resolution, it is very important that each culture in conflict with another tries to understand itself and the other. As in psychotherapy, this is with an aim of promoting understanding, respect, and good relationships.

> Humiliation, disrespect and unfair treatment of a community can be key factors in causing conflict and violence. I believe the way forward is to recognize each other as communities of real human beings who have their own thoughts, feelings, culture, background and hopes for the future. Then, there needs to be a progression toward respecting each other as individual human beings and as communities. Respect can then be entrenched in rights, and so violence and trauma can be reduced. The fundamental aim however is to create new and better relationships, not merely to put new legal commitments and regulations in place.[29]

Making Peace

The topic of making peace sometimes appears in the political public art in both Israel and Northern Ireland.

A pattern appearing in a person's behavior, or a rash or allergy breaking out on their body, is a symptom or an indicator. We can question: Is a surge of expression in political public art a symptom or indicator in the body politic? At times, it is an indicator of pain or need. At times is it an indicator of a drive toward war? At other times, is it an indicator of a drive toward peace?

In psychotherapy, part of healing is promoting inner dialogue; sometimes it is about finding ways to resolve intrapersonal and interpersonal conflicts; at other times it is more about helping the psyche find a moderate way rather than an extreme way, and opening up possibilities. When relevant, therapy aims to help a person be more realistic, rather than acting out of myths or cognitive distortions, and at times the need is to help a person be less self-focused, have more mutuality in relationships, and be more empathic about the needs of the other. While being compassionate, the therapist might need to take an ethical stance of not colluding with illegal or immoral power-based behavior.[30]

In relation to the war between Israel and Gaza and the other parties involved, where fighting is still going on, most Israeli banners and posters are about internal Israeli political issues, regarding the hostages, the government's policies, or soldiers' rights. For example, the poster in Figure 10 translates as "Go and then everything will be sorted" ("Go," referring to Benjamin Netanyahu).

Figure 10. Photograph of an Israeli poster that translates as "Go and then everything will be sorted" ("Go," referring to Benjamin Netanyahu).

Many in Israel will say that 'friendly' posters will not help, thus the decision to make the majority of posters blaming and accusing. Yet, there are posters such as those in Figure 11 which, from left to right, try and express hope more than anything (translation, "we all lose at war, we all win at peace"), or address an underlying issue and self-criticism (translation, "the fault is the fifty-seven years of occupation").

Figure 11. Photographs of an Israeli poster promoting peace (left), which translates as "we all lose at war, we all win at peace," and a poster noting the fault of the occupation (right), which translates as "the fault is the fifty-seven years of occupation."

Some more recent murals from Northern Ireland, made after the peace process and the Good Friday Agreement of 1998, depict images of peace, reconciliation, and integration. Some of this new art has over-painted some old conflict-related murals. Naturally, as relative peace is achieved, it can be easier to see the other and develop the stance of mutuality. In Figure 12, the mural on the left shows a child from each 'side' shaking hands in Belfast and includes the phrase "NO MORE"; the right mural depicts children and a banner being flown by a plane states, "Every child deserves the right to…" The latter image was part of an Arts Council sponsored initiative entitled "Building Peace Through the Arts: Re-Imaging Communities Programme" (2006–2009).[31]

Figure 12. Photographs of Northern Ireland murals promoting children's rights to peace.

In psychological terms, we would say this is creating a dialogue with the other, being less self-focused, being more empathic to the needs of the other and, in this case, to the needs of all children.

Shown in Figure 13, two Northern Ireland artists painted a re-creation of Picasso's 1930 anti-war painting *Guernica* in Belfast in 2007. The artists were from opposite 'sides' of the sectarian conflict (the Troubles). However, together they formed a collective, called Painting from the Same Palette, which advocated for the use of art as a healing mechanism to bring together the long-divided communities.

Figure 13. Photograph of a 2007 mural in Northern Ireland based on Picasso's 1930 painting *Guernica*.

As for psychotherapy, the psychotherapist helps the client to befriend extreme or opposing aspects to try to lessen intrapersonal and interpersonal conflict.

Some of the time, political public art is an impulsive cry, sometimes of pain, sometimes aggressive, and it is important that they can express themselves and communicate. But, as with clients, there can be the need for mediators to contain the conflict and try to heal it. Societies can need such mediators. In Northern Ireland, the peace process involved mediators both from the various communities and nationally and internationally.

Conclusion

We have tried to describe the type of political public art in conflict zones, both in Northern Ireland and in Israel. We question how helpful is it that there are murals or posters that can be offensive to the other 'side.' In psychotherapy, the therapist's role would be to bridge opposing sides of the inner self, yet there are situations where, according to certain schools of therapy, the therapist's role is also to highlight objectivity and a moral or ethical stance for the client.[32] As for our examples, we can question: Is it helpful to have enormous banners and posters displayed all over billboards in Israel showing pictures and slogans that depict the prime minster as a traitor (this is the word used) and guilty, mainly because of the fear that he is trying to change Israel into a dictatorship and that he is very inefficient concerning the war? Is it a moral or ethical stance, or is it creating more hostility between groups in Israel and toward the government? In relation to murals in Northern Ireland, most were created to be seen within one's own community and therefore were generally not designed to be oppositional to the other 'side.' We can question: Did they help to strengthen a sense of identity and deepen a sense of unity within those communities? If they did, did that make the people less open toward seeing the other 'side,' or did it strengthen and unite people and enable them to also think of ways to work toward peace and a resolution of the conflict? Having said all this, we need to note that the art is a response to a situation and not the situation itself. In addition, in discussions with people from the general public in Israel, some people said that the posters and banners are important, some said they will make the situation worse because they will divide the country even more, but some said they do not have any impact on them and are irrelevant. However, we know from research that advertising has an impact on us that we do not recognize consciously.[33]

It is also important to consider what images are put up and what images are not put up—both tell us something. Political public art can also be a response to crisis and can reveal new understandings of the crisis.[34] Currently, only about 4 percent of the protesting population in Israel walks around with posters asking for peace; the majority is about internal politics or about the hostages. This has declined from before the war when it was about 6 percent.

Israel does not have a 'therapist' to manage the situation at the moment. Not from within and not from without. In fact we fear, there seems to be no therapist for the world at the moment. If anything, there's a fear of the situation escalating. In psychotherapy, we would say that the client is in an unsafe state.

We noted that Minerva was chosen by CRIC as a symbol of the conference because she was a Roman goddess of war, wisdom, art, justice, etc. A symbol of Minerva or Athena is an owl, as shown in Figure 14. Hegel noted that "The owl of Minerva spreads its wings only with the falling of the dusk," meaning that that we come to understand only after it is too late.[35] How can we learn from experience? Or how, like an owl, can we see in times of darkness? How can we gain wisdom from political public art, and from psychotherapeutic understanding, in order to contribute to conflict resolution? Such wisdom also needs commitment from local leaders, communities, mediators, and wider parties to help work toward peace.[36]

Figure 14. Photograph of an Athenian coin (left) and a drawing by the second author used in the CRIC presentation (right).

In art psychotherapy, a therapist can be working with a couple who, for example, are in conflict and fighting over custody of children (like a country fighting for rights or land). In such work, it is important that the therapist aims to do a number of things with both parties and their art: treat them with respect; give space for each one's feelings, views, and hopes; address whether either or both had crossed a moral or legal line; not humiliate them or allow one to humiliate the other; and help to find a mutually acceptable way forward.

An example from art psychotherapy that might speak to our topic is when two people in conflict are invited to paint on either side of a window with opaque paint. This is depicted in Figure 15, which is a staged example with actors depicting an actual intervention with couples.[37] Each can ignore what the other person is doing and can paint their own picture, or they can co-create a painting from both sides of the glass. In other words, are they covering the other person's painting, or are they co-creating a joint picture? Are we going to get two completely different pictures on either side, or are we going to get a joint picture that shares the space and where both people can see their own and the other's painting? In the latter case, it is the same picture and yet some differences will be visible from either side due to reversing and some colors being more prominent on the side where they were painted. One or both people in a couple in conflict can engage with the activity in various ways. They can sit on either side and be indifferent to each other, due to being absorbed in painting or due to actual indifference to the other person. One or both can be aggressive and try to cover the other's painting. One or both can try to paint collaboratively and communicate, sometimes even mirroring each other's movements. A parallel can be made with how two groups in conflict can behave—they can be indifferent to each other, be aggressive to each other, or try to interact constructively with each other.

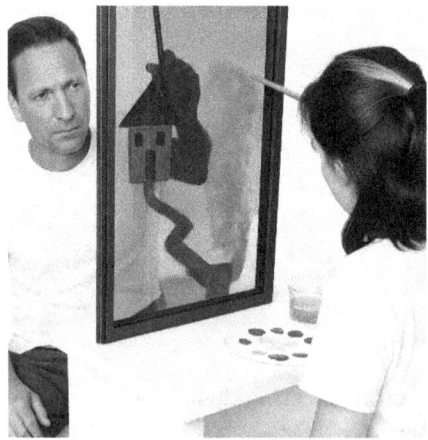

Figure 15. Photograph of actors depicting an intervention with couples.

Mediators, whether they are psychotherapists or people trying to help resolve conflict between two countries, need to let each party express, listen to, and see each other, to communicate respectfully and to co-create a resolution that is mutually acceptable and in which they can live together or alongside each other. All of this is usually a long process that demands patience, hope, love, and the belief that conflict can be resolved.

Notes

1. Deanna Petherbridge, *The Primacy of Drawing: An Artist's View* (South Bank Centre, 1991).
2. John, Lord Alderdice, "New Insights into the Psychology of Individuals and Large Groups in a World of Changing Conflicts," *International Political Science Review* 45, no. 1 (2023): 94–105, https://journals.sagepub.com/doi/full/10.1177/01925121231177444.
3. Carlo Strenger, *Individuality, The Impossible Project* (International University Press, 1998); Urie Bronfenbrenner, ed., *Making Human Beings Human: Bioecological Perspectives on Human Development* (Sage Publications, 2005).
4. Scott Atran, "The Devoted Actor: Unconditional Commitment and Intractable Conflict Across Cultures," *Current Anthropology* 57, no. S13 (2016): 192–203, https://www.jstor.org/stable/26545629.
5. Stephen Karpman, "Fairy Tales and Script Drama Analysis," *Transactional Analysis Bulletin* 26, no. 7 (1968): 39–43.
6. David Emerald, *The Power of TED* (*The Empowerment Dynamic)* (Polaris Publishing, 2016).
7. Leora Sotto and Eitan Gilor-Miller, *Politics – Therapy – Love, Community-Self, a Key for Understanding the Clinical Process* (Resling, 2021, published in Hebrew).
8. HM Government, *The Victims and Survivors (Northern Ireland) Order 2006*, https://www.legislation.gov.uk/nisi/2006/2953/part/1.
9. Sue Grand, *The Hero in the Mirror: From Fear to Fortitude* (Routledge, 2009).
10. Uri Hadar, *Psychoanalysis and Social Development: Interpretation and Action* (Palgrave Macmillan, 2013).
11. SAMHSA, *SAMHSA's Concept of Trauma and Guidance for a Trauma-Informed Approach* (Substance Abuse and Mental Health Services Administration, 2014); Angela Sweeney, Sarah Clement, Beth Filson, and Angela Kennedy, "Trauma-Informed Mental Healthcare in the UK: What Is It and How Can We Further Its Development?," *Mental Health Review Journal* 21, no. 3 (2016): 174–92, https://psycnet.apa.org/doi/10.1108/MHRJ-01-2015-0006.
12. Robert Heath, *Seducing the Subconscious: The Psychology of Emotional Influence in Advertising* (Wiley-Blackwell, 2012).
13. Yossi Ohayon, graphic designer, Israel.
14. Interview with Yossi Ohayon by the first author, Leora Sotto, 2024.
15. Wilfred Bion, *Learning from Experience* (Karnac Books, 1962); Donald W. Winnicott, "The Theory of the Parent-Infant Relationship," in *The Maturational Processes and the Facilitating Environment* (Karnac Books, 1990), 47; Rita Simon, *Symbolic Images in Art As Therapy* (Routledge, 1997), 14.
16. Bill Rolston, *Drawing Support: Murals in the North of Ireland* (Beyond the Pale, 1992).
17. Beatrice White, "The Writing on the Wall: The Significance of Murals in the Northern Ireland Conflict," in *Walking the Tightrope: Europe Between Europeanisation and Globalisation: Selected Papers Presented at European Studies Intensive Programme 2010, University of Groningen*, ed. Janny de Jong, Ine Megens, and Margriet van der Wall (Euroculture Consortium, 2011), 311; Bill Rolston, *Drawing Support 2: Murals of War and Peace* (Beyond the Pale, 1995); Bill Rolston, *Drawing Support 3: Murals and Transition in the North of Ireland* (Beyond the Pale, 2003).
18. CAIN Archive – *Conflict and Politics in Northern Ireland*, Abstracts on Organisations, https://cain.ulster.ac.uk/othelem/organ/iorgan.htm: "The Irish Republican Army (IRA) was the main Republican paramilitary group which was involved in the Northern Ireland conflict. . . . The

Provisional IRA [PIRA] was established when the IRA split in December 1969 between the 'Officials' and the 'Provisionals.'" The Irish National Liberation Army (INLA) is a smaller republican paramilitary group that was established in 1975.

[19] Judicial Communications Office, *Summary of Findings – In the Matter of a Series of Deaths That Occurred in August 1971 at Ballymurphy, West Belfast*, Summary of Coroner's Verdicts and Findings (Keegan J) (Belfast Lady Chief Justice's Office, 2021), https://www.judiciaryni.uk/judicial-decisions/summary-findings-matter-series-deaths-occurred-august-1971-ballymurphy-west.

[20] Eri Nakamura, "The Imperial Japanese Soldiers and Perpetrator Trauma," *New England Journal of Public Policy* 36, no. 2 (2024): Article 20, https://scholarworks.umb.edu/nejpp/vol36/iss2/20/.

[21] Hadar, *Psychoanalysis and Social Development*, 135; Grand, *The Hero in the Mirror*.

[22] Sotto and Gilor-Miller, *Politics – Therapy – Love*; Jessica Benjamin, *The Bonds of Love* (Pantheon, 1988); Georg Wilhelm Friedrich Hegel, *Phenomenology of Mind*, trans. J. B. Baillie (Harper & Row, 1967).

[23] Benjamin, *The Bonds of Love*, 37.

[24] Rhoda Kellogg, *Analyzing Children's Art* (Mayfield, 1970).

[25] *CAIN Archive – Conflict and Politics in Northern Ireland*, Symbols Used in Northern Ireland – Unionist and Loyalist Symbols, https://cain.ulster.ac.uk/images/symbols/unionloyal.htm.

[26] Simona Petru, "Red, Black or White? The Dawn of Colour Symbolism," *Documenta Praehistorica XXXIII*, vol. 33 (2006): 203–208, https://journals.uni-lj.si/DocumentaPraehistorica/article/view/33.18.

[27] Caryl Sibbett, "Creative Containment," in *Negotiating Power: Reprints and Transcripts, 31st Annual Summer Course*, ed. Penelope Hall (Champernowne Trust for Psychotherapy and the Arts, 2002); Caryl Sibbett, "Art Psychotherapy with Troubles Related Trauma – in Prisons & Wider Settings," presentation at the Annual Conference of the Centre for the Resolution of Intractable Conflict, Harris Manchester College, Oxford University, October 21, 2019.

[28] John Bowlby, *Attachment and Loss*, 3 vols. (Basic Books, 1983).

[29] John, Lord Alderdice, "Recognition – The First Step to More Human Relationships," *International Journal of Applied Psychoanalytic Studies* 15, no. 2 (2018): 72–75, https://doi.org/10.1002/aps.1568.

[30] Hadar, *Psychoanalysis and Social Development*.

[31] Independent Research Solutions, *Evaluation of the Re-Imaging Communities Programme: A Report for the Arts Council of Northern Ireland* (Belfast, June 2009), https://artscouncil-ni.s3-assets.com/Re-Imaging_Final_Evaluation.pdf.

[32] Hadar, *Psychoanalysis and Social Development*.

[33] Heath, *Seducing the Subconscious*.

[34] Stuart Andrews and Patrick Duggan, "Political Public Art as Performative Response to Crisis," *Liminalities: A Journal of Performance Studies* 20, no. 4 (2024), http://liminalities.net/20-4/performative-response.pdf.

[35] Georg Wilhelm Friedrich Hegel, *Philosophy of Right*, trans. T. M. Knox (Oxford University Press, 1967), 13.

[36] Bill Rolston, "Changing the Political Landscape: Murals and Transition in Northern Ireland," *Irish Studies Review* 11, no. 1 (2003): 3, https://ssrn.com/abstract=2638242.

[37] Leora Sotto, *Being in Touch* (Pardes, 2008, published in Hebrew), 88.

PREVENTING WAR AS ENDING WAR: THE EUROPEAN NETWORK REMEMBRANCE AND SOLIDARITY ON CHANNELING POTENTIAL CONFLICT THROUGH DIALOGUE ON HISTORY

Rafał Rogulski
European Network Remembrance and Solidarity

ABSTRACT

Dialogue about history is an important element in the processes of ordering social and international reality. In the nineteenth and twentieth centuries in Europe alone, we have experienced so many dramas that virtually every country and its citizens have issues in their history that call for prolonged and consistent dialogue, often in an international setting. Colonialism, wars, totalitarian and authoritarian regimes, genocide, forced displacement—we have a lot to talk about in Europe when it comes to history. The establishment and activities of the European Network Remembrance and Solidarity provide an example of how international discourse on history can be conducted and how it can be used to educate and defuse conflicts which, if left unaddressed, could develop into real threats.

Rafał Rogulski is a culture manager, a diplomat, and the director of the European Network Remembrance and Solidarity (ENRS).

This text is based on a talk delivered at the Conference on the Resolution of Intractable Conflict, CRIC 2024, Ending Wars, September 23-25, 2024, at Harris Manchester College, University of Oxford.

Dialogue about history is important in the processes of ordering social and international reality. Its importance increases especially in connection with crucial caesura, e.g., the end of an armed conflict or the fall of dictatorial or authoritarian governments. Indeed, reflection on history is a sine qua non for the formation of a lasting social order. Real open dialogue is only possible in a democratic order, but democracy does not guarantee it. What is needed is the political will and social expectation to carry out such a settlement. For it is through the decisions of the political class that the conditions necessary for this dialogue are created: the legal norms governing these processes; public and non-public institutions dealing with history and memory, which could be divided into research, educational, dissemination, and support institutions (financial programs); and consistent and different forms of funding. I will return to these issues in the following section.

In the nineteenth and twentieth centuries in Europe alone, we have experienced so many dramas that virtually every country and its citizens have issues in their history that call for prolonged and consistent dialogue, often in an international setting. Colonialism, wars, totalitarian and authoritarian regimes, genocide, forced displacement—we have a lot to talk about in Europe but the willingness to do so varies.

In those countries and societies that have made a consistent effort to come to terms with history, dialogue continues. Sometimes the temperature rises, sometimes it falls, and no one is fully satisfied with the results, but the important thing is that the dialogue continues, inter alia through its institutionalization, so that any resulting aggression is channeled, reducing the likelihood of internal an international conflict.

The following examples show a variety of issues. Due to the dictatorship of communism, it was very difficult for the societies that remained on the other side of the Iron Curtain to discuss the experiences of World War II, and some topics were not discussed at all in the public domain. It was only after the restoration of independence, i.e., after 1989, that a real dialogue had a chance to begin, which must be linked to the discourse on the communist past, which was in a way a consequence of World War II. These processes are still going on in the post-communist countries and, although they are proceeding at different speeds, they are largely shaping the political scene, including in Germany. After World War II, when it was occupied by four victorious powers and then divided into two states, democratic West Germany (the Federal Republic of Germany) and communist, undemocratic East Germany (the German Democratic Republic), the process of coming to terms with the Nazi dictatorship took very different paths. Then, after German reunification, this ongoing process was compounded by the issue of coming to terms with the communist dictatorship in the former East Germany, which, as a communist country, ceased to exist and became a post-communist area of reunified Germany, which based its functioning on the democratic heritage of West Germany. This created completely different conditions for coming to terms with the communist dictatorship and its legacy, from those of other countries behind the Iron Curtain. The process of coming to terms with Nazism and communism is still ongoing, especially in the academic and political spheres, and sometimes in the legal sphere, with certain issues also resurfacing on the international stage.

The situation is different in the countries of the former Yugoslavia, where the war of the 1990s left such deep and still-unhealed wounds that the willingness to engage in dialogue about twentieth century history remains limited. A different example is Spain, where, after the fall of Franco's dictatorship, an attempt was made to dispense with historical settlements and accountability and now, for several years, there have been attempts to conduct this processes and dialogue, mainly internally, but including steps made on the international level.[1] The situation differs even more in Ireland, where skillfully initiated and consistently conducted dialogue first led to the abandonment of terrorism and now allows the current state of affairs to be maintained. The memory of the fate of the Irish people, especially in World War I, but also in World War II, is still one of the most important aspects of the dialogue on history, although it also concerns later periods. One of the key participants in this dialogue is the Glencree Centre for Peace and Reconciliation. All of these examples are only a brief overview of much deeper and more complex processes. It is not my aim in this text to present the history of the dialogue on history in these countries or to show its complexity, but it is important to show, even if only briefly, that in Europe we have different approaches to talking about history and memory, that there is no single model that can be applied everywhere, and that even those that are applied require patience and do not always produce the desired effect.

Sooner or later, a link must be established between the dialogues taking place in different countries. This gives an international dimension to the internal discussions, and this can be useful both internally and internationally. First, most often some potential conflict over history and its memory involves a neighbor or neighbors. Second, most often the parties involved see the same aspect differently. Dialogue helps to find this out, and this knowledge in the long run allows one to look at one's own history with more detachment. The dialogue about history is never-ending; current events in Ukraine and the Middle East show what can happen when it is lacking and history is falsified and used instrumentally.

Dialogue requires appropriate laws, institutions, and funding, and this applies as much to domestic issues as to international ones. Institutions (universities, museums, and foundations) focused on the 'internal market' can and should cooperate across borders. A number of programs within the European Union allow for the funding of such cooperation. But first, not everyone is a member of the European Union, and second, not all institutions are able to benefit from these programs. That is why institutions of an international nature, whose task is to implement projects with partners from different countries, have an important role in shaping dialogue. There are several of them, differing in legal status, scope of action, size, and organizational and financial capacity. The most visible include the Platform of European Memory and Conscience,[2] an association based in Prague that brings together institutions from many countries and has an important concept for the creation of a memorial to the victims of totalitarianism in Brussels; EUROM,[3] an institution affiliated with the University of Barcelona focused mainly on academic projects; Euroclio,[4] an association based in The Hague that brings together teachers and educators and runs projects on teaching history; the Observatory on History Teaching in Europe (OHTE),[5] an institution within the Council of Europe based in Strasbourg that brings together twenty countries, mainly in southern Europe, and publishes reports on the state of history teaching in those countries; and the largest and oldest is the European Network Remembrance and Solidarity (ENRS),[6] whose unique formation and programs I will describe below.

Not only are the activities of the ENRS worth learning about, but so is the process of its creation. It exemplifies what was at the time an innovative way of dealing with the problem of remembering relatively recent events in European history, namely World War II and its aftermath. Its various types of projects can be broadly described as forms of social discourse on history. Individual projects involve different social groups and do not always follow the same paths in expanding knowledge about twentieth century history, the processes that shaped it, and its actors.

The Formation of the European Network Remembrance and Solidarity

The European Network Remembrance and Solidarity grew out of an international conflict over the memory of World War II and its consequences, a conflict that swept across central Europe at the turn of the twentieth and twenty-first centuries. For many, it came as a surprise, as it became clear that despite more than fifty years having passed since the end of World War II, and despite the fall of communism and deeper cooperation in many areas, we still know so little about each other in Europe. Above all, it became clear that we remember and want to remember differently. At the heart of this conflict was a discussion about commemorating the fate of the German population who, following the Potsdam Agreement and the shifting of Poland's borders to the west against the will of the legitimate Polish authorities, had to leave the former eastern territories of the Third Reich.

The flashpoint of this conflict was the resolution of the German Bundestag of May 29, 1998, recalling the fate of the 'German expellees' and, somewhat later, the project of the so-called Association of Expellees to establish an institution commemorating their tragic fate. In Poland and other countries in the region, the narrative used at the time by these circles, which separated causes from effects, caused outrage. It focused on the suffering of Germans who lost their homeland after the war, but almost completely ignored the fact that it was Germany that caused the war, resulting in the deaths of millions of people, trauma for the survivors, forced border changes, resettlements, and all the drama that this entailed.

These events sparked a debate that raged for several years with varying intensity in the media, diplomatic circles, and politicians' offices. As a result of the intergovernmental negotiations that took place at that time, the European Network Remembrance and Solidarity was established, an international initiative whose aim was and still is to support international dialogue on the history of Europe in the twentieth century. The idea was to create an institution that would support cooperation between institutions from different EU countries involved in researching and disseminating twentieth-century history, by establishing cooperation between them and implementing joint projects.

In February 2005, the ministers of culture of Germany, Hungary, Poland, and Slovakia signed a declaration of intent to establish the ENRS. It took several more years to work out a mutually acceptable formula for the functioning of the Network and its Secretariat, which formally began its activities on April 1, 2010. During these fifteen years, Romania and the Czech Republic joined the Network, while Austria, Albania, Georgia, Lithuania, and Estonia were granted observer status. The ENRS Secretariat, organizing an increasing number of projects, has gradually grown from one employee at the beginning to a team of more than thirty people in 2025. We have established cooperation with more than five hundred institutions in Europe and beyond, and together with them we have organized more than two hundred and fifty projects. They have always been international in nature and always concern the history of more than one country. Most ENRS projects are periodic in nature so that they can be continuously developed and as many people as possible can participate in them.

The ENRS always carries out its projects in cooperation with public and non-public institutions from across Europe and sometimes beyond, such as research and academic institutions, national memory institutes, think tanks, archives, museums, memorial sites, cultural centers, educational institutions, schools, government and local government bodies, diplomatic missions, and cultural institutes. The Network fulfills its mission by disseminating historical knowledge and supporting research, in particular by organizing conferences, symposia, seminars, and workshops; implementing research, cultural, and educational projects; and publishing and translating scientific and popular science works. These initiatives are aimed at representatives of institutions and organizations dealing with twentieth-century history, cultural managers, scientists, researchers, teachers, educators, students, and graduates (mainly in history, sociology, political science, philosophy, and law), young people, politicians, opinion leaders, journalists, and anyone else who is interested.

Selection of European Network Remembrance and Solidarity Periodic Projects

From the beginning, most ENRS projects were designed with the aim of being organized periodically. On the one hand, this provides opportunities for their organizational development, on the other hand, it allows the number of participants to increase and the geographical scope to expand. I briefly outline the main ones below. Details of the various editions can be found on our website and in the electronic or printed ENRS catalogues.[7]

ENRS Educational Projects

Sound in the Silence

Sound in the Silence[8] is a project for secondary school students, with young people and teachers from four schools in different European countries participating in each edition. Together with artists from the US, Slovakia, and the United Kingdom, they visit places marked by difficult history—former death camps, concentration camps, labor camps, or places associated with genocide and systematic humiliation of people. Participants learn about the history of these places and then, in collaboration with the artists, prepare performances that they present at the end. The final, often very moving act is a discussion with the participants, during which they share their impressions of the project. A parallel methodological program is organized for teachers and educators, as well as teachers from nearby schools. By combining history lessons with collaboration with artists from various fields of art, participants have the opportunity to understand historical processes and reflect together on questions concerning the present.

Between 2011 and 2025, Sound in the Silence took place at the Neuengamme concentration camp memorial site (Germany) in 2011, at the former military camp in Borne Sulinowo (Poland) in 2012, in Gdańsk, the place where World War II began and the cradle of Solidarity, a symbol of the fight against communism (Poland) in 2015, in Auschwitz-Birkenau and in Żylina (Poland, Slovakia) in 2016, at the memorial site of the former Ravensbrück death camp (Germany) in 2017, in Warsaw, the city of two uprisings—the Warsaw Ghetto Uprising (1943) and the Warsaw Uprising (1944) (Poland) in 2018, at the Submarine Bunker Valentin in Bremen (Germany) in 2019, at the Kaunas Ninth Fort Museum (Lithuania) in 2022, at the Gusen and Mauthausen memorial sites (Austria) in 2022, in Berlin at the House of the Wannsee Conference (Germany) in 2023, at the memorial site of the former Jasenovac death camp (Croatia) in 2023, in Bucharest and at the Pitești Prison, site of crimes committed by the Romanian communist regime (Romania) in 2024, and at the memorial site for the victims of the Dulag 121 transit camp in Pruszków (Poland) in 2025.

In Between?

In Between?[9] is a series of study visits for young students. Participants from different countries, selected through a recruitment process, first take part in workshops where they learn how to use oral history methods, photograph and describe documents and artifacts, and prepare podcasts. They then visit European border areas in small groups, where they conduct research, learn about the history of the region and, under the guidance of professionals, prepare a podcast together. Since 2016, In Between? has taken place in twenty-six border regions or cities in Europe, including Lower Silesia on the German-Polish-Czech border, Transylvania and Bukovina in Romania, the city of Pécs in the border region of Hungary and Croatia, southern Styria on the Austrian-Italian border, in the city of Gorizia on the Italian-Slovenian border, in the border region of Poland and Lithuania, on the Slovak-Czech-Austrian border, in Catalonia on the Spanish-French border, in Alsace on the German-French border, in several border regions in the western Balkans, on the former Polish-German border in Masuria in Poland, and on the borders of Estonia and Finland. The project received a special mention in the Europa Nostra Awards in 2018.

Hi-story Lessons

Hi-story Lessons[10] is a constantly evolving interactive online platform in six languages (English, German, Polish, Hungarian, Slovak, and Romanian) supporting the teaching and learning of twentieth-century European history. It is used by more than 50,000 users annually, and around 1,000 teachers participate in webinars and workshops organized by the ENRS. The platform also includes materials to help recognize false historical information and disinformation in this field.

Annual ENRS Conferences and Seminars

European Remembrance Symposium

The European Remembrance Symposium[11] is an annual international networking event for representatives of institutions involved in disseminating knowledge about twentieth-century European history and research. Participants take part in discussions, presentations, and turbo presentations (90 seconds) of projects, workshops, and visits to memorial sites. Previous symposia have been held in Gdańsk, Berlin, Prague, Vienna, Bucharest, Brussels, Budapest, Paris, Dublin, Tallinn, Barcelona, Warsaw, and Helsinki. Coming Symposia are planned in Bratislava (2025) and Vilnius (2027).

Genealogies of Memory

Genealogies of Memory[12] is an annual international academic conference on memory research methodology, bringing together scholars and different research schools from across Europe and beyond to engage them in debates, seminars, and workshops on twentieth-century European history. Between 2012 and 2024, it took place in Warsaw, in 2025 it will be held in Berlin, in 2026 in Jassy (Romania), and in subsequent years, the venue will change each time to make the event more accessible.

Exhibitions

Between Life and Death

Between Life and Death[13] is a traveling exhibition that presents the personal stories of Holocaust survivors and rescuers from several countries. Each panel is devoted to one country and, in addition to individual stories, provides historical background and a description of the situation in that country during World War II. A separate panel is devoted to diplomats from various countries who helped Jews in different ways in their countries of service.

After the Great War. New Europe 1918–1923

After the Great War. New Europe 1918–1923[14] is an outdoor traveling exhibition presenting the history of the first five years after the end of World War I, a time when a new European order was taking shape. The exhibition presents not only historical processes, facts and figures, but also the different ways in which different countries remember that period. Between 2018 and 2024, the exhibition was presented in twenty seven cities across Europe, and from 2025 it will be available online.

Educational Campaigns

Memento. 27 January

Memento. 27 January[15] is a campaign commemorating International Holocaust Remembrance Day. As part of the campaign, we publish short films on social media dedicated to the victims of the Holocaust, including the film *Memento* directed by the Hungarian author Zoltán Szilágyi Varga and a film composed of drawings by Mieczysław Kościelniak, a prisoner of Auschwitz, created by Piotr Kornobis.

Remember. 23 August

Remember. 23 August[16] is a campaign commemorating the European Day of Remembrance for Victims of all Totalitarian and Authoritarian Regimes. Activities include the distribution of postcards with metal pins and an educational campaign on social media. An important element of the campaign are short films and poster campaigns depicting victims of totalitarianism.

Conclusion

The European Network Remembrance and Solidarity is the only international institution in Europe operating on the basis of an intergovernmental agreement, financed by membership fees, open to other countries, and cooperating with several hundred institutions active in the field of research and dissemination of knowledge about the history of Europe in the twentieth century, and not embedded in the structures of any other international organization. It combines the characteristics of an international institution with those of a non-governmental organization, which allows it to be a reliable partner both for ministries responsible for historical (memory) policies in individual countries and for all kinds of institutions active in this field. One of the fundamental reasons for the creation and maintenance of the ENRS is to support dialogue on history, especially its difficult aspects, in order to channel potential conflicts and defuse tensions that arise from different interpretations of the same historical processes. Whether such activities can prevent war or help to end it once it has broken out is another question, but they are an indispensable aspect of building lasting peace.

Notes

[1] Committee on Culture, Science, Education and Media of Council of Europe, "Multiperspectivity in Remembrance and History Education for Democratic Citizenship," text adopted by the Parliamentary Assembly on January 29, 2025, https://pace.coe.int/en/files/33942/html; and resulting Recommendation 2290 (2025), https://pace.coe.int/files/34121/pdf.
[2] Platform of European Memory and Conscience, https://www.memoryandconscience.eu/.
[3] EUROM, https://europeanmemories.net/.
[4] Euroclio, https://euroclio.eu/.
[5] Observatory on History Teaching in Europe, https://www.coe.int/en/web/observatory-history-teaching.
[6] European Network Remembrance and Solidarity, https://enrs.eu/.
[7] ENRS catalogues, https://enrs.eu/publication/list?publication_list_filter_form%5Bsearch%5D=&publication_list_filter_form%5Bauthors%5D%5B%5D=176&publication_list_filter_form%5Bsubmit%5D=.
[8] Sound in the Silence, https://enrs.eu/sound-in-the-silence.

9. In Between? https://enrs.eu/inbetween.
10. Hi-story Lessons, https://enrs.eu/hi-story-lessons.
11. European Remembrance Symposium, https://enrs.eu/european-remembrance-symposium.
12. Genealogies of Memory, https://enrs.eu/genealogies.
13. Between Life and Death, https://enrs.eu/between-life-and-death.
14. After the Great War. New Europe 1918–1923, https://enrs.eu/afterthegreatwar.
15. Memento. 27 January, https://enrs.eu/january27.
16. Remember. 23 August, https://enrs.eu/august23.

www.ingramcontent.com/pod-product-compliance
Lightning Source LLC
Chambersburg PA
CBHW080224100526
44583CB00020BA/2555